The author would like to thank all those who have helped in the preparation of this book. In particular, thanks go to Peter Green for providing so many of the photographs and so much encouragement. Thanks, too, to the Editor of the Grimsby Evening Telegraph *for providing ready access to the newspaper's extensive photographic library and to the photographic department for the help in copying borrowed prints. And a special thanks to all the people of Lincolnshire for their response to appeals for information carried in the county's local newspapers.*

Lancaster M-Mother of 100 Squadron pictured at Waltham in the summer of 1944.

LINCOLNSHIRE AIRFIELDS IN THE SECOND WORLD WAR

Patrick Otter

COUNTRYSIDE BOOKS
NEWBURY, BERKSHIRE

First Published 1996
© Patrick Otter 1996
Reprinted 1997

COUNTRYSIDE BOOKS
3 Catherine Road
Newbury, Berkshire

ISBN 1 85306 424 6

The cover painting shows Lancasters of No 9 Squadron at
RAF Bardney preparing for take off and is reproduced from an
original painting by Colin Doggett

Design by Mon Mohan

Produced through MRM Associates Ltd., Reading
Typeset by Techniset Typesetters, Merseyside
Printed by Woolnough Bookbinding Ltd., Irthlingborough

CONTENTS

LINCOLNSHIRE WORLD WAR II AIRFIELDS

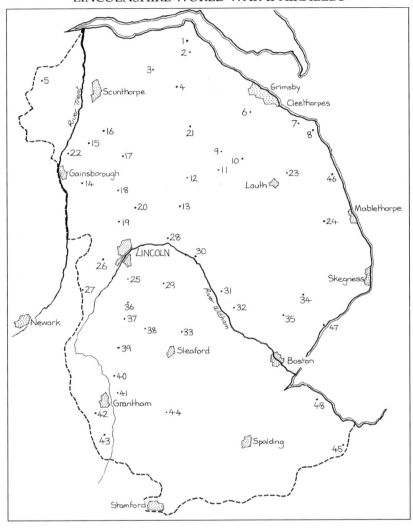

KEY TO MAP (*Opposite*)

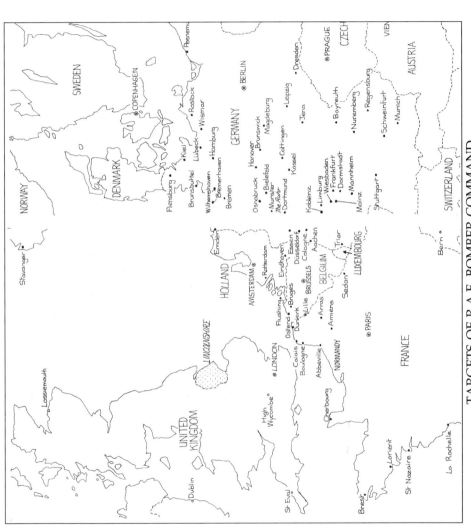

TARGETS OF R.A.F. BOMBER COMMAND

1
SETTING
THE SCENE

You have to look closely these days for the evidence, but half a century ago Lincolnshire was at the very heart of Britain's air power.

Now the markers are hard to find. A distant view of a hangar roof, now perhaps a warehouse or grain depot; a crumbling building in the corner of a wheat field; a stretch of unexplained concrete; the hump back of a rotting Nissen hut; the overgrown ribs of what might have been an air raid shelter. Then there are the memorials to the men and machines which packed into this green backwater of England between 1939 and 1945. They range from simple roadside plaques to the dramatic memorial at Woodhall Spa to the country's most famous airmen of all, the Dambusters.

So many airfields were to be found in the country's second largest county that it was estimated there was, on average, only seven miles between each of them. They covered an estimated 30,000 acres of Lincolnshire, accommodating around 80,000 RAF personnel at any one time. Big though Lincolnshire skies are, the county was so crowded with military airfields that circuits overlapped and flying operations had to be curtailed in the Lincoln area. At the peak of wartime aviation, there were some 46 military airfields plus numerous ancillary sites in the county. Now that figure has shrunk to a handful with only two, Coningsby and Waddington, still operational.

So how did Lincolnshire, which is far from the pancake-flat country strangers believe it to be, become the base for over 1,000 aircraft and home to tens of thousands of young airmen and women? We have to go back to the days of wood and wire, castor oil and dope to find the answer to that.

A year before Archduke Ferdinand was assassinated in Sarajevo and the world was plunged into the bloodiest war in history, the fledgling Royal Flying Corps was busy expanding. The RFC was then a tiny organisation, based mainly in Hampshire, but the infant corps was spreading its wings and this included the setting up of a new base at Montrose on the east coast of Scotland. In those days, Farnborough to Montrose could be a week's journey by air. The RFC's aircraft, which had advanced little from the time of Bleriot, had a very limited range and it was necessary to set up a series of staging posts for aircraft on cross-country flights. These involved advance parties of ground personnel, equipped with fuel and spares, who would scout ahead for suitable landing grounds, make the necessary arrangements with farmers or landowners, refuel and service the aircraft, and then move on by road for the next site. Lincolnshire, with its broad fields, was ideal for this purpose.

It was the Royal Naval Air Service which was initially charged with the aerial protection of Britain when the First World War began, but the Zeppelin raids of 1915 and 1916, which included the bombing of a number of Lincolnshire towns, were to lead to some rapid changes. Home defence switched to the Royal Flying Corps, which was authorised to form ten new squadrons to combat the Zeppelin menace. With just about everywhere on the east coast vulnerable, it was decided that one of these squadrons should be based in Lincolnshire. 33 Squadron had its headquarters in the Trentside town of Gainsborough, with its aircraft spreading across three airfields (then known as 'flight stations') at Elsham, near Brigg, Kirton Lindsey and Brattleby, four miles north of Lincoln. It was no coincidence that all three sites were close to what would become major Second World War airfields. In addition to these, a series of relief landing grounds were set up for the short-range FE2b aircraft then in use.

The expansion of the RFC necessitated a rapid growth in primary and advanced training. Where better to train these pilots than at the flying stations then scattered across the country, and Lincolnshire proved to be no exception. As the Zeppelin threat diminished, so Lincolnshire's training role grew so that, by 1918, the county had some 37 airfields of one kind or another, the third highest total in the country.

The Royal Naval Air Service also had a considerable presence in Lincolnshire, with a seaplane base at Killingholme on the Humber estuary (later to be used by the United States Navy) and the major airship training centre at Cranwell. The city of Lincoln was also one of the principal manufacturing centres for aircraft and Handley Page and Vickers Vimy bombers, Sopwith Gunbuses and BE2s were all flown from aircraft acceptance parks on the outskirts of the city.

The pace of this wartime expansion was matched only by the evaporation of military flying after the war. Some training units were preserved but, by 1925, Lincolnshire was left with just four airfields, none at all north of Lincoln.

This, however, was the nadir of aviation in Lincolnshire. In 1927 a Special Reserve Bomber Squadron was formed at Waddington, the site of one of the First World War airfields. 503 Squadron initially had just ten aircraft, three Avro 504s and seven Fairey Fawns, but their arrival signalled the beginning of an association between the county and the bombing arm of the RAF which was to last until the 1980s. Special armament training camps were also established at Sutton Bridge on the Wash, and at North Coates, just south of the Humber.

When the decision was taken in 1935 to expand the RAF in the face of the growing threat from Germany, Lincolnshire was high on the list of areas for that expansion. Waddington was modernised, Hemswell and Brattleby (now known by the name of the adjacent village of Scampton) were reoccupied and plans drawn up for new airfields at Kirton Lindsey, Swinderby, Digby, Coningsby, Manby and Binbrook.

These airfields all exist today, although only Coningsby and Waddington remain operational, and are all easily identifiable by their large brick hangars and air of permanence. Not all of them were occupied by the time German troops invaded Poland, but several were, and some of the first operational sorties of the war were to be flown from the bomber airfields at Scampton, Waddington and Hemswell and Digby, Lincolnshire's major fighter station. Training was also well established with major centres at the RAF College at Cranwell, at Manby, Grantham, North Coates and Sutton Bridge. But the real expansion was yet to come.

In 1940 a steady stream of new airfields came into use. Fighters moved in to Kirton Lindsey, Wellingore and Coleby Grange; Fairey Battle light bombers flew into Binbrook where the builders were still at work, and Polish bomber crews began operating from the grass strip at Swinderby.

Elsewhere the surveyors were hard at work, looking for more sites on which to build the airfields the RAF would need. They examined first those First World War air stations and relief landing grounds, and then they extended their search for suitable sites for a whole chain of bomber airfields planned for Lincolnshire.

There were a string of radar stations just inland from the coast, at Stenigot, Langtoft, Ingoldmells, Skendleby and Orby, along with

11

wireless stations at Humberston and South Elkington, near Louth.

The county's bomber role also led to the creation of major supply facilities in the county. These included a large fuel depot at the Trentside village of Torksey, which was served by rail, road and barge, and bomb and ammunition dumps at Norton Disney, near Lincoln, South Witham, near Stamford, and Market Stainton, near Louth. The latter, which supplied most of the munitions to Bomber Command's 1 Group, occupied an enormous area of the Lincolnshire Wolds with bombs piled high alongside a section of the Caistor High Street, which was closed to civilian traffic in parts. It was supplied by rail heads on the Lincoln-Louth line and later at Brocklesby. At the height of the bombing offensive, several trains a day were needed to feed the appetite of the 1 Group aircraft and a staff of 270 was needed to run the Market Stainton depot.

Of equal importance to the county's bomber squadrons was the 22 Marine Craft Unit, which operated an air-sea rescue service from the tidal basin at the entrance to Grimsby docks. It was equipped with eight launches at the height of its operation and had a staff of 150 RAF personnel. Many airmen were to owe their lives to 22 MCU.

The Airfields

When the surveyors began looking for new sites for airfields, they were not drawn to the flat Fenlands around the Wash, but to the rolling farmlands of the Lincolnshire Cliff, the fertile plain south of Lincoln and the uplands on the edge of the Wolds. It was here that most of the county's wartime airfields were to be found.

It is easy to see why these areas were chosen. Sites along the Cliff (as a geographic description, this is not strictly accurate; it is a natural limestone escarpment, but its steep west-facing edge earned it the name 'Cliff' long before the RAF came) were well drained and sat astride the Ermine Street, the main arterial road through Lincolnshire. The farmland south of Lincoln was well-drained and free from obstruction while the Wolds sites, some of which were over 400 feet above sea level, were able to make full use of the prevailing south-westerly winds.

By a quirk of planning and geography, the city of Lincoln found itself at the hub of an almost complete circle of airfields. There were some 16 airfields within a ten mile radius of the city centre (including Wigsley, just across the county boundary in Nottinghamshire). So crowded did the sky become at one stage that a Lancaster squadron had to be moved to an airfield in the east of the county to relieve the congestion. Circuits still overlapped to such an extent that one airfield, Dunholme Lodge, eventually closed for operational flying. The situation was almost as bad in the north of the county where clusters of airfields were so close that there was a real, and sometimes realised, risk of collision.

The airfields themselves ranged from the very good pre-war stations to the jerry-built wartime-only ones. Not all the wartime-built airfields were bad, but most were. Accommodation was spartan, mostly in Nissen huts where the only running water was supplied by leaking roofs or condensation. Most were without electricity and all had just a single coke stove to keep the occupants warm. Medical officers issued dire warnings about the threat of illness and disease while, outside, hastily-laid concrete runways broke up under the weight of the aircraft using them.

It was noticeable that Australian bomber squadrons serving in Lincolnshire enjoyed some of the best conditions. Three RAAF squadrons served with 5 Group and one in 1 Group and each was to spend most of its time in Lincolnshire on one of the pre-war airfields. One Australian pilot interviewed by the author some years ago suggested this was because of a gentleman's agreement between the governments of the two countries: Australia would provide the squadrons on the understanding they got the best accommodation going. Both sides appeared to have stood by the agreement.

When the war began there were just two airfields in Lincolnshire with a paved runway, North Coates and Manby, both of which were used then primarily for training. Grass strips at other airfields were thought to be perfectly acceptable for the light bombers and fighters then in use. However, by the winter of 1940 these were clearly inadequate to provide all-weather conditions for the expanding bomber force, which was now using heavier aircraft with the prospect of even heavier ones to come. So a major programme of runway construction was put into operation to provide almost all existing and planned bomber airfields with either concrete or asphalt runways. Teams of navvies, employed by half a dozen contracting firms, were kept busy for several years on this work. When new airfields were being built, it was always the runways which went down first. They were invariably laid in an A-pattern with the longest running from south-west to north-west (although there was a notable exception at

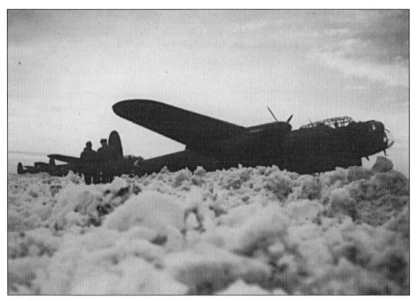

Men and women who served in Lincolnshire always remember the winters. This was a typical scene as 467 Squadron Lancasters are prepared for action at a snow-bound RAF Waddington, 1944.

Ludford Magna).

The runway programme inevitably meant that the major pre-war stations were closed for lengthy periods for operational flying. Scampton, for instance, was shut for almost a year not long after the epic Dams raid and took no part in the Battle of Berlin or the operations to support the Normandy invasion. The RAF, however, made full use of the facilities at these airfields by bringing in ground schools while the runway work was going on. Many RAF cooks learned their trade at Coningsby during the eleven months it was closed for operational flying.

Hardened runways were restricted only to those airfields used by heavy bombers. The county's fighter airfields, whose roles diminished in the later stages of the war, and those used for primary training had to make do with grass strips. On a number of heavily-used training airfields pierced steel matting, an innovation brought to England by the Americans, was used to replenish worn-out grass strips.

The pre-war airfields were all built with large brick C-type hangars, together with substantial brick-built accommodation sites. The wartime

14

airfields came with an array of building types, B-, J- and T-type hangars with wooden, concrete or corrugated iron huts. Watch towers came in a variety of shapes and sizes, some were simple observation points on top of flying control buildings, while from 1943 onwards, a standard design was adopted with the balcony and rail familiar from those wartime films.

Today, almost all the wartime airfields have all but disappeared. Some buildings do remain, pressed into use for agricultural or industrial uses. Their style, however, still betrays them for what they were, utilitarian buildings hastily constructed to house a very sizeable proportion of the RAF's front-line wartime strength.

The Bombers

Of the 46 airfields in use in Lincolnshire in 1945, 24 were principally concerned with the bombing campaign, although several of these had combined their offensive role with one of training. Some, like Swinderby and Blyton, had begun as bomber airfields and had then become the home of heavy conversion units. Others alternated between the two; Hemswell, for instance, served as home for bomber squadrons for both 1 and 5 Groups and spent some time providing Lancaster training for 1 Group squadrons.

During the war years, Bomber Command roughly divided Lincolnshire in half; the southern part of the county (together with a number of airfields in Nottinghamshire) was allocated to 5 Group, the northern half to 1 Group. By the time the war ended the county was home to one of the most potent striking forces in the world. In April 1945 the two groups between them had on strength 720 Lancaster bombers spread over 32 squadrons, 18 of them in 5 Group's area alone.

When the war began Lincolnshire was Bomber Command's 5 Group territory. 1 Group was in the south Midlands and went to France as the Advanced Air Striking Force where its light bomber squadrons were cut to ribbons by the Luftwaffe in the Battle of France.

5 Group, which then had its headquarters at St Vincent's House in Grantham, had a strong presence in Lincolnshire before the war began and six of its squadrons were based at the county's three major airfields, Waddington, Scampton and Hemswell. They all flew Hampdens and were to take part in the very first bombing operations

Post-op debrief. A scene familiar to all those who flew in Lancasters from Lincolnshire during the war. This one was at Ludford Magna in 1944. (Redfearn Collection)

of the war. Five of those six squadrons were still serving with 5 Group in Lincolnshire when the war ended.

After Dunkirk, 1 Group was reformed with its headquarters at Hucknall, near Nottingham. It had just four squadrons, two of these going to the new airfield at Binbrook, near Grimsby, and the other two to Newton in Nottinghamshire. It was later to be strengthened by the formation of two Polish squadrons at another new airfield, Swinderby. 1 Group's squadrons were equipped initially with Fairey Battles, but these were exchanged in the autumn of 1940 for Vickers Wellingtons. These two groups were to play different, but complementary roles, in the conflict to come.

5 Group already regarded itself as the elite of Bomber Command and the events of the next six years were to underline that position still further. It was to host arguably the war's most famous bomber squadron, 617, which breached the Ruhr dams, pioneered new marking and bombing techniques, dropped the Tallboys and Grand Slam bombs and, in concert with another 5 Group squadron, 9, sank the *Tirpitz*. 5 Group was also the first to use the outstanding bomber aircraft of the Second World War, the Lancaster, receiving its first

machines a full year ahead of its neighbours in north Lincolnshire. Nine of the 32 Victoria Crosses awarded to RAF personnel in the Second World War went to men serving with 5 Group. It supplied the nucleus of the revolutionary new Pathfinder Force and was later rewarded by being allocated its very own Pathfinder units so that it could operate as a separate entity within Bomber Command.

5 Group carried out the greatest number of bombing raids, 70,357 sorties in all, including the first and last attacks of the war, and suffered the highest number of casualties, 11,990 men killed and 1,888 aircraft lost in action.

1 Group started its war in earnest almost a year after 5 Group. But once it had received the aircraft with which to operate and the airfields from which to fly, it became very much the workhorse of Bomber Command, losing 1,429 aircraft in action and with them the lives of 8,577 aircrew.

Tirpitz bound. This was the Tallboy bomb about to be loaded onto WS-J of 9 Squadron at Bardney, prior to the Tirpitz raid in November 1944. On the right is the pilot, Flt Lt W. Scott with his two gunners, F. Gray and Les Jepson. They were ordered to stand in front of the tail of the bomb to protect from view one of its secret elements. (Via Les Jepson)

A word of fatherly advice from Air Commodore 'Hoppy' Wray, who commanded 1 Group's No 12 Base at Binbrook, for two young airmen just returned from operations. (Author's collection)

1 Group also had its notable squadrons. 460, the Australian squadron which was to fly from Binbrook for the last two years of the war, set all kinds of Bomber Command records, including the highest tonnage of bombs dropped (24,000) and the most Lancaster sorties flown (5,700). And, in 101 Squadron, 1 Group had the RAF's first electronic counter measures unit.

Both 5 and 1 Groups regarded Lincolnshire as their wartime home, but both spread their wings beyond the county's boundaries. 1 Group was to move its headquarters to Bawtry Hall, just south of Doncaster, and several of its early stations were in Nottinghamshire or Yorkshire. 5 Group had a number of airfields around the Newark area, although its headquarters were always in Lincolnshire, moving later in the war from St Vincent's to Morton Hall, near Swinderby.

Towards the end of 1943 all bomber airfields in Lincolnshire were reorganised into the Base structure, each Base headquarters station having two or three 'satellite' airfields for which it provided the major administration and servicing facilities. This led to the creation of six Base units within 5 Group and five in 1 Group. This was followed by a further reorganisation in the autumn of 1944 which saw the Base units

Ops are on! The Base operations centre at Ludford Magna, from where operations from Ludford, Faldingworth and Wickenby were co-ordinated. Among those pictured are Group Capt King, the station commander (second left) and Air Commodore Bobby Blucke, the Base commander (third right). Standing is Sqdn Ldr Thompson of 101 Squadron. (Redfearn collection)

dealing with training transferred to 7 Group while one of 5 Group's Bases was transferred to 1 Group.

The units were as follows (headquarters stations first) – **1 Group**: 11 Base: Lindholme (South Yorkshire), Blyton, Faldingworth, Sandtoft. 12 Base: Binbrook, Grimsby, Kelstern. 13 Base: Elsham Wolds, Kirmington, North Killingholme. 14 Base: Ludford Magna, Wickenby, Faldingworth (from January 1944). 15 Base (from October 1944): Scampton, Dunholme Lodge, Ingham, Hemswell, Fiskerton.

5 Group: 51 Base: Swinderby, Syerston, Wigsley, Winthorpe (Nottinghamshire). 52 Base (before October 1944): Scampton, Dunholme Lodge, Fiskerton. 53 Base: Waddington, Bardney, Skellingthorpe. 54 Base: Coningsby, Woodhall Spa, Metheringham. 56 Base: Systerton (Nottinghamshire), Fulbeck, Balderton (Nottinghamshire).

Both groups had, certainly during the critical stages of the bombing campaign, a different style of leadership. Early in 1943 the Hon Ralph Cochrane took over as Air Officer Commanding 5 Group and it was under his leadership that the group was to achieve its pre-eminence.

Flying Officer Peggy Burnside and Sqdn Ldr Bruce Derner pictured at North Killingholme plotting the track for 550 Squadron's role in an attack on Nordhausen, April 1945. (Via Rowland Hardy)

He was an outstanding leader, full of energy and zest, a man who had begun his service career in the Royal Navy in 1912 and had served with distinction in the RNAS before embarking on a new career in the RAF when it was formed in 1918. He also had the full confidence of Bomber Command's Commander in Chief, Arthur Harris, himself a former 5 Group AOC.

In the same period 1 Group was led by Air Commodore Edward Rice, a man brought back from the obscurity of a command in West Africa by Harris. He was a former soldier who had transferred to the Royal Flying Corps and then served with distinction in the post-war RAF and, like Harris, had spent some time as station commander at Hemswell. He may have lacked Cochrane's charisma, but he was an ideal man for the job given to him by Harris, ensuring that 1 Group never fell below the high standards he set for it. Rice was determined to get the absolute maximum out of the squadrons under his command and ordered trials to be carried out to determine what was the heaviest bomb load his Lancasters could carry. The result was that, Lancaster-for-Lancaster, 1 Group squadrons carried a higher tonnage of bombs than other groups. It was a policy which, some believe, resulted in higher than average losses in 1 Group operations.

It was the efforts of men like Cochrane and Rice, those they led and particularly the 22,000 men from both groups who were to lose their lives between 1939 and 1945 that led Lincolnshire to earn its title as Bomber County.

The Fighters

In 1940, Lincolnshire was the northern outpost of the Battle of Britain. Its fighter airfields were used to provide respite from the fighting in the south-east for the battle-weary squadrons and, later in the conflict, it supplied aircraft for the Duxford Wing. And, just as it did in the First World War, it provided fighter protection for the industrial cities in the North and Midlands and for the East Coast ports. Night fighters were in action from Lincolnshire during the Blitz of 1940 through to 1942 and it was only when the threat from the Luftwaffe subsided that the country's role as a base for fighter operations began to diminish.

The two major fighter airfields in Lincolnshire were Digby, near Sleaford, and Kirton Lindsey, just south of Scunthorpe.

Digby had been used in the First World War and extensively between the wars as a training airfield. In 1937 it was incorporated into 12 Group of Fighter Command, which had responsibility for aerial defence north of a line running roughly from Lowestoft into the Midlands. Sorties were mounted from Digby on the first day of the war and it was the first Lincolnshire fighter airfield to see action against German aircraft operating over the North Sea.

Satellite airfields for both Digby and Kirton were opened and were to be used mainly for night fighter operations. It was when operating from one of these that Lincolnshire's most famous wartime airman, Guy Gibson, was to shoot down the first of three German bombers he claimed as a night fighter pilot.

Both Kirton and Digby played host to numerous fighter squadrons during the war, many drawn from overseas. Kirton was used by the American Eagle squadrons, which flew with the RAF prior to America's entry into the war, while Digby became the main centre of operations for Canadian fighter squadrons, spending some consider-

WAAFs played a vital part in almost every aspect of life on operational stations in Lincolnshire. Here four young women service a Mk V Spitfire of 411 Squadron at Digby, June 1941. (RAF Digby)

able period of the war as RCAF Digby.

Once Fighter Command switched from defensive to offensive mode, the role of the Lincolnshire airfields began to diminish. Some fighter sweeps were flown from Lincolnshire, along with bomber protection operations. But the county was too far north to play an effective role in operations over France and the Low Countries and in 1943 Kirton was passed to Flying Training Command and the following year Digby found itself reduced to the status of an operational training unit.

Coastal Command

The link between air and sea in Lincolnshire goes back to the very early days of aviation in the county. During the First World War, Cranwell was officially HMS *Daedalus* and was used for the training of naval pilots. It later expanded into the nation's largest military airfield with the bulk of the RNAS based there. Further north the RNAS had a seaplane base at Killingholme which was so large it boasted England's biggest aircraft hangar (part of which still exists as a bus depot in Grimsby).

Killingholme had long since closed and fallen into disrepair when the Second World War began, but there was an ideal airfield a little further south for Coastal Command purposes at North Coates. It had been established in the First World War as North Coates Fitties and used in the inter-war years for training. It was situated just a few yards from the North Sea in a strategically important position and had a single concrete runway, making it suitable for all-weather operations.

It was passed to Coastal Command in 1941 and, together with its satellite airfield at Donna Nook, went on to play a vital role in strike operations against German shipping in the southern North Sea, so much so that by 1944, the North Coates Wing of three Beaufighter squadrons caused the Germans to halt all shipping movements by day off the Dutch coast.

In April 1944, as the need increased to suppress German shipping, the new airfield built for Bomber Command at Strubby, near Mablethorpe, was used briefly to supplement the activities of the North Coates Wing up to and beyond the D-Day invasion.

Training

A third of all the wartime airfields in Lincolnshire were devoted almost entirely to training. These ranged from the heavy conversion units, where new bomber crews would train and fly together for the first time in four-engined aircraft, to basic training for RAF cooks and clerks.

There were special courses for gunners, for bomb aimers, for navigators and wireless operators. Battle of Britain fighter pilots were trained at Sutton Bridge, there was an Air Commando School in Lincolnshire, while even the docks and local swimming baths in Grimsby were pressed into use to train bomber crews how to use their emergency dinghies.

Flying training was central to the operation of the county's bomber squadrons, particularly later in the war. In the early days crews joined together at Operational Training Units, flew on twin-engined aircraft and were then posted to squadrons operating very similar aircraft. The advent of the four-engined bombers saw a radical rethink of training methods. Initially this was done at squadron level with the creation of conversion flights. But it was soon evident this was insufficient and specialist training was needed. This led to the creation of heavy conversion units, which specialised in four-engined training for new crews, units which were often bigger (and suffered greater losses) than some of the squadrons their pupils were destined for.

With both 5 and 1 Groups eventually operating all-Lancaster squadrons, there was an acute shortage of these aircraft. HCUs operating Lancasters were stripped of them and received elderly Halifax or Stirling replacements. Crews then had to pass from their heavy conversion units through Lancaster Finishing Schools (5 Group's was at Syerston in Nottinghamshire, 1 Group's at Hemswell) for their final training before going on to join their squadrons.

The major centres of wartime training in the county were at Cranwell and Manby, both major pre-war training centres. Manby was the premier training centre for air armament while Cranwell hosted a huge range of training courses, from basic pilot training to pay clerks.

The Americans

Five of Lincolnshire's wartime airfields were to be occupied at one time or another by the United States Army Air Force, four as transport airfields used to lift troops into the invasion zones in Europe, and the fifth as a training base for fighter pilots.

This was at Goxhill, the most northerly of all Lincolnshire's airfields. It had been planned as a bomber airfield but the main runway was directly downwind of the barrage balloons moored to barges in the Humber as protection for the docks at Hull. In 1942 it was occupied by the US 8th AAF and used to provide acclimatisation training for fighter pilots freshly arrived from the United States.

Four airfields in the south of the county, Fulbeck, Barkston Heath, Folkingham and North Witham, were used by the American 9th Air Force, whose C47s were to play such a key role in dropping paratroops behind the invasion beaches on D-Day and again for the attack on the Rhine bridges in Holland.

It was from North Witham, the most southerly airfield in Lincolnshire, that the first Pathfinder units of the American 81st and 101st Airborne were dropped into Normandy shortly after midnight on 6th

June 1944. By some strange quirk of fortune, an airfield at the opposite end of the county, North Killingholme, provided the aircraft which was later credited with dropping the very first stick of bombs which heralded the start of the D-Day operations.

All four airfields played an important part in later airborne operations in Europe (Fulbeck was then to revert to Bomber Command control and was taken over by 5 Group) and, together with Goxhill, accounted for most of the 5,000 USAAF personnel listed as serving in Lincolnshire in April 1944.

The Aircraft

When war was declared operational squadrons in Lincolnshire were already equipped with the latest aircraft available, Hampdens for the six bomber squadrons and Hurricanes for the fighter units. But both types were outnumbered by the large array of biplanes still in service with the RAF in Lincolnshire. These included a number of fine aircraft, like the Hawker Hart, which had given sterling service to the RAF in the inter-war years but which were completely unsuitable for the task which lay ahead. These were quickly relegated to training and ground instruction roles and within 18 months most had disappeared completely.

Bombers were to be Lincolnshire's stock-in-trade over the next six years and just about every type in service with the RAF was to fly from Lincolnshire.

5 Group began its war with Hampdens and progressed on to the Manchester, to become the first to be equipped with the Lancaster, an aircraft Lincolnshire was to adopt as its own. Over half of all the 8,000-plus Lancasters built served at one time or another with Lincolnshire-based squadrons and some 2,500 were lost on operations from the county. 5 Group, which also had its own target marking force, also operated a limited number of Mosquitos plus a handful of American-built Mustangs and Lightnings in this role.

Neighbouring 1 Group started operations with the obsolete Fairey Battle light bomber, which it soon exchanged for the Vickers Wellington, an aircraft which was superior in most respects to both the Hampdens and Manchesters of 5 Group. It was perhaps for this reason that 1 Group did not begin re-equipping with Lancasters for a

The eyes have it. Bomb cameras being serviced in the 14 Base workshops at Ludford Magna. (Redfearn collection)

full year after 5 Group had received its first Lancasters. Wellingtons were to fly on operations with 1 Group until the late autumn of 1943 and it was the spring of the following year before it became an all-Lancaster group.

1 Group had been scheduled to re-equip with the Halifax, which was already going into service with 4 and 6 Groups in Yorkshire. The first aircraft were, in fact, delivered to 103 Squadron at Elsham Wolds and conversion training began before Bomber Command decided that 1 Group should re-equip with Lancasters. It was a decision welcomed by crews at Elsham who had already found to their cost that the Halifax, certainly in its early variants, could be an unpleasant aircraft to fly and, in the wrong hands, a dangerous one.

Halifaxes, however, remained part of the aerial scene in Lincolnshire. They were used to equip 1 Group's heavy conversion units until sufficient Lancasters were available later in the war. 5 Group had begun its conversion training with Lancasters, but the demands from operational squadrons for these aircraft led to them being replaced by MkIII Stirlings, the RAF's first four-engined heavy. The Stirling was a much more accommodating aircraft to fly than the Halifax but its limited bomb-carrying capacity and inability to operate at the heights

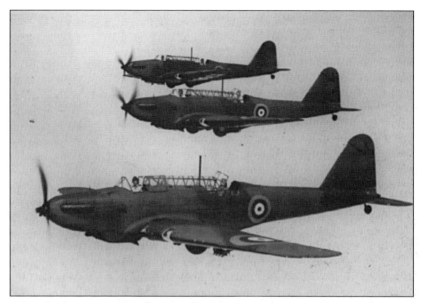

Fairey Battles were used as front line bombers by 1 Group squadrons in 1940. (RAF Museum)

achieved by the Halifax and Lancaster led to it being withdrawn from operational service. At least two Stirlings also served with one of 1 Group's conversion units.

During the war Lincolnshire's main fighter airfields at Digby and Kirton were host to large numbers of squadrons. These operated mainly Spitfires and Hurricanes, although a few did bring the occasional odd-ball aircraft with them, including the mid-engined American built Airacobra. Night fighter squadrons also served in Lincolnshire and these initially operated in Blenheims and Defiants, later switching to Beaufighters and Mosquitos.

Beaufighters were also the favoured aircraft of the powerful Coastal Command strike wing which flew from North Coates. This was made up of three squadrons, the aircraft carrying a mixed armament of torpedoes, rockets and cannon. Coastal Command also flew air-sea rescue operations from Lincolnshire, using Walrus flying boats and later Warwicks, a Wellington derivative which could carry a large lifeboat in its bomb bay.

The many training units in Lincolnshire operated a large and varied array of aircraft. Several training airfields had over 100 aircraft in their

Comradeship existed between air and ground crews and many scrapbooks contain snapshots of the two. This one, showing Flt Lt Wedderburn, his crew and ground crew, was taken during Wedderburn's second tour at Ludford with 101 Squadron. (Redfearn collection)

charge at any one time, ranging from Tiger Moths to Harvards, Ansons to Blenheims, Audaxes to Masters.

The Americans brought still more new types to Lincolnshire. Twin-boomed Lightnings became a common sight in north Lincolnshire as they flew from Goxhill, along with Thunderbolts and Mustangs, while, in the south of the county, they flew large fleets of C46 Curtis Commandos and C47 Dakotas.

Lincolnshire was famous for its 'big' skies. Between 1939 and 1945 it needed them.

2
BARDNEY

In the centre of the quiet Lincolnshire village of Bardney is a most impressive memorial. It incorporates the propeller and spinner from a Lancaster bomber and a piece of stone which once rested on the shores of a Norwegian fjord. The reason why those two items came together in a war memorial can be found a mile and a half away – the still recognisable form of RAF Bardney.

The airfield was just one of the chain of bomber stations built across the county in the early part of the war, yet it achieved lasting fame as home of one of Bomber Command's premier squadrons.

It was from Bardney that 9 Squadron operated as part of a devastating precision bombing team with 617 Squadron. Between them they delivered monster bombs onto key targets across Europe. 9 Squadron helped blast hitherto indestructible U-boat pens, key railway bridges, V-weapon sites and, of course, the *Tirpitz*, the German battleship which, by its very presence, affected the whole strategy of the Royal Navy.

Bardney was also the airfield from which a young Scottish wireless operator won a posthumous Victoria Cross in one of the supreme acts of bravery in Bomber Command.

The Air Ministry surveyors first identified a flat site for a bomber airfield north of the village of Bardney early in 1941. Bardney stands on the flat plain which stretches north from the true Fenlands of Lincolnshire towards Lincoln and the rising land of the Wolds. It is rich, fertile farmland, interspersed with woods. It was between two of these, Austacre and Scotgrove, that the airfield was built to the standard pattern of three concrete runways and three hangars by a number of contractors, both national and local. Work had begun in the spring of 1942 but a shortage of building material, particularly hard core and concrete, meant that the completion was delayed. Bardney was just one of a dozen airfields then being built in Lincolnshire and

Dinghy drill at Bardney, autumn 1943. (Via J B Blanche)

the building supply industries were stretched almost to breaking point.

The airfield was finally ready for opening by the beginning of April 1943 and allocated to 9 Squadron, then at Waddington. 9 had been in action continuously since the outbreak of the war, initially operating Wellingtons within 3 Group at Honington in Suffolk. It transferred to 5 Group in August 1942 and moved to Waddington where it converted first to Manchesters and then to Lancasters, which it flew operationally for the first time in September 1942 in an attack on Bremen. 9 Squadron's move was somewhat unusual. On the evening of 13th April its aircraft took off for a long-distance raid on port facilities at La Spezia in northern Italy. As soon as the aircraft were clear of Waddington, the ground staff began moving to their new station and almost everything was in place at Bardney by the time the aircraft arrived back from Italy. 9 Squadron was to remain at Bardney until the war ended.

The move to Bardney coincided with the growing pace of what was to become known as the Battle of the Ruhr. Lancasters were still in short supply and those in service with 5 Group were constantly in action. One of those at Bardney was W4964, which had arrived at the airfield from the Metropolitan Vickers factory in Manchester a few days after the squadron's move from Waddington. It was assigned the

Bardney's most famous Lancaster, WS-J (J-Johnny), after its first operation to Stettin in April 1943. (Via J. B. Blanche)

squadron codes WS and the letter J and flew for the first time on the night of 20th/21st April when it went to Stettin.

Now known as J-Johnny, it soon began sporting a nose-art painting depicting the trademark of Johnnie Walker whisky and the company's logo, 'Still Going Strong'. It was to prove remarkably prophetic for J-Johnny was to fly 106 operations with 9 Squadron before being finally retired in the autumn of 1944. And it was J-Johnny which was credited with dropping the 12,000lb Tallboy bomb which hit the *Tirpitz* in an attack in September 1944, the aircraft's 100th operation. Although J-Johnny was scrapped four years after the war it lived on again when the Battle of Britain Memorial Flight adopted its codes and nose-art in the early 1990s for the last remaining flying Lancaster.

9 Squadron had already lost four Lancasters over the Ruhr in the two weeks prior to its move to Bardney and the losses were to go on, seven Lancasters being lost in the next ten weeks. Thirty-six men were killed while just 13 survived. Two Bardney Lancasters were lost in the raids on Hamburg while a third, W4133, which was the first Lancaster assigned to the squadron in its time at Waddington, was written off after crashing on its return from Hamburg. The squadron was heavily

31

involved in the attack on the rocket research station at Peenemunde on the Baltic coast, an attack which cost Bomber Command 40 aircraft, 17 of them from 5 Group alone.

Six nights later the first of 17 Lancasters took off from Bardney shortly after 7.45 pm. The target was Berlin and, although those 17 crews were not to know it, they were participating in the opening of what was to become known as the Battle of Berlin. It would go on for eight long, bloody months and would almost bring Bomber Command's Main Force to its knees. That night 56 aircraft of the 727 sent failed to return, the heaviest loss on any single night so far for the RAF. All the 9 Squadron aircraft returned safely.

Two aircraft which later didn't quite make it back to Bardney were WS-Y, which crashed close to the village of Minting, near Horncastle on 7th September 1943 on its way home from Munich, and WS-D which crashed into the sea off Skegness following a raid on Bochum three weeks later.

The attack on Berlin was the first of 20 raids on the German capital carried out by 9 Squadron, involving some 254 sorties from which they lost seven aircraft, the second lowest casualty rate of any squadron in

The crew of Y-Yoke of 9 Squadron, early in December 1943. In the centre is the pilot, P/O R A Blaydon. On his right is the navigator, F/O Bernard Otter, father of the author. (Author's collection)

Bomber Command. They lost two Lancasters on the night of 18/19th November, one in a crash-landing at Scampton with the loss of six of its crew on 24th November, another on 2nd/3rd December, and two more on the night of 16/17th December. One of those, DV293 Y-Yoke, was probably involved in a mid-air collision over Brandenburg in the heart of Berlin with a Lancaster from 619 Squadron at Woodhall Spa. The 14 crew members of the two aircraft are buried side by side in the Berlin War Cemetery. The navigator on Y-Yoke was the author's father.

Two more Lancasters were lost from Bardney on 1st/2nd January 1944 and on 27/28th January. The pilot of the last Lancaster lost was Flight Lieutenant S. James, who died along with three of his crew. He was just 19 years old.

One of the aircraft involved in the final attack of the Battle of Berlin was WS-L, which was to complete 97 operations with the squadron (the last was on Kiel in April 1945) before being scrapped.

It was during the Berlin period that 9 Squadron began establishing its credentials for accurate bombing. In an attack on the railway tunnel and marshalling yards at Modane on the French-Italian border, aircraft from 9 Squadron brought back photographs showing they had hit the tunnel entrance, a remarkable feat in the very early days of Pathfinder marking.

By now Bardney, previously a satellite of Waddington, had assumed full station status within 53 Base and its first commanding officer was Group Captain A. C. Evan-Evans. He went to Coningsby as Base commander and was replaced at Bardney by Group Captain Pleasance, a former CO at Swinderby. Soon after he arrived at Bardney he opted to fly on a raid to Frankfurt with Flying Officer Manning and his crew. Theirs was to be one of 26 Lancasters lost that night. Group Captain C.C. Mullen arrived soon after to take command at Bardney.

9 Squadron was still operating as a two-flight Main Force squadron and, as such, sent 16 aircraft on the ill-fated Nuremberg raid at the end of March. One was lost with its crew, who were on their 25th operation. Another was attacked by two night fighters before it reached the target. The Lancaster managed to evade the first attack but, just as the crew thought they had escaped, they were caught by a second which raked the bomber with cannon fire, killing the rear gunner and starting a fire. The pilot, Pilot Officer Forrest, dumped his bomb load somewhere south of Cologne and dived steeply to put out the blaze. Rather than turn the empty bomber and return to England alone, Forrest regained height and elected to stay with the stream and flew over the target with empty bomb bays.

Targets were now shifting to France as preparations began for the invasion. On 10/11th April 9 Squadron carried out a highly successful attack on the railway marshalling yards at Tours, although several aircraft were unable to bomb because of thick smoke.

There was a similar experience for 9 Squadron later in the month when 16 aircraft took part in a raid on an explosives factory at St Medard-en-Jalles, near Bordeaux. After the first 26 aircraft bombed, the target became shrouded in smoke from fires started by marker flares which dropped in a nearby wood and the Master Bomber ordered the remaining 62 aircraft, including those from 9 Squadron, to abort. But there was no respite for the factory. The following night 9 Squadron, along with 52 other 5 Group Lancasters, was back and this time the target was well and truly hit. On the night of 5/6th June 9 Squadron attacked gun batteries on the Normandy coast and the following night hit a railway target at Argentan. For the next few weeks French targets came up with regularity at briefings at Bardney. In the meantime, however, plans were being drawn up at 5 Group headquarters for a new role for the squadron.

617 Squadron, whose exploits over the Ruhr dams a year earlier were still being talked about, was being used now as a precision bomber squadron. But it had become clear that a single squadron was not enough for some of the targets selected and so 9 Squadron, which had earned itself a good reputation for navigation and bombing, was elected to partner 617 on specialised attacks.

617 had been using 12,000lb Tallboy bombs that summer, mainly in an effort to penetrate the thick concrete protecting V-weapon sites in France. By the time 9 Squadron joined 617, Tallboys were in short supply. The British factory was turning out only one a day while American factories were producing around 30 a week but the bombs then had to be shipped across the Atlantic. When 9 joined 617 for the first time for a daylight attack on a railway bridge at Etaples its Lancasters were all armed with standard 1,000lb bombs. It was not an auspicious start. Bombs from all 27 Lancasters, 13 of them from 9 Squadron, fell around the bridge, leaving it damaged but still usable.

9 flew with 617 again on 13th August, the Bardney Lancasters carrying 1,000lb armour-piercing bombs for an attack on Brest where the old French warships *Clemenceau* and *Gueydon* were the targets. It was feared the Germans would use them to block the harbour and both were hit in the attack.

There was another failure on 16th August when bad weather prevented 9 Squadron dropping 2,000lb bombs on U-boat pens at La

Pallice, but the Bardney boys made up for it later in the month when they were credited with hits on merchant shipping in the port of Brest.

The first Tallboy bombs were delivered to Bardney at the end of the month just as plans were being prepared for the squadron's most daring attack yet – on the *Tirpitz*. The Tallboy-armed Lancasters flew first to northern Russia and from there they attacked the battleship at its anchorage in Kaa fjord. Two Tallboy bombs hit the ship, the first dropped by Flying Officer Melrose in 9 Squadron's J-Johnny. Although the *Tirpitz* was to survive this attack, it was crippled and was never again to pose a threat to Allied shipping in the North Atlantic. The battleship was towed south to Tromsö where it was intended for use as a floating gun battery. On 29th October 617 and 9 Squadrons, this time operating from Lossiemouth, attacked for a second time but bad weather prevented a repeat of the successes in September.

A third raid was mounted on 12th November and this time there was to be no escape for the *Tirpitz*. At least two Tallboys, both dropped by 617 Squadron Lancasters, hit the battleship and several more, including two 9 Squadron bombs, fell close by. Soon after the raid finished a magazine inside the ship exploded and she capsized, killing up to 1,000 of her crew. One 9 Squadron Lancaster was badly damaged by flak and was forced to land in Sweden but the others returned safely, thanks in no small way to an enormous blunder by the Luftwaffe which had not been told the *Tirpitz* had moved and directed its covering fighters to Kaa fjord.

9 Squadron, in the meantime, was still playing its full part in Main Force attacks and in one, on Munich, dropping 12,000lb bombs on the city.

The Dortmund-Ems canal had been a target for Bomber Command throughout the war and early on the morning of 1st January 1945, 102 5 Group Lancasters left their Lincolnshire bases to attack the recently repaired section near Landbergen. One of the aircraft was U-Uncle of 9 Squadron, flown by New Zealander Flying Officer Harry Denton. His wireless operator was a young Scotsman, Flight Sergeant George Thompson, who had been in the RAF since 1941 and at Bardney since October 1944.

U-Uncle had just dropped its twelve 1,000lb bombs when the aircraft was hit by an 88mm flak shell, which tore away part of the nose and set fire to the port inner engine. A second shell hit the fuselage, severing hydraulics, leaving the bomb doors open and starting another fire.

Thompson quickly saw the plight of the gunners, trapped in the fire which engulfed the centre section of the bomber. Despite the flames and exploding .303 ammunition, Thompson dragged the mid-upper gunner from his turret and used his bare hands to beat out the man's burning clothing before carrying him past the gaping hole in the fuselage to the relative safety of the front of the aircraft. Despite his own severe injuries, he then went back a second time to extricate the rear gunner from his turret, again beating out the flames with his hands before pulling the injured gunner clear.

Thompson, now in intense pain from his own burns and the effect on them of the icy blast blowing through the open nose of the Lancaster, crawled to the cockpit to report what had happened to the pilot. Denton later said his wireless operator was so badly burnt that he hardly recognised him.

Over the Rhine the Lancaster was hit for a third time by flak and, as Denton struggled to keep it flying, its plight was noticed by a flight of Canadian Spitfires which attempted to direct the Lancaster to an Allied airfield in northern Holland, at one point flying in front of the bomber to warn the pilot of high tension cables. Finally, Denton was forced to put the aircraft down in open country.

Six of the crew, including Denton and Thompson, were taken to hospital in Eindhoven and it was there that the mid-upper gunner, Ernie Potts, died that night. George Thompson was later transferred to a British military field hospital where he appeared to be recovering well from his injuries. But, three weeks later, he was found to be suffering from pneumonia and he died on 23rd January. A month later he was awarded a posthumous Victoria Cross. The citation said: 'Flight Sergeant Thompson might have devoted his efforts to quelling the fire and so have contributed to his own safety. He preferred to go through the fire to succour his comrades. He knew that he would then be in no position to hear or heed any order which might be given to abandon the aircraft. He hazarded his own life in order to save the lives of others. Young in years and experience, his actions were those of a veteran.'

Bardney, in the meantime, was still going about the business of bombing and in April was host to a second squadron, 189, which had been formed at Fulbeck the previous autumn.

It was 189 which was to be the last occupant of Bardney. 9 Squadron returned to Waddington shortly after the war ended while 189 remained until October 1945 before moving to Metheringham.

Bardney itself had another brief operational period as a Thor missile base in the late 1950s before being used by a glider club and a crop spraying company.

3

BARKSTON HEATH, FOLKINGHAM AND NORTH WITHAM

A group of airfields in the south of Lincolnshire, built initially as bomber bases, were used as the springboard for two of the biggest airborne operations of the Second World War, the landings in Normandy and the assault on the bridges at Nijmegen and Arnhem.

Four airfields close to Grantham were used for the attacks, Barkston Heath, Folkingham, North Witham and Fulbeck, with the air element being provided by the American 9th Army Air Force. For three of the airfields these attacks were to be their major contribution to the war effort while the fourth, Fulbeck, also spent some time as an RAF 5 Group bomber airfield and will be dealt with in a separate chapter.

Barkston, which stands on the edge of the Lincolnshire Cliff a few miles north-east of Grantham, was in use as a relief landing ground as early as 1936 by the Hawker Harts, Furys and Audaxes from nearby Cranwell and it was still used in this capacity when the war began. The Luftwaffe thought it sufficiently important to attack in May 1941 when several bombs landed on the grassed area used by Cranwell. There was little else there to damage. But it was not to remain that way for long. The site had been selected for airfield development and construction began on a standard pattern bomber airfield, initially minus the hardened runways, which were to follow a year later. There were three T2 hangars and a single B1 hangar but it was to be some time before they were used for the purpose for which they were intended.

Barkston Heath had been built for Bomber Command's 5 Group and initially it was planned as a satellite of RAF Swinderby and was to house a heavy conversion unit, equipped, most likely, with Stirlings.

The lack of hardened runways, however, meant its early days were spent, as before, as a relief landing ground for Cranwell. In April 1943 part of Cranwell was closed for flying while runways were laid and the displaced aircraft, mainly Airspeed Oxfords, were transferred to Barkston from where they flew regular circuits-and-bumps until Cranwell reopened and they returned to their home airfield.

Barkston had also been the home of 5 Group's Aircrew Commando School, which moved in from Winthorpe in Nottinghamshire and provided fitness and evasion training for 5 Group air crew before they were posted to HCUs. This particular unit remained at Barkston until March 1943 when it was moved to Morton Hall, near Swinderby, the headquarters of 5 Group.

The departure of the Cranwell Oxfords saw a temporary end to flying at Barkston while concrete runways were laid and it was not to officially reopen until January 1944 by which time the airfield had been allocated to the United States 9th Army Air Force.

Planning for the coming invasion of France was by then well under way and from the outset it was intended that part of the assault would be from the air.

The 9th Army Air Force had responsibility for transport and it was its 52nd Troop Carrier Wing which took responsibility for Barkston. It assigned the 61st Troop Carrier Group, then stationed in Sicily, to Barkston and early in February 1944 its four squadrons, 14, 15, 3 and 59, began arriving with their C47s, the superb aircraft the RAF operated as the Dakota.

The 61st was commanded by Colonel Willis W. Mitchell, a forceful leader, who quickly began putting his squadrons through their paces, training them for the task which lay ahead of them. The arrival of the Americans brought major changes at Barkston Heath. Four more T2 hangars were erected by the arrow-straight Ermine Street, which ran alongside the airfield. Those hangars, which are still there today, were needed to accommodate the C47s and to erect and store Horsa and Hamilcar gliders.

Colonel Mitchell was keen to build good relations with the people of Lincolnshire and, although his command was to be a relatively brief one at Barkston, it is still remembered with some affection in the nearby villages. Regular visits were organised to the airfield for local residents and, as almost everywhere else in Britain where US forces were stationed, the generosity of the Americans was astonishing.

A little over a week before D-Day the 52nd TCW mounted a public demonstration of its capabilities. The troops it had been allocated to carry to Normandy were the 507th Parachute Infantry, 101st Airborne, who had been quartered for some time on the Players tobacco sports field in Nottingham where their natural generosity and ample supplies of everything the British were starved of guaranteed them a happy stay. They arrived at Barkston Heath for the first time on 1st and 2nd June and many watched with interest on 3rd June as teams of ground crew swarmed over the C47s, painting broad black and white 'invasion' stripes around the fuselages and wings.

It was soon after 22.00 hours on 5th June that the first of the heavily-laden paratroopers began climbing on board the 72 C47s lined up at Barkston Heath and at eight minutes before midnight the first aircraft, flown appropriately by Colonel Mitchell, lifted off from the Lincolnshire airfield. The invasion was under way. The four squadrons carried a total of 1,167 paratroops to Drop Zone T, close to the Normandy village of Ste Mère-Eglise. One of the aircraft was shot down by light flak over Normandy, another six were damaged, including the aircraft flown by Mitchell who was wounded by shrapnel. All the damaged aircraft made it back to Barkston, where the first aircraft touched down at 4.15 am on D-Day.

The following day 52 aircraft flew from Barkston to drop supplies to the American troops. It was, by necessity, a low-level operation and no fewer than 20 aircraft were damaged by the light flak guns with which most German army units were equipped. Three of the aircraft later ditched in the Channel, their crews picked up by the network of rescue craft which extended from the beaches right up to the English coast.

During the summer the Americans at Barkston repaired the damage to their C47s and continued their training. And, as the Allies broke out of the Normandy bridgehead, another mission was found for them. In September the greatest airborne assault in history took place to capture the Rhine bridges ahead of the advancing Allies and Barkston Heath was to play a key role in the operation.

The 61st TCG at Barkston and the 314th TCG at Saltby, just over the county border in Leicestershire, were tasked to carry the first lift of the British paratroops whose mission it was to seize the bridge at Arnhem. The 71 C47s which the 61st had available were to carry 1,166 men, including the 1st Battalion of the 1st Airborne Division along with the divisional and brigade headquarters elements, Royal Engineers, a field ambulance unit, and other units for the attack on the last of the bridges needed to break across the Rhine.

The 1st Battalion included some of the British Army's most experienced and seasoned paratroops, men who had already seen service in Tunisia. They were led by Lieutenant Colonel David Dobie

Members of the 1st Parachute Battalion at Barkston Heath on 9th September 1944 shortly before take-off for Arnhem. (Humberside APS via Peter Green)

and, before arriving at Barkston, had been based in nearby Bourne.

The aircraft began taking off from Barkston at 11.20 on the morning of 17th September 1944, just a minute after the first C47 had lifted off from Saltby. By 11.30 all 143 aircraft from both airfields were airborne and climbing to their assembly point over March in Cambridgeshire. There they were joined by other elements which made up the air armada before crossing the coast at Aldeburgh in Suffolk where they were joined by the aircraft and gliders which had taken off from airfields in the south of England. Flying at just 1,500 feet, the aircraft presented an awesome sight, even to those used to seeing large numbers of aircraft flying over Britain's east coast.

The Barkston aircraft all dropped their paras according to schedule and returned to Lincolnshire without loss. It is interesting to note that the men carried were involved in the thick of the fighting which was to take place in and around the town of Arnhem over the next nine days. Dobie was captured and then escaped from the Germans before swimming the Rhine to help arrange the escape of many of his men.

Over the next few days the Barkston C47s flew 158 sorties in support of Operation Market Garden, this time towing gliders carrying equipment and reinforcements for the US 81st and 101st Airborne around Nijmegen. Four of the Barkston aircraft were shot down.

The 61st spent much of its remaining six months at Barkston Heath flying supplies into France and later Belgium, with some of its aircraft converted to carry fuel. It finally left early in March 1945, moving to a new airfield in France. The group was immediately replaced by the 349th Troop Carrier Group, which flew Curtis C46s. It was commanded by Colonel Leonard Barrow Jnr who, at 28, was one of the youngest commanding officers in the 9th AAF.

They were to stay at Barkston for just two months. The war had now ended and the need for large fleets of transport aircraft was diminishing. Barkston was officially returned to the RAF on 1st June 1945 and, after a short period as a training centre for RAF Regiment personnel, it was closed. The RAF, however, decided to retain the airfield and its hangars were used to store equipment. In 1954 it reopened in its original role, as a relief landing ground for RAF Cranwell.

What remains of Folkingham airfield can be found just off the A15 between the villages of Folkingham and Aslackby. It was first used for military purposes in 1940 when a number of fields were requisitioned by the Air Ministry and pressed into use as a decoy airfield. It came complete with half a dozen dummy Battles and a few scattered buildings to make it look real from the air. There are records showing that the airfield was bombed on a number of occasions, usually by single aircraft looking for the scattering of real airfields which then existed in Lincolnshire.

It was in August 1942 that the Ministry decided that the time for pretence at Folkingham was over and went ahead with plans to build a standard-pattern bomber airfield on the site, complete with hardened runways and the usual three hangars. But, between that decision and the completion of the airfield in the autumn of 1943, things had changed. Plans were being drawn up for the invasion and Folkingham was one of the airfields chosen for use by the Allied airborne forces. It was allocated to the US 9th Army Air Force which, in turn, made it the responsibility of the 52nd Troop Carrier Wing. As Air Station 484, it was allocated to the 313th Troop Carrier Group, which comprised 29, 47, 48 and 49 Squadrons, operating a total of 70 C47s.

The airfield was officially opened on 5th February 1944 and the Group, which was under the command of Colonel James Roberts, began arriving the following week from airfields in Sicily.

All the aircraft and squadron personnel were in place by 5th March and from that point on there was a concentrated programme of training to prepare the 313th for the role it was to play in the D-Day operations.

41

Its task was to carry the 508th Parachute Infantry, part of the American 82nd Airborne, to Normandy, more specifically to a drop zone three miles from Ste Mère-Eglise.

Take off was at 23.40 on 5th June and at 2 am on D-Day, the first of the 1,181 paratroops the C47s had carried from Lincolnshire, began landing in Normandy. The route determined for the Folkingham aircraft took the C47s low over known flak concentrations. It was the price which had to be paid for getting the 82nd Airborne men into place on time. Three of the aircraft were shot down and at least another 20 damaged, but the paratroopers were landed in the right place and at the right time thanks to the skill and determination of the C47 crews. For its work on D-Day, the 313th was later awarded a Distinguished Unit Citation — effectively, a medal for the entire group.

Their work, however, was not finished and the following day they were back over France in an effort to drop supplies to the paratroopers. Again, a number of aircraft were damaged while bad weather meant that all the supplies did not get to the men who needed them.

It was the 82nd Airborne which were to be Folkingham's passengers again later in the year when the 313th carried paratroops to Nijmegen.

Originally, Folkingham was to have been one of the 'first-lift' airfields for the British 1st Airborne. But this role was later given to the 314th TCG at Saltby and, instead, the 313th carried American troops for their part in Operation Market Garden, joining other groups from Cottesmore in Leicestershire and Spanhoe, near Northampton.

It was a faultless operation by the American troop carrier groups, although the 313th was to lose four aircraft in resupply drops in the days to come. In all, it flew 303 sorties during the Nijmegen operation, a quarter of which involved towing gliders to the battlefield.

For the remainder of its stay at Folkingham, the 313th was involved in resupply and medical evacuation flights from recently liberated areas of France, Belgium and Holland. It remained at Folkingham until the end of February 1945 when, in common with other troop carrier groups, it was moved to France.

There were to be no further American occupants at Folkingham, much to the dismay of some of the local inhabitants who, after an uncertain beginning, had come to like having the well-paid, well-dressed and, in the main, well-mannered young Americans in their community. Once the Americans had gone, the RAF moved in for the first time since the days when the site was occupied only by dummy aircraft. Like Barkston, it became a training depot for the RAF Regiment and, like Barkston, it did not retain this role for long. The last of the trainees moved out in May 1946 and the station closed a month later.

The redundant airfield was used in the late 1940s and early 1950s for the trials and development of the BRM racing cars, which were built a few miles away down the A15 in Bourne.

Folkingham reopened as one of the string of Thor missile bases across Lincolnshire in 1959, large concrete bunkers being built for the three ballistic missiles the airfield held. This was at the height of the Cold War and, like all other military establishments in Britain, Folkingham reached a high state of readiness at the time of the Cuban missile crisis. The missiles, which were manned by 223 Squadron, were removed in 1963, much to the relief of most of those who lived in the area. Within four years virtually all the land was back in the hands of local farmers and over the years most of what comprised Air Station 484 has disappeared.

The first of the Lincolnshire airfields to be occupied by the 9th Army Air Force was the newly-built North Witham, just off the A1, south of Grantham. It was a virgin site when the airfield contractors moved in during November 1942 to build a standard-pattern bomber airfield. It was only a mile or so away from the RAF's Maintenance Unit at South Witham, which was to become one of the biggest bomb dumps in England.

Work finished in the autumn of 1943 by which time it had already been decided to allocate North Witham to the Americans for their airborne transport units. As such, it became Air Station 79 and an advance party from the 9th AAF Support Command arrived in December 1943 to begin the task of opening up the airfield. Apart from operating transport aircraft, North Witham was also to become a Tactical Air Depot, the American equivalent of an RAF Maintenance Unit. It would be the depot's task to prepare new aircraft for squadron service, stockpile and supply spares to its feeder units, and carry out major servicing of aircraft.

North Witham also had a key operational role to play in the forthcoming invasion. It was to become the base for the 9th AAF's Troop Carrier Group's pathfinders, an elite force who would be dropped ahead of the main body of paratroopers to find and identify drop zones and set up beacons for the airborne forces to follow.

The men selected for this task had already been chosen and had begun their training at Cottesmore, just across the boundary in the old county of Rutland. They were moved to North Witham in March 1944, putting a further strain on the facilities and accommodation there, where the airfield was already staffed by 75 officers and 1,256 men of the 33rd and 85th (later renumbered 29th) Air Depot Groups. Much to their chagrin, many of the Air Depot Group personnel were moved out of their hutted accommodation into tents on the northern edge of the airfield to make way for the newcomers. Despite being an almost new airfield, facilities at North Witham were rudimentary and the strain was beginning to show by April, by which time the airfield was occupied by 3,600 USAAF and Army personnel plus a detachment of 86 men from the RAF.

The airfield had been built with just two T2 hangars. During the spring of 1944 a further six hangars were erected, with one being taken over by the Pathfinder units for the training of small groups of men.

On 5th June North Witham became the first airfield to mount an operation in support of the coming invasion when 20 C47s took off soon after 21.30 hours heading for Normandy, the first aircraft being flown by Lieutenant Colonel Joel Crouch, Commandant of the Pathfinder School. The aircraft carried 200 troops drawn from both the 82nd and 101st Airborne Divisions and they began landing at just 15 minutes after midnight on 6th June. All but one of the C47s returned safely to North Witham.

During the summer of 1944 the airfield continued to fulfil its supply and maintenance role while the Pathfinder School trained elements of the 1st Independent Polish Airborne Brigade before the school was moved to Hampshire.

The Allied advance through France and Belgium in the late summer and autumn of 1944 led to the capture of numerous airfields, from which better support could be provided than the more distant airfields in eastern England. The Americans began moving out of North Witham in December 1944 and they had gone completely within three months when the airfield was handed back to the RAF. It was to spend another year as an RAF Maintenance Depot, its runways and buildings being used to store everything from unused bombs to redundant ambulances before it finally closed in 1948.

Today what remains at North Witham can be glimpsed through the trees of the new Twyford Forest planted by the Forestry Commission. There is precious little else left to record the vital part this airfield played in the success of the D-Day operation.

4
BINBROOK

To many people who grew up in north Lincolnshire in the post-war years Binbrook was the Royal Air Force. The airfield, perched high on top of the Wolds with views across the Humber estuary and out into the North Sea, was the home of a succession of Lancaster, Lincoln, Javelin, Canberra and finally Lightning squadrons, all visible reminders of the county's aviation history.

Now Binbrook is closed. Its green hangars are still visible for miles around, its housing areas have been turned into a new 'village'. Where once engine and radar mechanics worked, cottage industries turn out bird tables and wrought iron gates.

Fifty years or so ago it was all so different. Binbrook was still unfinished when the war broke out, yet by June 1940 had become the first airfield in Lincolnshire to host elements of Bomber Command's 1 Group. It became one of the biggest Wellington bases in the country and was later home to the premier bombing squadron in the Royal Australian Air Force, which flew more Lancaster sorties and dropped a greater tonnage of bombs than any other unit in Bomber Command. It also suffered some of the heaviest losses.

Binbrook was one of the chain of pre-war airfields planned as part of the expansion scheme and was among the last to be started. It was still far from finished when the airfield formally opened in June 1940, when the advance elements of 12 and 142 Squadrons arrived with their Fairey Battles. Both had been part of the Advance Air Striking Force which had been sent to France in 1939 only to be almost shot out of the sky by the Luftwaffe in the May blitzkreig. The Battles had proved hopelessly inadequate in France, yet they had to remain in front-line service until the arrival of bigger and better aircraft.

The Battles were quickly put to work, flying patrols over the North Sea and along the East Coast. It was one of these which led to the loss of the first of 277 aircraft to be shot down over the next five years while flying from Binbrook. Unfortunately, the Battle lost was shot down by a Lincolnshire-based Spitfire while flying in the Mablethorpe area. The three-man crew were later buried with full military honours in Binbrook churchyard.

At the height of the invasion scare, Binbrook's squadrons were detached to the south from where they carried out attacks on barges massed in French, Dutch and Belgian ports. They returned in mid-September by which time construction work at Binbrook was almost complete. There were, however, serious problems with the airfield, so serious that it was to be another seven months before it could begin to play an effective part in the bombing war.

Although it is built on top of the Wolds, the airfield itself lays in a natural 'saucer' and, even in the summer of 1940, the grass runways became unusable after only moderate rain. The problems increased dramatically in that first winter, particularly when 12 and 142 Squadrons happily exchanged their Battles for Merlin-engined Wellington MkIIs. The first Wimpeys arrived in November and by early 1941 both squadrons were re-equipped. But the marshy condition of the airfield meant it was almost impossible to take off with any appreciable bomb load. Conditions became so bad that in March one

Flt Sgt Wheeldon and his 12 Squadron crew pose beside their Wellington in 1941. (G R Wheeldon via Peter Green)

Wellington sank several feet into the Binbrook mud.

The spring brought better conditions and on 9th April 1941 12 Squadron was able to send four of its Wellingtons to Kiel. One, piloted by the squadron commanding officer, Wing Commander Blackden, failed to return. His was to be the first of many empty dispersals in the years to come.

By now Binbrook was playing a key role in the bombing campaign, which was beginning to gain momentum. The two squadrons were able to send 10, 12, 14 or 15 aircraft a night to raid distant targets. These were the days before bomber streams, when aircraft headed off independently, choosing their own routes to and from the targets. These were also the days before the German defences became the formidable hurdle future bomber crews would have to overcome. Losses did occur, but the weather, darkness and lack of navigational aids were equally serious problems facing the Wellington crews at Binbrook.

In September 1941 the Binbrook squadrons attacked Stettin, their longest trip yet. It involved flying to Mildenhall in Suffolk before refuelling for the long haul to the Baltic coast and back, an eight-hour flight for the Wellingtons.

In the autumn of 1941 Binbrook took over the new airfield at

Bombing up a 12 Squadron Wellington in the summer of 1941. (Via Stuart Scott)

Waltham, just outside Grimsby, as a satellite. It had paved runways and meant that heavily-laden Wellingtons could take off in just about any weather conditions. 142 Squadron moved to Waltham in November, their place at Binbrook taken by the 1 Group Target Towing Flight, with its Lysanders. Later the Flight, by now renumbered 1481 Target Towing and Gunnery Flight, acquired four Whitleys and a Wellington, and added air gunnery training to its role. These aircraft, although intended purely for training, were pressed into use by Binbrook at the end of May 1942 when the station and its satellite at Waltham provided 53 of the 1,047 aircraft which attacked Cologne in the first 1,000-bomber raid of the war.

Earlier in the year 12 Squadron at Binbrook had been the first Wellington squadron in the RAF to drop the 4,000lb blast bomb, known to all as a 'cookie', in an attack on Hamburg. Six aircraft were specially modified for the raid and, in one aircraft at least, the bomb-aimer actually sat on the bomb during take-off. In the event, Hamburg was cloud-covered and the Wellingtons dropped their cookies on the port of Emden with some success. It was not long before the cookie became a standard part of the bomb load of most Bomber Command heavies for their area attacks on German cities. The remainder of the bomb load was usually made up of canisters of incendiaries, the idea being that the cookie would blow off the roofs of buildings which would then be left at the mercy of the incendiaries. It proved to be a deadly combination and was directly responsible for the firestorms which destroyed Hamburg and later Dresden.

Another new 'weapon' dropped by 12 Squadron's Wellingtons proved not to be successful. 'Razzle' was the name given to strips of celluloid containing phosphorus-impregnated cotton wool. They were dropped over heavily-wooded areas of Germany in the hope that the phosphorus would ignite, set fire to the celluloid and, hopefully, the surrounding vegetation. It was a comic-book idea of how to wage war and there is no evidence that it did more than disturb a few Black Forest squirrels. But, laughable though it may seem today, it ought to be remembered that many young men risked their lives to drop Razzle.

Another bizarre use found for the Wellingtons of 12 Squadron in the summer of 1942 concerned the Dieppe raid which, apart from the losses sustained by the army, cost the RAF 100 aircraft. On 11th June 16 aircraft from 12 Squadron were sent to Thruxton in Hampshire where, two days later, the crews found large holes had been cut in the fuselage floor and then covered in two semi-circular flaps. It soon transpired they were being pressed into use as paratroop transports, as later exercises over Salisbury Plain were to prove. Each of the Wimpeys carried ten soldiers and they were briefed to drop paras onto a big coastal battery which commanded the beaches at Dieppe. Then the raid was postponed and in the interim the planners had a change of mind and 12 Squadron's Wellingtons returned to Binbrook. When the raid did take place the paras' place was taken by sea-borne commandos.

In the meantime 12 Squadron had resumed its work over the Ruhr and of the 16 aircraft sent to Thruxton, only four still survived. The summer of 1942 was a terrible period for Binbrook. Twelve aircraft were lost in July and the following month saw the airfield's worst night of the war when nine Wellingtons, five of them from 142 Squadron, were lost in a raid on Kassel. September saw the two squadrons lose another 17 aircraft. The only thing which stopped the attrition was a decision by the Air Ministry to lay paved runways at Binbrook. 12 Squadron moved to Wickenby, 142 left Waltham for the Middle East and 1481 Flight moved to Blyton.

Flying stopped at the airfield until the following spring when Binbrook was allocated to 460 Squadron (RAAF), which had been formed a year earlier within 1 Group and had operated from Breighton in East Yorkshire. Like 103 Squadron at Elsham, it had been included in the Wellington squadrons to convert to Halifaxes but the order was cancelled and it was re-equipped with Lancasters.

The squadron's chosen method of transfer from Breighton to Binbrook was a reflection of its extrovert nature – by Horsa glider. All the ground crew were given the option of taking the train or the glider to Binbrook. Remarkably, 868 of them took the second option!

Their arrival was greeted initially with some reservation by the people of Binbrook. At least one child mistook the blonde Australian newcomers with their strange uniforms and even stranger way of talking for Germans and rushed home to tell her mother the invasion had begun! But it was to be the start of a long and happy association between the men of 460 and the villagers of Binbrook, a bond which still exists today. The squadron was to lose more than 800 aircrew in the following two years when it suffered one of the highest casualty rates in Bomber Command.

460 made its bow from Binbrook with the traditional mining trip. Its first bombing operation was an attack on Dortmund, which cost the squadron two Lancasters. This was the summer of the Battle of the Ruhr and 460 was to lose 15 of its Lancasters. Two more Lancasters were destroyed in an airfield accident in July when an entire bomb load fell from a Lancaster which had just been prepared for a raid on

Cologne. The incendiaries caught fire and the heat quickly detonated a number of the high explosive bombs, setting fire to two other Lancasters and damaging six more. One of the burning Lancasters was destroyed but the fire on the second was extinguished by the squadron commanding officer, Wing Commander Martin, and Flight Sergeant Kan. The station commander, Group Captain Hughie Edwards, an Australian who had won the Victoria Cross two years earlier while flying with 2 Group, ordered the unexploded bombs to be moved to allow 17 other Lancasters to take off for Cologne.

Four aircraft were lost in two consecutive Ruhr raids but the crew of one Binbrook Lancaster, hit by flak over Wuppertal, all managed to bale out. The rear gunner was injured and two other crew members, one of them British, were quickly picked up. But the other four, including the pilot, Sergeant George Stooke, made good their escape and were eventually picked up by the French resistance only to be discovered hiding in Paris by the Gestapo.

460 lost three Lancasters and with them the lives of 21 young men in the Hamburg raids, when 'window', thin strips of radar-blinding aluminium foil, was used to great effect. Great store was placed by all in Bomber Command on the use of window, not least by the Commander in Chief himself, Air Chief Marshal Arthur Harris, who visited Binbrook during August and saw a demonstration of window dropping.

Mid-August of 1943 coincided with a period of full moon, conditions highly unfavourable for bomber attacks on heavily defended targets. This was traditionally the time for a 'stand-down' and the Australians at Binbrook planned to mark it with a huge party to celebrate the squadron's 1,000th Lancaster sortie. It was to be held in the dance hall on Cleethorpes Pier and an 'advance party' had already left on the nine mile journey when the squadron was put on stand-by for ops. Service police, aided by the local constabulary in Cleethorpes, rounded up the airmen who had already begun celebrating and returned them immediately to Binbrook, where the squadron was about to be briefed for the raid on the rocket research establishment at Peenemunde. That night Binbrook provided 24 aircraft for the attacking force, a figure only surpassed by 12 Squadron, now at Wickenby (which put up 25 aircraft). The Binbrook Lancasters all bombed and returned safely and the night of 18th August saw one of the most riotous parties of the year on Cleethorpes Pier, so riotous in fact that the then Mayor of the Borough wrote to Wing Commander Edwards to tell him his men were no longer welcome in the town!

In the late autumn Binbrook became the headquarters of 12 Base, with responsibility for sub-stations at Waltham and Kelstern. The base commander was Air Commodore Arthur Wray, a First World War veteran who walked with the aid of a stick and liked nothing better than flying with his crews. Though officially barred from operations, he would often appear in 'mufti' at dispersals and beg a ride in a Lancaster with the crews ordered not to breathe a word about it.

If the Ruhr was bad for Binbrook, what became known as the Battle of Berlin was even worse. 460 Squadron was to fly more sorties, 385, than any other squadron in Bomber Command and to suffer the highest casualty rate in 1 Group – 23 aircraft shot down, five crashed, 135 men killed.

The worst night of the battle came on 2nd/3rd December 1943 when 460 lost five of its Lancasters. Among the 30 men who died that night were two war correspondents, Nordahl Greig of the *Daily Mail* and Norman Stockton, of the *Australian Associated News*. They were among four war correspondents given permission to fly to Berlin that night by Harris. The other two were Americans Ed Murrow and Lowell Bennett, who both flew with 50 Squadron at Skellingthorpe. Murrow was the only one to return.

One of the 460 Squadron casualties in the Berlin raids was Flying Officer F. A. Randall, an Australian pilot whose aircraft was badly damaged by a fighter over the German capital on the night of 3rd/4th September. One of his crew baled out almost immediately and Randall ordered the rest out as they were crossing Denmark. One disappeared in the sea, two others were picked up by the Germans in Denmark, another escaped by boat from Denmark, while Randall and one of his gunners were rescued from the sea by a Swedish boat. After being landed in Sweden he was quickly repatriated and returned to Binbrook where he picked up a new crew and began flying again. He was to die on the night of 16/17th December when his Lancaster crashed into a bomb dump at Market Stainton, near Louth, on his return from Berlin.

There was little respite even after the Berlin raids ended. Three 460 Squadron Lancasters went down on the disastrous Nuremberg raid, one of them piloted by one of the squadron's flight commanders, Squadron Leader Utz, who was on the 18th operation of his second tour. One of his crew did manage to bale out after his Lancaster was attacked by a fighter near Fulda, one of only four men to survive from the three aircraft lost. Even worse came six weeks later when the squadron lost five aircraft in the debacle over Mailly-le-Camp.

Soon after this, Binbrook was visited by the Australian Prime

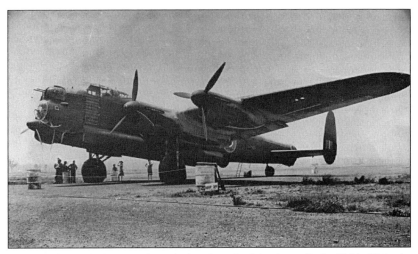

460 Squadron's G-George, pictured after it arrived in Australia in 1944. (Grimsby Evening Telegraph)

Minister, Mr John Curtin, who was in Britain on a morale-boosting visit for Australians serving here. While he was at Binbrook he was shown over the squadron's veteran G-George, which by then had completed 90 trips with the squadron. The aircraft was flown to Australia in October 1944 and today is preserved in the Australian War Memorial Museum in Canberra. It is interesting to note that no other Lancaster which served with 460 Squadron exceeded 90 operations, a measure of the loss rate the squadron suffered while flying from Binbrook.

Binbrook became the home of 1 Group's own Pathfinder unit in the late spring of 1944. The 1 Group Special Duties Flight was made up of six Lancasters and highly-experienced crews drawn from Binbrook itself, Waltham, Ludford, Elsham, Wickenby and Kelstern. It was under the command of Squadron Leader Bill Breakspear and flew operationally for the first time on 30th April when it led over 100 1 Group Lancasters in a successful raid on Maintenon. It operated until early August by which time it had played a key role in the group's operations, particularly against French targets.

Breakspear was a highly respected airman at Binbrook and, in his excellent book *Massacre Over The Marne*, Oliver Clutton-Brock recounts a delightful story about an acrimonious meeting Breakspear had with Harris after the Mailly-le-Camp raid, which the squadron leader had warned would be suicide in the moonlit conditions predicted. He stormed out of the meeting without saluting, only to be called back by Harris who demanded: 'Don't you salute Air Chief Marshals?' Breakspear responded: 'Not stupid ones, sir!'

The winter of 1944 and spring of 1945 saw 460 in action almost continuously and, despite mounting losses, morale remained high. An indication of this came one night as the squadron's aircraft taxied out for a raid on the Ruhr. One suffered engine problems soon after it left its dispersal. The crew pulled it off the perimeter track, climbed out and hitched a lift in a passing lorry to 460's spare Lancaster and managed to take off in time to join the raid.

460 took part in the final raid of the war, the daylight attack on Berchtesgaden, Hitler's Bavarian headquarters. Just two of the 359 Lincolnshire-based Lancasters were lost, including one flown by Pilot Officer Payne from 460 Squadron. He and the other six men in the Lancaster were the final casualties in what had been a long and costly war for RAF Binbrook.

5

BLYTON, SANDTOFT AND STURGATE

There are many who believe the unsung heroes of Bomber Command were those who trained the crews to operate heavy bombers.

After their initial training, airmen were sent to Operational Training Units where the nucleus of the bomber crew was formed and learned to work together, mainly on obsolete aircraft which had passed out of squadron service. In the early days heavy conversion was carried out at squadron level but, as pressure grew for better trained crews, conversion units were set up to bring crews up to standard on four-engined aircraft. Until the formation of 7 Group late in the war, which had specific responsibility for training, the HCUs were the responsibility of the groups. They were staffed largely by experienced aircrew who acted as instructors as a means of 'resting' between operational tours. In reality, instructing could prove to be just as dangerous as operational flying, mixing as it did well-used aircraft and inexperienced hands.

In 1 Group training was centred on RAF Lindholme in South Yorkshire, with additional HCUs located on satellite airfields, including Blyton and Sandtoft.

Blyton was an agricultural village which lay five miles north of Gainsborough on the Scunthorpe road. The airfield was built on land north-east of the village and was completed late in 1942. It was pressed into use long before the contractors had finished work. 18 (Polish) Operational Training Unit moved to Blyton in the late summer of 1942 soon after work on the runways had been completed and began training crews for the Polish squadrons then flying with 1 Group. They operated Wellingtons from the airfield, the same aircraft used by the operational squadrons, so no further transition was required. They shared the spartan conditions at the half-finished airfield for a few weeks with 1481 Bomber Gunnery Flight, which moved in from Binbrook with a mixed bag of aircraft, including at least one Whitley along with some Martinets and Lysanders.

Early in November 1942 the airfield officially opened and 199 Squadron was reformed at Blyton, taking over Wellingtons released by 12 Squadron at Wickenby, which was re-equipping with Lancasters. It operated for the first time on the night of 6/7th December when six aircraft took part in an unsuccessful attack on Mannheim.

199, which had served briefly at Harpswell, close to Hemswell, in the First World War, flew a number of bombing and mining operations from Blyton before it moved to Ingham in February 1943. Its place was taken by 1662 HCU, which was equipped with a mixture of Manchesters, Halifaxes and a small number of Lancasters. The Lancasters were mainly straight from the factory, but the remainder of 1662's aircraft were squadron hand-me-downs and it wasn't long before the remains of them began littering the Lincolnshire countryside.

Flying at Blyton went on almost around the clock as the pressure was on for new crews to fill the gaps caused by battle losses on 1 Group squadrons. The Lancasters, too, were needed by the operational squadrons and Blyton's were reformed into B-Flight of the 1 Group Lancaster Finishing School and moved the few miles to Hemswell late in 1943, leaving 1662 HCU with 32 of the unloved Halifaxes, an aircraft which was never as easy to fly as the Lancaster and could prove fatally unforgiving in the wrong hands.

Losses were frighteningly high for a training unit: eight aircraft were written off in crashes in a matter of a few weeks in the spring of 1944 while at least one more, with the experienced Wing Commander Tait on board, disappeared over the North Sea on a training flight.

Blyton itself was ill-equipped to handle the large number of service personnel stationed there at any one time. Conditions in some of the accommodation sites were primitive, with no electricity or running water, while the runways and technical sites were in a constant state of repair from a combination of heavy use and poor construction. During the summer of 1944 Blyton housed some 1,600 men and women and its throughput reached a peak in August that year when 44 crews were trained.

Blyton was transferred along with other training airfields in Lincolnshire to 7 Group in November 1944 as part of the reorganisation of Bomber Command, but its role continued unchanged.

There were now sufficient Lancasters to meet Bomber Command's

Happy landing for a Halifax. But they were not always easy machines to master, as many of those who flew with HCUs at Blyton and Sandtoft will remember.

operational requirements and gradually they were reintroduced into 1662 HCU, a move which coincided with the running down of the Lancaster Finishing School at Hemswell. Some Halifaxes did remain with 1662, however, until it was finally disbanded in April 1945.

Blyton was used by No 7 Aircrew Holding Unit and during the summer and autumn of 1945 some 5,000 men passed through it before being demobbed. The airfield itself was closed soon after the war, only to be reopened briefly in the early 1950s as a relief landing ground for training units at Finningley. Today it has almost completely reverted to agriculture, although a few brick buildings and some of the concrete perimeter tracks and dispersals remain.

Sandtoft, which now stands alongside the busy M180 motorway just across the Lincolnshire boundary from South Yorkshire, was built as a bomber airfield and officially opened in December 1943. But it was to be another two months before it received aircraft of its own, 34 Halifaxes of 1667 Heavy Conversion Unit from Faldingworth, near Market Rasen. 1667 had operated from there, initially with a mixture of Lancasters and Halifaxes, from August 1943 but had moved out to make way for 300 (Polish) Squadron, which was moving from the grass runways at Ingham and exchanging its Wellingtons (the last in operational service in Bomber Command) for Lancasters. Sandtoft lay only a few miles from its base headquarters at Lindholme and, with Blyton only 15 miles away across the Trent, it made sense to bring together 1 Group's training airfields in the north-east corner of Lincolnshire.

Stories still abound in the Isle of Axholme villages about the pilots who flew their Halifaxes low across the rich farmland and the even more daring ones who skimmed the Trent. And there are those who claim to have seen a Halifax fly under the road and rail bridge at Keadby, but nothing exists in the records of 1667 to substantiate this. Certainly, a number of Halifaxes were left embedded in the rich soil of the Isle. One of the first to go down was a Halifax from 1667 at Haxey less than a fortnight after the unit arrived. After that crashes came at such regular intervals that the airfield was dubbed 'Prangtoft' by those who served there. The records show, in fact, that most of the villages in the Isle, including Crowle, Owston Ferry, Epworth, Belton and Westwoodside, all had their 'own' crashes from Sandtoft.

During the summer of 1944 a fourth flight was formed at Sandtoft

A new crew at 1667 HCU at Sandtoft early in 1944. They are (left to right) Vernon Wilkes (bomb aimer), Gordon Markes (pilot), Bill Mann RAAF (navigator), Frank Petch RAAF, (wireless operator), Ken Brotherhood (flight engineer), Danny Driscoll (rear gunner), Les Buckell (mid-upper gunner). (Vernon Wilkes)

and was used to train 1 Group instructors in an attempt to standardise the quality of training among the various conversion units.

Like Blyton, Sandtoft was transferred to 7 Group, but its work continued unabated. It, too, began to exchange its Halifaxes for Lancasters and these were still in service when the war came to an end. Flying continued until the autumn when 1667 was disbanded and Sandtoft closed.

Today limited private flying still continues from Sandtoft, where much of the old airfield is used for light industrial purposes, including the storage of cars imported through the Humber ports.

A third airfield used for limited training purposes towards the end of the war was Sturgate, which was one of the last Lincolnshire airfields to be built. It was opened as a 1 Group airfield at the end of March 1944 but there was no immediate use for it. Its runways were used by 1 LFS at Hemswell and it was to be September of that year before it received its first resident unit, 1520 Beam Approach Flight, which brought its Airspeed Oxfords from Leconfield in East Yorkshire. No 1 Group Aircrew School was moved in from Lindholme and remained there until the end of the war. It was not, in fact, until the war was over that Sturgate received its first operational squadrons, 50 and 61, which later moved to Waddington after the fitting of Rose turrets made in nearby Gainsborough.

Curiously, Sturgate was one of the airfields selected for the installation of FIDO (also see the chapters on Fiskerton, Ludford and Metheringham). Work started on the installation some months before the airfield was completed, a two and three-quarter mile fuel pipeline being laid from rail sidings near the village of Lea.

The fog dispersal equipment was first used on 21st December 1944 when ten Lancasters from 625 Squadron at Kelstern landed there on their return from an attack on Pölitz. Conditions were very bad indeed and the records show that over 138,000 gallons of fuel were consumed in the two hours in which FIDO was lit. The fog persisted and FIDO was lit again on Christmas Eve to allow the 625 Squadron aircraft to take off once again, this particular operation consuming a further 126,000 gallons.

After the war the airfield was used for several years by the United States Air Force, who finally moved out in 1964, ending Sturgate's brief operational history.

6

COLEBY GRANGE AND WELLINGORE

The attractive Lincolnshire Cliff villages of Coleby and Wellingore gave their names to two airfields, both of which were to serve for much of the war as satellites to the fighter airfield at nearby Digby.

Coleby and Wellingore villages stand astride the A607 Lincoln-Grantham road but the airfields were to be found further west, bordering onto the A15 Ermine Street, from where their remains can still just be seen.

Wellingore had been used in the First World War as a relief landing ground for the Royal Naval Air Service station at Cranwell and it was in a similar capacity that both it and neighbouring Coleby Grange were first used in the Second World War.

The site at Coleby was acquired in 1939 and work began on laying out a small airfield. The road between Boothby Graffoe and Metheringham was closed and part of it incorporated in the concrete perimeter track laid around the site. There were no concrete runways but a T1 hangar was constructed across the A15 from the airfield site and eight Blister hangars – canvas covered affairs – erected. Later seven more were to be sited at Coleby. The airfield was named RAF Coleby Grange after a nearby country house, which was to be used to house aircrew soon after it became operational.

It was used briefly by Cranwell and by RAF Waddington as a landing ground before its first Fighter Command occupants, 253 and 264 Squadrons, moved in. Both came from Kirton Lindsey in north Lincolnshire whose own satellite at Hibaldstow was not yet completed, and the latter was to remain at Coleby until mid-September 1940 before moving north again with its Defiant night fighters.

It was the following summer before Coleby received its first permanent squadron, 409 of the Royal Canadian Air Force, which

59

moved in from Digby with Defiants in late July 1941. The squadron, nick-named the Nighthawks, quickly converted to Bristol Beaufighters. The Beaufighter, which had already proved itself a potent night fighter, albeit a difficult one to fly, was fitted with the RAF's new A1 radar and packed a fearsome punch through its nose-mounted guns.

The squadron began to work up on its new aircraft but suffered a set-back early in October when its commanding officer, Wing Commander Petersen was killed when his aircraft crashed. It was the squadron's first fatality and more were to follow. In December two Beaufighters collided over the airfield and a third crashed while attempting to land three days later. Two more were lost in crashes early in 1942.

But by this time the Nighthawks were in business as a fighter unit, the new commanding officer, Wing Commander Davoud shooting down a Dornier 217 over the North Sea. This was followed by a He111 the following March, the first of a series of 'kills' notched up by the squadron, five German aircraft falling to their guns.

409 Squadron remained at Coleby until February 1943 when it was replaced by another Canadian squadron, 410, which moved down from Acklington in Northumberland with its Mosquitos. 410 mixed its defensive duties with a series of intruder operations over occupied Europe, its aircraft being given the job of attacking targets of opportunity and paying particular attention to German night fighter airfields.

410 flew from Coleby until October 1943 when it moved to West Malling in Kent. It was replaced by another Mosquito squadron, 264, but it remained for less than four weeks before leaving. Coleby Grange had now become a transit station, with squadrons moving in and out rapidly. Other occupants at this time included 288 Squadron (Defiants), 68 Squadron (Beaufighters) and 307 (Polish) Squadron, which was flying Mosquitos.

By the autumn of 1944 Fighter Command had no further use for the tiny grass airfield at Coleby Grange and it was transferred to 27 Group as a satellite of 17 Service Flying Training School at Cranwell, which brought its Harvards and Oxfords from Caistor to Coleby at the end of October. They were joined by 1515 BAT Flight which arrived in February 1945 from Peplow with still more Oxfords. And the final arrival at Coleby during its wartime career was 107 Elementary Glider School, which moved in during the spring of 1945 to provide training for Lincolnshire Air Cadet units.

After the war Coleby was to have a further brief operational period when it was used to house a detachment of Thor missiles. These were removed in 1963 and the airfield quickly reverted to agriculture.

Wellingore had been used during the First World War and in the intervening years as a landing ground by aircraft from Cranwell and it was no surprise to people living nearby when contractors moved in during the winter of 1939-40 to carry out some limited expansion work. This involved laying a concrete perimeter track, erecting eight Blister hangars and building a number of pillboxes for airfield defence.

On 9th July 1940 29 Squadron, a fighter unit which has a long association with Lincolnshire, moved in from Digby with its Blenheim night fighters. Among its pilots was Flight Lieutenant Guy Gibson, who had joined the squadron at Digby. He had already completed a tour of operations – 39 sorties in all – with 83 Squadron at Scampton and was one of a number of experienced former bomber pilots to be converted to a night fighter role.

When he arrived the airfield was still known as Wellingore Heath, the name used in the First World War. The officers' mess was in the oak-panelled Wellingore Grange, and it was commanded by Squadron Leader Charles Widdows, an experienced airman who was to survive a crash near Sleaford later in the year in the squadron's first Beaufighter.

It was during the squadron's first few weeks at Wellingore that it was asked to test a novel idea of illuminating German aircraft at night. It was allocated two Fairey Battles to tow powerful flares which were supposed to show up the intruders, which would then be at the mercy of the night fighters. The idea was dropped after two brief sorties which left the fighter pilots almost blinded and nearly resulted in a collision with the flare-towing aircraft. A similar idea, this time using a powerful light mounted in an aircraft's nose, was used with some success in the months to come (see the chapter on Hibaldstow).

Gibson and his wife, Eve, lived in the village pub in Wellingore which, after the life they had been used to, they found very uncomfortable. There was no electricity, the rudimentary toilets were outside and they were certainly not made to feel welcome. The Gibsons soon moved to the neighbouring village of Navenby where they found a comfortable room in the Lion Inn. This, at least, had electricity and the luxury of a hot bath.

They were the lucky ones. Other airmen billeted in Wellingore itself found some resentment amongst villagers to their presence and many billets were cold and uncomfortable. One unfortunate airman was allegedly evicted from his quarters in the village for having the temerity to ask for an extra blanket.

29 Squadron, which had already brought down at least five enemy

aircraft in operations from Wellingore, were beginning to exchange their Blenheims for the new Beaufighters. The first of the new twin-engined Bristol fighters arrived in September and was promptly written off in a heavy landing by the squadron's commanding officer.

Shortly before Christmas, Gibson and his navigator came across a German aircraft, later identified as a Ju88, over the Louth area of Lincolnshire and began to stalk it, using their aircraft's A1 radar. Before they could move in for the kill, the anti-aircraft gunners at Manby opened fire and brought the intruder down. Two days after this the Luftwaffe struck back when another Ju88 shot down one of 29 Squadron's remaining Blenheims in the Wellingore circuit, the aircraft crashing at Leadenham.

Gibson was to be thwarted again early in February 1941 as he tried to shoot down his first German aircraft. Circling Mablethorpe at 10,000 feet, there was near-perfect visibility over a snow-covered Lincolnshire when he was ordered to intercept a raider which had been seen in the mouth of the Humber between Grimsby and Spurn point. Gibson's Beaufighter found the German aircraft but, after an inconclusive engagement, the raider dropped its bombs in the Humber and turned for home.

There were more successes for 29 Squadron in March when Widdows shot down a Ju88 near Hull and Pilot Officer Bramham shot down a Do215 off Skegness. Gibson, however, did not have long to wait for his first 'kill', a He111 which he shot down into the sea close to Skegness pier. The following morning he drove to Skegness and picked up a dinghy from the Heinkel and returned to Wellingore with it as a squadron souvenir.

Soon after this victory, 29 Squadron moved to Kent and, with Digby now officially a Canadian station, Wellingore received its first RCAF squadron, 402, which arrived with its Spitfires, remaining for a little over two months. It was later replaced by another Canadian squadron, 412. Two other Spitfire squadrons, 154 and 81, also had short spells at Wellingore before the end of the year.

There was a new type of aircraft at Wellingore in March 1943 when 613 Squadron arrived with its North American Mustangs. Its job was to provide fighter cover for the Coastal Command strike squadrons at North Coates which it carried out before leaving Wellingore in May, when it was replaced briefly by 349 Squadron, operating Spitfires.

Wellingore's future as a fighter airfield was now in doubt and it was to have only brief operational spells over the next 18 months, control alternating between Digby and Cranwell, which used the airfield's

A Spitfire VB of 402 Squadron undergoing a routine 60-hour inspection in one of Wellingore's Blister hangars late in 1941. (R Jones via Peter Green)

grass strips as a relief landing ground for its huge fleet of training aircraft.

Among the operational squadrons to serve at Wellingore in this period were 416 and 439, which arrived with Hurricanes before leaving for Dyce, Aberdeenshire to re-equip with Typhoons. 402 Squadron had another brief spell at Wellingore in the spring of 1944 before leaving the airfield to the Harvards and Oxfords of 17 SFTS at Cranwell.

After the war the airfield was used briefly to accommodate German prisoners of war before it reverted to agriculture.

7
CONINGSBY

The past and present of the RAF in Lincolnshire are today embodied at RAF Coningsby, one of only two operational airfields left in the county. The past is found in the form of the Battle of Britain Memorial Flight, which has its home in a corner of the Lincolnshire airfield. The present is represented by a Tornado F6 fighter aircraft squadron, operating from an airfield which first opened on 4th November 1940.

During the war, Coningsby was at the very hub of 5 Group's operations from the county. It first saw service as the home for a Hampden squadron. Later it saw the introduction of the Manchester and was the second airfield to receive the new Lancaster bomber only a matter of months later. It was one of the airfields from which 617 Squadron operated and, in the latter stages of the war, was home to 5 Group's own target marking force. Guy Gibson and Leonard Cheshire both commanded squadrons which flew from Coningsby and it is fitting that it should be one of the few airfields to survive the post-Cold War defence cuts.

The Lincolnshire Fens begin at Coningsby. There are no Wolds here to interrupt the view of Boston's famous Stump, ten miles away. In wartime, this was a landscape dotted only with village churches, windmills and the odd historical building, including nearby Tattershall Castle.

Work had begun on what was to be a substantial airfield late in 1937 as part of the second phase of the RAF's expansion in Lincolnshire. The work took four years to complete, with frequent interruptions caused by drainage problems encountered by the contractors. The airfield was built with two large J-type hangars and extensive administration, accommodation and technical buildings, but no hardened runways. These would come later in the war, together with a further expansion of the facilities.

Coningsby's first occupants were to be 106 Squadron, which had been with 5 Group since the beginning of its wartime operations. 106 began arriving on 23rd February 1941 from Finningley, just south of Doncaster. It began operations on the night of 1st/2nd March when five aircraft took part in an attack on Hamburg. Two nights later 106 Squadron went to Hamburg again and this time one of its aircraft failed to return. It was later found to have crashed in Belgium and the four men on board became the first of many to be lost on operations from Coningsby.

A second squadron arrived on 15th March, 97 (Straits Settlement) Squadron, which had begun the war flying Whitleys with 4 Group. It was reformed at Waddington and then moved within a month to Coningsby from where it initially flew the new twin-engined Manchester.

The poor reliability of the Manchester meant that it was 106 which was to bear the brunt of operations from Coningsby during those first few months. The squadron lost some 45 Hampdens on operations before it, too, converted to Manchesters in the spring of 1942. It is interesting to note that such was the unreliability of the Manchester, that 97 Squadron crews occasionally flew 106 Squadron Hampdens on operations and at least two were lost, one when their aircraft plunged into the sea off Plymouth Hoe after hitting the port's balloon barrage while returning from a mining operation to Brest.

106 was to have a harrowing time in 1941 with its Hampdens. On the night of 10/11th April two of the aircraft sent on a small-scale raid on Düsseldorf were lost, both shot down by night fighters over Holland. Today, the eight men from those aircraft lie side by side in the same Dutch cemetery. Fifteen aircraft were lost in July and August alone, the equivalent of the whole squadron wiped out in a matter of weeks. Two Hampdens went on yet another attack on Düsseldorf, two more on the same mining trip to Oslo fjord.

There was a bizarre end to an attack on Karlsruhe for one 106 Squadron crew in October 1941. On the return trip they became disorientated and finally baled out of the aircraft when it ran out of fuel over the mountains of Donegal. They landed safely and were interred by the Irish authorities.

Two Hampdens were lost on near-suicidal daylight raids over northern Germany. The attacks, in December 1941, were both carried out in heavy cloud. In the first attack on Gelsenkirchen, three of the six aircraft sent turned back and only three dropped their bombs, one of these crashing near Oberhausen, killing all four on board. The second raid was aborted, but not before a 106 Squadron aircraft crashed in

Holland. Three of the men on board survived.

Four men from 106 Squadron had one of the most remarkable escapes of all Bomber Command crews. The crew of AE193 were homeward bound from Duisburg in late August, 1941 when both engines failed 40 miles out over the North Sea off the island of Texel. The pilot, Sergeant Lyon, managed to land his aircraft on the sea and there was just time for the crew to scramble into the dinghy before the aircraft sank. For two days the four sergeants endured rough seas, heavy rain, cold and seasickness. Then the weather changed and they had to endure two days under a hot sun as they tried to paddle towards the Dutch coast, using their parachute harnesses as paddles and flying jackets as sails.

Several times they spotted aircraft or ships but no one saw their frantic signals. Two of the men became seriously ill. Finally the dinghy was capsized by a series of big waves and, much to their surprise, the men found they were ashore. But their ordeal was still far from over. With no fresh water and only raw mussels to eat, it was to be another day before they were found by Dutch fishermen who eventually handed them over to the Germans so that the four airmen could receive medical treatment.

97 Squadron was faring little better with its Manchesters at Coningsby. It operated its new aircraft for the first time on the night of 8/9th April 1941 when three joined what was then the largest raid of the war by Bomber Command on Kiel.

The Manchester was beset by technical problems from the start and several were lost in accidents, among them one of the squadron's original aircraft which crashed on take-off at Coningsby when an engine failed. Just as serious as the technical problems was the mistrust crews had in the Manchester. This was compounded in the early hours of 16th May when a signal was picked up from a 97 Squadron aircraft, returning from a raid on Berlin. The pilot gave his position as off the island of Borkum and reported: 'Starboard engine cut, other giving trouble ...' Nothing more was heard from the Manchester. The squadron was also to lose its popular commanding officer, Wing Commander Balsden, in a tragic incident in December 1941. Balsden's Manchester had been damaged by flak during a daylight raid on Brest and the rear gunner badly wounded. Rather than bale out and abandon his gunner, Balsden tried to land back at Coningsby but the Manchester stalled as he was trying to overshoot and crashed on the airfield, killing all eight men on board.

Despite the problems 97 was having with its aircraft, 106 Squadron began re-equipping with the Manchester early in 1942. They had several false starts, with crews aborting missions, before the squadron's first operational sortie in a Manchester was completed on the night of 20th March 1942, Warrant Officer Merralls and his crew successfully planting mines off Kiel. A week later this same aircraft, with a different crew, failed to return from an attack on Lübeck.

106 operated Manchesters for less than three months before it began re-equipping with the infinitely superior Lancaster. 97 Squadron had received the first of its new four-engined heavies on 14th January 1942 but was not to fly them operationally from Coningsby. The airfield was clearly unsuitable for heavy bomber operations and plans were already in hand to move 97 to the newly-completed airfield at nearby Woodhall Spa. Indeed, the runway there was already being used by Coningsby's Hampdens and Manchesters during times of particularly bad weather.

The arrival of the Lancaster had also created training problems for crews used to twin-engined aircraft and 97 formed a heavy conversion flight at Coningsby of two Manchesters and two Lancasters. When 97 Squadron finally moved to Woodhall at the beginning of March, this flight remained behind to continue conversion training. A second conversion flight was formed to retrain 106 Squadron crews before their change to Lancasters in May 1942 and eventually both flights

Telephone switchboard staff at work at Coningsby, 1st June 1942. (Brian Robinson via Peter Green)

moved to Swinderby where they formed the nucleus for the new 1660 Heavy Conversion Unit.

106 Squadron received its first Lancaster at the end of April and was operational within a month, just in time to take part in the first 1,000 bomber raid on Cologne. Its first aircraft off that night was L7579, which was to survive the war before being scrapped in October 1945. Among its pilots during its time with 106 was the squadron's new commanding officer, Wing Commander (acting) Guy Gibson. At just 23, he was the youngest squadron CO in Bomber Command and a man already marked out for great things. Gibson had joined the squadron during its Manchester days and his biography records that during a 30-day period in the late spring of 1942, the squadron took part in 18 raids, including six on consecutive nights.

He flew a Lancaster operationally for the first time on 8/9th July in a raid on Wilhelmshaven when a young Australian pilot officer, Dave Shannon, went with him to gain experience. Shannon, like Gibson, was later to find fame with 617 Squadron. The aircraft he flew was lost a month later over Essen in the hands of a different crew.

Gibson was a somewhat unpopular figure at Coningsby where he was regarded by some as a glory-seeker (his nick-name was 'The Boy Emperor'), but there was no denying his courage. In a special attack mounted by nine aircraft of 106 Squadron on the port of Gdynia where the new German aircraft carrier *Graf Zeppelin* was being fitted out, Gibson made twelve runs over the haze-covered target in an attempt to locate the carrier and drop his special 5,600lb anti-shipping bomb. The *Graf Zeppelin* survived, although it was never to be used, as did all the 106 Squadron Lancasters.

106 Squadron had been the first to drop one of the new 8,000lb blast bombs although the aircraft which carried the weapon to Düsseldorf failed to return. The squadron was now under notice to move to Syerston, but, before it did, took part in an attack on Bremen from which three of its aircraft failed to return, one flown by one of the flight commanders.

The departure of 106 heralded the start of a major construction programme at Coningsby, which included the laying of three runways and the erection of four more hangars. The station was to be closed for operational flying for almost a year but full use was made of its facilities. It became the temporary home for a number of ground schools, including the 5 Group Training School, 5 Group Gee Equipment School and Bomber Command's Field Cookery School. Its runways were also put into use in the spring of 1943 with the arrival of

1514 BAT Flight with its Ansons and Oxfords.

It reopened as an operational bomber airfield at the end of August 1943 and its first occupants were 617 Squadron, which moved from Scampton where flying had ceased for runway laying.

An advance party from 617 arrived at Coningsby on 25th August, with the squadron flying in five days later. At its new home, 617 continued its role as a specialist bombing squadron and its first target following the move was the Dortmund-Ems canal, and in particular a stretch near Greven which was thought to be particularly vulnerable. A first sortie was mounted on 14th September and eight Lancasters left Coningsby armed with 12,000lb high capacity bombs. However, a reconnaissance Mosquito reported bad visibility over the target and the aircraft were recalled. At the time they were flying low over the North Sea and one, flown by Squadron Leader Dave Maltby, crashed, its wing-tip hitting a wave and the big bomber cartwheeling into the water. There were no survivors.

The raid was mounted again the following night, the eight aircraft splitting into groups of four for a low-level approach. Twenty miles from the target one of the group was fired on by light flak. The petrol tank on Squadron Leader George Holden's Lancaster was hit and the aircraft crashed into a farmhouse, its bomb exploding, killing a number of civilians as well as the crew.

Over the target, visibility was poor and although two 12,000lb bombs hit the canal, little visible damage was recorded. The flak defences were formidable and four of the attacking Lancasters were hit and brought down. Several men survived and one evaded capture, returning to England some months later. Among those killed were the six men with whom Gibson had flown on the Dams raid.

Despite the mauling it had taken, 617 was back in action the following night, joining forces with 619 Squadron from Woodhall for an attack on the Antheor viaduct on the French Riviera. It was another failure although, on this occasion, all the aircraft returned. 617 attacked the viaduct again in November and, although hits were observed, it again survived, as did the aircraft although one crashed into the sea on their return flight from North Africa, where they had landed to refuel. Soon afterwards, Leonard Cheshire was appointed 617's commanding officer. He had been commanding officer of a station in 6 Group but was itching to get back to operations and dropped a rank to Wing Commander to join 617.

617 mounted several more raids from Coningsby before it moved in January 1944 to what was to prove its final home of the war years,

Woodhall Spa. It changed places with 619 Squadron which itself was to spend only four months at Coningsby before going to Dunholme Lodge. The change coincided with the formation of 54 Base headquarters at Coningsby, which had Metheringham and Woodhall Spa as its satellite airfields. 1514 BAT Flight also left at this time, moving to Fiskerton, and it was replaced by 61 Squadron, which came from Skellingthorpe.

Both squadrons were to play a role in the final stages of the Battle of Berlin from their new home. 61 lost two Lancasters in a raid on 27/28th January, although four men were rescued from one of the aircraft, which had ditched in the North Sea. Both squadrons were each to lose two more aircraft in Berlin raids and both were to suffer losses in the Nuremberg raid at the end of March. Two of 61's 14 aircraft were shot down and one from 619 crash-landed at Woodbridge in Suffolk after suffering battle damage. The crew survived. 61 lost 14 men killed in their two aircraft with two more being killed after baling out from their damaged aircraft over the North Sea.

A major change in Bomber Command policy in the spring of 1944 had particular significance for RAF Coningsby. It resulted from an attack by 144 Lancasters from 5 Group on an aircraft factory at Toulouse. The group provided its own marking force and the small target was hit very successfully. Sir Arthur Harris was so impressed that he gave 5 Group's AOC Air Vice-Marshal Cochrane permission for his squadrons to act in a semi-independent role. Two of 8 Group's Pathfinder squadrons, 83 and 97 (both former 5 Group squadrons) were released to rejoin 5 Group along with a specialist Mosquito marker squadron, 627. This went to Woodhall Spa to join 617, and 83 and 97 went to Coningsby, from where they were to operate with great success for the remainder of the war. The change was not welcomed by the crews of the two squadrons. After the relaxed life of 8 Group's PFF, they found themselves back amidst the 'bull' of 5 Group and, still worse, found their role was to be one of illuminators for the target-marking force of Mosquitos.

The switch was well timed to meet the demand for precision bombing brought about by the invasion and 5 Group, led by its Coningsby-based Pathfinders, was to play a key role in the months to come. The new system was not, however, an immediate success. It was used in an attack on Schweinfurt, but smoke generators on the ground made accurate marking almost impossible. Then on 1st May a devastating attack on an aircraft repair factory at Tours proved just what could be done.

OF-D of 97 Squadron at Coningsby, early in 1945. Note the outline of Tattershall Castle directly underneath the port outer engine. (Eric Brown)

There was some resentment among other groups about what had become known as 'Cocky's Fifth Air Force' and these were to be heightened by a tragic night early in May 1944 over the former French army training area at Mailly-le-Camp, 80 miles south-east of Paris. Mailly was being used as a training area for units of a German panzer division, soldiers and tanks which could pose a serious threat to the invasion, then just a month away.

The attack was planned as an all Lincolnshire affair, with the bombers split into two waves, 5 Group first, followed by 1 Group. The marking would be carried out by four Mosquitos led by Leonard Cheshire and 1 Group's own Special Duties Flight, with 97 Squadron acting as target illuminators.

The initial marking was accurate and the Main Force Controller, Wing Commander Deane of 83 Squadron, called in the 5 Group aircraft, which were orbiting some 15 miles away. His VHF transmissions were drowned out by an American forces network broadcast and only a few aircraft responded. However, others followed the first attackers in and their bombing was reasonably accurate.

While all this was going on the 1 Group aircraft had been arriving at their holding point, marked by yellow target indicators. Night fighters had begun to arrive, attracted by the bombing and the yellow TIs. As the attacks began, angry exchanges could be heard over the radio network as Squadron Leader Neville Sparks of 83 Squadron ordered the 1 Group aircraft to maintain their holding pattern. By now Lancasters were being picked off one by one in the bright moonlight. Some pilots had used their initiative and moved away from the TIs, but most obeyed orders and many would pay with their lives for doing so.

It was an aircraft piloted by Flying Officer Edwards of 97 Squadron which finally marked the second aiming point and then Sparks ordered the 1 Group aircraft in. The target was immediately inundated with bombs as the Lancasters sought to do their job and get away from Mailly as quickly as possible. They were harried all the way to the coast by the night fighters and among the last aircraft to be shot down was that flown by Squadron Leader Sparks. He managed to bale out and escape capture and was back at Coningsby within seven weeks.

Many other men, however, were not so lucky. Forty-two Lancasters were lost in the raid, 28 of them from 1 Group. Many of those who flew to Mailly that night and survived found it to be the most frightening experience of their time with Bomber Command, not least because of the confusion which appeared to reign, albeit briefly, over the target.

Mailly, thankfully, proved to be an isolated incident. 83 and 97 Squadrons were to serve 5 Group well over the months to come, their marking techniques helping bring about an accuracy in bombing hitherto thought almost impossible.

Guy Gibson returned to Coningsby in the summer of 1944, this time as 54 Base Air Staff Officer, a desk job he hated. He still managed to fly occasionally and flew operationally at least three times from Coningsby in marker aircraft, twice in a Lockheed P-38 Lightning and once in a Mosquito. It was in his capacity as 54 Base ASO that he chose to fly from Woodhall Spa in a Mosquito of 627 Squadron as master bomber in a raid on München Gladbach on 19/20th September 1944, his aircraft crashing in Holland on its return flight, killing Gibson and his navigator.

One of the great characters at Coningsby at the time was the station commander, Group Captain Anthony Evan-Evans, a big cheerful man who had commanded Bomber Command airfields for most of the war. He flew occasionally but his rank, his age and his sheer size were against him. Evan-Evans did manage an occasional trip in a Lancaster and, sadly, that is how he met his end, shot down in an 83 Squadron Lancaster over the Mitteland Canal in February 1945.

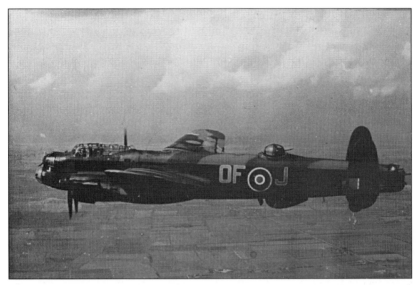

A magnificent shot of OF-J of 97 Squadron, airborne near Boston in the spring of 1945. At the controls was Wing Cmdr Baker DFC. (Eric Brown)

The Coningsby squadrons ended their war on the night of 25/26th April 1945 in an all-5 Group attack on an oil refinery at Tonsberg in southern Norway. Accurate marking enabled the target to be almost completely destroyed in what proved to the last major Bomber Command operation of the war.

Coningsby remained a bomber station until 1964, housing, at various times, squadrons equipped with Lancasters, Lincolns, Washingtons (the RAF version of the B29), Canberras and Vulcans. In 1969 it became a fighter airfield, home initially to Phantom squadrons and eventually to the F4's replacement, the Tornado.

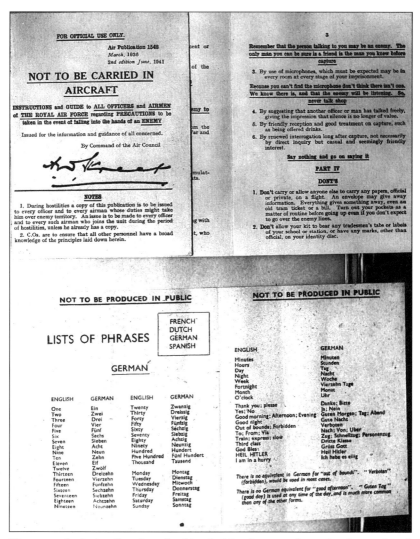

These were the instructions issued to Lincolnshire air crew to be read and remembered. (J. W. Wright)

8

CRANWELL, GRANTHAM AND HARLAXTON

On 3rd September 1942 a service was held to mark the National Day of Prayer at RAF Cranwell. Some 7,000 airmen and women, together with around 3,000 civilian staff, were drawn up on the parade ground of what had been the pre-war RAF College, an indication of the sheer size of what was almost certainly the biggest RAF station in Britain.

Cranwell had originally been a First World War Admiralty airfield, when it was known as HMS *Daedalus*. It was there that naval pilots, for both aircraft and airships, were trained and so large did it become that it was split into two, known as the South and North camps. The airfield covered some 3,000 acres and survived the post-war defence cuts to become the home of the RAF Cadet College and School of Technical Training. It was renamed the RAF College in 1929 and the present magnificent college buildings were erected soon afterwards, being formally opened by the Prince of Wales in 1934. Cranwell was now at the very heart of the Royal Air Force and its airfield was used to launch many of the RAF's long-distance record-breaking flights of the 1930s.

On the day war was declared in 1939, the RAF College formally closed and reopened again as the RAF College Service Flying Training School as part of 21 Group, whose AOC, Air Vice Marshal J. Baldwin, was also commandant at Cranwell. Both camps were packed to capacity and the total RAF complement may well have exceeded the figure of 7,000 noted in the station records in 1942. The population was boosted by the retention of most of the pre-war civilian staff, who were drafted into the RAF and kept in their old jobs.

1940 was to see the beginning of still further expansion, with the

HRH the Duchess of Gloucester arriving at Cranwell to open the new YMCA, 1941. (E W Chorley via Peter Green)

establishment of numerous new courses and 'schools'. Cranwell was passed to 26 Group, which controlled technical training, in June of that year, with 21 Group headquarters and the RAF College SFTS remaining as lodger units. At the same time, the airfield was home to the RAF Hospital (later moved to nearby Raunceby), the No 1 Electrical and Wireless School, the School of Clerk Accounting, the Specialist Signals Course, the Supplies Depot Course and, by September, the No 2 Flying Instructors Course. The following year the clerks' course moved to Penarth, equipment training to Bridlington and 2 FIC to Church Lawford, Warwickshire, their departure making way for more newcomers, one of which was No 3 (Coastal) Operational Training Unit, which brought with it a mixed bag of Whitleys, Wellingtons, Lysanders and Ansons.

These additional aircraft brought new air traffic control problems in and around Cranwell. Accidents were inevitable, and in one of the worst an Oxford collided with a Westland Wallace biplane 'owned' by the No 1 Signals School, killing all those on board.

No 3 OTU, which had arrived from Chivenor under the command of Wing Commander J. B. M. Wallis, was involved mainly in training

A Miles Master at Cranwell in 1942. (A S Thomas via Peter Green)

crews for the long-distance flying required in Coastal Command. A typical flight (though with an untypical conclusion) was undertaken by Flight Lieutenant Crawford and his six-man crew in May 1942. Their Whitley left Cranwell at 8.40 pm, flew to the tiny blip of land at Rockall, turning at 4.30 the following morning to head down the west coast of Scotland. Thirty minutes later the elderly Whitley developed a coolant leak in its port engine and the crew sent out a Mayday before ditching. They were located in their dinghy by a Hudson at 6.15, picked up within 20 minutes by a destroyer, transferred to an RAF launch off Greenock and landed at Abbotsinch where an aircraft was waiting to fly them back to Cranwell in time for lunch.

Not all mishaps had such happy endings. In March 1943 a Whitley crashed onto the roof of the RAF College building, killing the three-man crew and setting the building on fire.

The Coastal Command OTU crews had been using the newly-completed paved runways at Skellingthorpe for night flying but in June 1943 the unit was moved to the less congested air space over Haverfordwest. In its time at Cranwell 22 complete courses had passed through the training unit.

Around this time one of the hangars at Cranwell was allocated to General Aircraft Ltd for glider development while, in another, the Gloster Aircraft company was involved in development work on two

77

top secret projects. One was the completion of the Gloster E28/39, which had arrived at Cranwell by road on 14th May 1941 under the watchful eye of Air Commodore Frank Whittle. The following day the tiny aircraft, with test pilot P. E. G. Sayers at the controls, took off for the world's first flight of a jet-powered aircraft. Two years later development work on a second jet, the F9/40, led to its maiden flight at Cranwell on 5th March 1943 with M. Daunt at the controls. This aircraft later went into service with the RAF as the Gloster Meteor.

Back on the ground, training was going on at a furious pace and there were constant changes to keep pace with technical developments. The No 1 Signals School became the No 1 Radio School, the No 1 Radio Operators' School became the No 1 Radio Direction Finders' School. In March 1944 the Officers' Advanced Training School was created at Cranwell, its purpose being to train men for command, with courses covering flight, squadron and station command.

At various times Cranwell had a series of satellites and relief landing grounds, all with the purpose of relieving pressure on the flying from the main airfield itself. This had become so intense that the South camp had to be closed for flying while the grass runways were relaid. More room was made with the move of 17 SFTS, formerly the RAF College SFTS, to RAF Spitalgate in March 1945.

The very size of Cranwell created an administrative and logistical nightmare for those charged with running the station. The large numbers of personnel did, however, have some advantages. During one of the several severe wartime winters endured in Lincolnshire, the station commandant hit on a novel way of keeping snow-bound runways open for flying. Large groups of airmen, sometimes eight deep, were simply marched up and down to keep the snow flat!

With the war over, the RAF College reopened and continues today to train officers for service in the Royal Air Force.

RAF Grantham was another First World War airfield which, like its neighbour at Cranwell, was to play an important wartime training role. The airfield stands at the top of Somerby Hill, overlooking Grantham. For the first eleven years of its life it was known as RAF Spittlegate, was renamed RAF Grantham in 1928, and renamed yet again in March 1944. It had played an important role during the inter-war years (the RAF's best-loved training aircraft, the Tiger Moth, first went into service there in 1931) and had a short spell as a 5 Group bomber airfield before becoming the home to 12 Service Flying Training School in 1939, which flew another famous training aircraft, the North-American Harvard. Its complement of around 1,000 personnel was quickly

North American Harvards at Grantham with 12 FTS, 1939. (Seymour Feldman via Geoff Gardiner)

expanded following the outbreak of war and was eventually to peak in 1942 at around 2,800, most of whom were accommodated in a large number of hastily-erected Nissen huts.

12 SFTS was transferred to 21 Group Flying Training Command soon after the outbreak of war and it was this unit which was to occupy the airfield overlooking Grantham for the next few years. The airfield's proximity to Grantham, where 5 Group had its headquarters in St Vincent's House, made it ideal for the group's communications flight of Tutors, Oxfords and Magisters.

Oxfords also joined the Harvards of 12 SFTS in 1941 and the following year the unit was reformed as 12 (Pilot) Advanced Flying Unit. Its role was expanded to take in night-fighter training and up to 60 Blenheims were added to the station strength, mainly at the expense of the Oxfords, to take on the extra work.

The Grantham area was favoured by Luftwaffe intruder pilots and the airfield itself was attacked in February 1941, when a number of buildings were damaged and one airman killed. Two Fairey Battles, on the strength of 12 SFTS, were shot down by intruders during the summer. In another incident in October, a Ju 88, which had earlier unsuccessfully attacked a Wellington off Filey, was spotted circling Grantham, looking no doubt for easy pickings amongst the training

A Blenheim 1F of 12 (P) AFU at Grantham outside A-Flight. (Geoff Williams via Geoff Gardiner)

aircraft using the airfield and its relief landing ground at Harlaxton. A favoured tactic of the intruders was to switch on their navigation lights and join the unsuspecting training machines in the circuit. This happened on this occasion before the Ju 88 was seen to open fire on an unarmed Oxford. What happened next was never ascertained, but the Oxford and the German aircraft collided, killing instructor Sergeant Tom Graham and his pupil and the three German airmen. If Graham did, indeed, ram his attacker, his actions were worthy of the highest traditions of the RAF.

The grass runways at Grantham soon began to suffer from all the extra use they were getting. Some flights were moved out to Harlaxton and steel mesh laid to help strengthen the grass strips. Although this method of runway strengthening had worked well on many airfields, it caused almost as many problems as it solved at Grantham, proving particularly hard on the Blenheims' tyres.

It wasn't the only problem afflicting the aircraft. Most of the Blenheims had seen much misuse while in squadron service and, in his book on the airfield, Grantham author Geoff Gardiner records the loss of 28 of these aircraft and the lives of 15 men with them during 1943 alone. The Blenheims were eventually replaced by Bristol Beauforts but almost immediately 12 (P) AFU moved, one element going to Hixon, Staffordshire, and the second to Cranage, Cheshire.

In the meantime, RAF Grantham had been renamed yet again, this time becoming RAF Spitalgate, the change in spelling from the original 'Spittlegate' being attributed to an Air Ministry typing error! The latest name-change was made necessary to avoid confusion with other military establishments in the Grantham area.

Spitalgate, as it now was, was briefly put on a care and maintenance basis until the arrival in the last days of the war of 17 Flying Training School from Cranwell. RAF training was to continue there until 1975 when the airfield was handed over to the Army as a Royal Corps of Transport Territorial Army depot.

Harlaxton was another First World War airfield virtually within sight of the graceful church spire which dominates the sky-line at Grantham. It had been opened in 1916 to train fighter and reconnaissance pilots but was closed in 1920, most of its wooden buildings disappearing over the next decade. The build-up of training in the late 1930s, particularly at Cranwell and RAF Grantham, led to the site being reopened as a relief landing ground. A small practice bombing range was also established close to the airfield.

The airfield, known locally as simply 'the landing ground', was expanded with some new brick buildings being constructed together with a wooden-hutted accommodation site. Eight Blister hangars were also erected and by the spring of 1942 Harlaxton was officially opened as a satellite of Grantham, housing a detachment from 12 (P) AFU, operating a variety of aircraft including Ansons, Battles, Oxfords and, finally, Blenheims.

The airfield was to suffer the same problems as Grantham and Cranwell, its grass runways deteriorating under the weight of the training aircraft using them. The Blenheims were eventually moved to Balderton in Nottinghamshire and steel mesh strips laid for the aircraft which remained. It was only a temporary solution, however, and by the autumn of 1944 all resident aircraft were withdrawn. Harlaxton continued to be used as a relief landing ground for what was now Spitalgate until the war ended. The airfield was retained by the Air Ministry until the late 1950s when the land was sold and returned to agriculture. Most of the wartime buildings have long since disappeared, the few that do remain being used for storage purposes.

9
DIGBY

Lincolnshire's only true Battle of Britain airfield can be found a few miles south of Lincoln between the villages of Scopwick and Digby. Spitfires and Hurricanes based at RAF Digby played a minor role in the air battles waged over south-east England in the late summer and early autumn of 1940, supporting the squadrons based in East Anglia in the 'Big Wing' tactics employed in the later stages of the campaign. Later Digby was to become the only airfield in Lincolnshire to be directly under the control of the Royal Canadian Air Force and of the 36 fighter squadrons to serve there during the war, no fewer than eleven were Canadian.

The airfield dates back to the First World War when open fields near the village of Scopwick were used as a relief landing ground by the RNAS at Cranwell. Between the wars it was used extensively for training (its commanding officer was, for a few months in 1920, Squadron Leader A. T. Harris, later to become Commander in Chief of Bomber Command; others included Wing Commander Tedder and Group Captain T. Leigh-Mallory) and was upgraded and extensively modernised as part of the RAF expansion programme in 1935–36. Following the completion of that work it passed to the control of 12 Group of Fighter Command and was to remain a fighter airfield for much of the war.

In September 1939 its two resident squadrons were 46 and 73, both of which had recently re-equipped with Hawker Hurricanes. At 21.34 hours on 3rd September 46 Squadron was scrambled for the first time, but the alarm, like everything else that day, was premature.

The Digby Hurricanes had their first brush with the Luftwaffe a week later when a squadron relatively new to Digby, 611, attacked German seaplanes (almost certainly He 115s) over the North Sea in an inconclusive engagement. Later the same day, the Germans were not to escape so lightly. A Flight of 56 Squadron were on patrol when they were ordered to intercept German aircraft which were believed to be heading for either Immingham or Hull. According to the station history, seven German aircraft were confirmed destroyed, an action which earned a DFC for 46's commanding officer, Squadron Leader Barwell. A month later 46 Squadron shot down three He 115s and damaged a fourth as they tried to attack a convoy.

Back at Digby there were constantly changing faces in the mess as fighter squadrons came and went in the ceaseless rotation that was part of life in Fighter Command. Digby was ideally located as a night fighter station, guarding as it did much of the North Midlands and Yorkshire industrial areas and the Humber ports. The first of many night fighter units to be stationed there was 229 with its Blenheims, followed by 29 Squadron in June 1940. This latter unit was converted to Beaufighters at Digby and was to operate most successfully from the airfield and its satellites. Among its pilots was Flight Lieutenant Guy Gibson. He had

Waiting for the off. A night fighter pilot whiles away the hours with a game of cards, Digby 1941. (RAF Digby)

already completed a tour with Bomber Command and later in the year was to receive his DFC from George VI on a Royal visit to Digby.

Digby was used by several squadrons which had been heavily involved in the air battle over Dunkirk. In Lincolnshire, they were given time to re-equip and assimilate replacement pilots into squadron life before moving south again.

The Royal Canadian Air Force made its bow at Digby at the end of 1940 when 2 Squadron RCAF arrived with its Hurricanes and was reformed as 402 Squadron (RCAF) in line with the adopted policy giving Dominion squadrons 400-numbers.

402 was later to move to Wellingore, but was followed by 401 which re-equipped with Spitfires and began flying offensive sweeps and patrols from Digby before it, too, moved in October 1941 to Biggin Hill. Two more Canadian squadrons, 409 and 411, were formed on the same day at Digby, the former flying Defiants in a night-fighter role from Coleby Grange, and the latter operating Spitfires.

By now there was a constant stream of squadrons passing through Digby. Some remained while others, like 92, moved on quickly, in its case to Egypt. 54 Squadron went to Australia, 611 to Malta and 242 to North Africa. Others, like 228, 609 and 421, were intended for duties in England.

Spitfires of 411 Squadron lined up at Digby in June 1941. (RAF Digby)

The Canadian Prime Minister, McKenzie King, visited the airfield in September 1941 and a year later the airfield became officially Canadian under its commanding officer, Group Captain McNab of the RCAF. Earlier in 1942, 411 Squadron was one of the Canadian fighter units used to provide cover for the ill-fated Operation Jubilee, the landing of a largely-Canadian force at Dieppe.

Among the notable pilots to serve at Digby during this period was the Belgian ace Jean Offenburg whose published diaries, *The Lonely Warrior*, remain one of the classics of Second World War literature. He was a Spitfire pilot with 609 Squadron when he arrived at Digby and was killed in a training accident, his Spitfire colliding with another aircraft from 92 Squadron close to the airfield. Offenburg is buried in Scopwick churchyard, close to Digby, as is another pilot who was to find literary fame and then meet his death at Digby. Pilot Officer John Magee, a 19 year old American, was serving with 412 Squadron when he was killed flying a Spitfire on 11th December 1941. Magee wrote what is still one of the finest poems to capture the majesty of aviation. It began:

Oh! I have slipped the surly bonds of earth
And danced the skies on laughter-silvered wings;

Ready for action. A Canadian fighter pilot in his Spitfire, Digby 1942. (RAF Digby)

and it ended:

And while with silent, lifting mind I've trod
The high, untrespassed sanctity of space,
Put out my hand and touched the face of God.

A number of new types of aircraft began to arrive at Digby, including Hawker Typhoons, with which 198 Squadron re-equipped before moving north to Northumberland. In February 1943, 410 Squadron arrived with Mosquitos, moving soon afterwards to Coleby Grange. And in March the same year 613 (City of Manchester) Squadron arrived with North American Mustangs. It, too, remained only briefly before going to Coleby Grange.

Digby-based squadrons were playing a major role in the increasingly offensive daylight operations of the RAF over northern Europe. Anti-shipping strikes were flown from Digby itself and from Coleby Grange, while in the summer of 1943 416 and 402 Squadrons formed the Digby Wing, giving close support to tactical bomber attacks on targets in Holland, Belgium and northern France.

During the winter of 1943 and the early spring of 1944 Digby was used to prepare squadrons being honed for the forthcoming invasion. 438 Squadron went to Digby in November 1943, worked up on Spitfires and left early in 1944 for Wittering. They were followed by three more new Canadian fighter squadrons, 441, 442 and 443, all of which formed at the Lincolnshire airfield before moving south for the invasion. They were joined by three other squadrons, one RAF, one Belgian and one Czech, which all completed their training and flew offensive patrols from Digby before joining the Allied Tactical Air Force in readiness for the invasion.

The last offensive missions were flown from Digby by 310 (Czech) Squadron in July 1944, the Spitfires spending much of their time operating along the Dutch coast. By the late summer of 1944 Digby's war had all but come to an end. The airfield was to be used by three further squadrons, 116 which flew Oxfords on air-sea rescue duties and 527 and 528, whose Blenheims were used for radar calibration purposes.

Early in 1945 the run-down at Digby began. 527 and 528 Squadrons were amalgamated and the station organised classes in nearby Lincoln for airmen who were expecting to be demobbed in the next few months. The Canadian influence was still strong, however, and airmen who hailed from Alberta were allowed to take part in elections for the provincial government there, a special polling station being set up at the camp. And RCAF Digby's proudest moment of the year came when

Canadian pilots with what was possibly Digby's communications Magister. (RAF Digby)

a team from the station finished as runners-up in the Canadian overseas ice hockey championship.

A few days before the war ended the Canadian commanding officer at Digby since September 1942, Group Captain McNab, was posted away and was replaced by an RAF officer, Group Captain Bristow, and early in May the RAF resumed control of the station again. Digby was to play a long and active role in the post-war Royal Air Force as a training establishment. Its proud wartime record, however, was never forgotten and a Canadian maple leaf provided the central motif in the station badge.

10
DUNHOLME LODGE

RAF Dunholme Lodge was a place of desolation on the morning of 19th July 1944. The previous night one of its squadrons, 619, had sent 13 Lancasters on what looked like being a routine attack on marshalling yards near the French town of Revigny.

It was an all-5 Group attack and followed two previous attacks on recent nights by Lancasters from neighbouring 1 Group. Neither had been successful. On the first only half the aircraft involved had reported bombing the target and, in doing so, ten Lancasters had been lost. Two nights later 1 Group was sent back to finish the job. This time conditions made it impossible to identify the target and, rather than bomb blind and hit nearby civilian areas, the raid was abandoned, but not before another seven aircraft were lost.

5 Group was then given the task of eliminating the railway junction and on the night of 18/19th July 109 Lancasters took off to do just that. Dunholme Lodge was then the home of two Lancaster squadrons, 44 (Rhodesia) and 619 and it was the latter, a squadron which had been in being for a little over a year, which was to suffer so grievously that night.

The route took the Lancasters straight in, with no attempt to deceive the defenders, as had been the case on the two previous raids. Despite other operations (a successful attack on another railway junction by 3 Group, attacks on flying bomb sites by Halifaxes of 4 Group and raids by 1 and 6 Groups on synthetic oil plants) the fighters were waiting for the 5 Group Lancasters as they approached their target east of Paris.

Twenty-four of the attackers were shot down, five of them from 619 Squadron. Four of the first five to go down were from Dunholme with another following soon afterwards. Only two men, the bomb-aimer from Flying Officer Begernie's crew and the rear-gunner from Flying Officer Morcan's Lancaster, survived.

In his outstanding account of the three Revigny raids, *Massacre Over*

The Marne, Oliver Clutton-Brock recalls the feelings of the rear-gunner of the only surviving A-Flight Lancaster. After the post-flight briefing he went to bed and tried to sleep but he was still too frightened to close his eyes. 'We really thought our time had come that night,' he said.

One of the 619 Squadron casualties, the Lancaster flown by Flying Officer Donnelly, was later credited with shooting down a night fighter, but five for one was scant reward to a close-knit community like a 5 Group bomber squadron. It could have been even worse. Two other 619 Squadron aircraft reported brushes with night fighters, one escaping only after a violent corkscrew manoeuvre threw off its attacker.

The disaster over Revigny was the worst of many bad nights suffered at Dunholme Lodge, a station which was never a stranger to tragedy.

The site of the airfield, three miles north-east of Lincoln and close to the villages of Welton and Dunholme, had first been used by the RAF in the early days of the war when Hampdens from nearby Scampton were dispersed in fields overlooked by the large house known locally as Dunholme Lodge. Like so many other airfields in Lincolnshire, it came about virtually by custom and practice. The fields continued to be used as and when necessary and, gradually, evolved into a satellite airfield of Scampton.

Some rudimentary buildings were provided, accommodation sites developed (mostly in and around the village of Welton) and by the summer of 1942 it had achieved official satellite status. The Lodge itself was pressed into use to accommodate airmen, although washing facilities were initially limited to an ancient pump which stood outside the building. There were no local mess facilities and lorries were sent to take the station staff to Scampton to eat.

Conditions gradually improved and soon Dunholme Lodge had its own facilities though to those used to Scampton, they must have seemed very inadequate. Dunholme's first occupants were the crews and aircraft of 1485 Target Towing and Gunnery Flight, moved from Scampton with its collection of aircraft, which included several Manchesters, a Battle, Lysander and a single Wellington. Its name was changed to 1485 (Bomber) Gunnery Flight and it was to move to Fulbeck before the end of October 1942.

Before it did, there was a near-tragedy involving one of the flight's Manchesters. It was due to take part in a fighter affiliation exercise over Skegness and the crew invited one of the young airmen in the station headquarters, George Black, along for a trip. He had never flown before and he readily agreed. He was issued with a badly-packed parachute, part of which was trailing behind him as he climbed into the bomber, and he later recalled sitting on the navigator's table for take-off. Once airborne the pilot started to climb over Welton when the port engine suddenly cut out. The undercarriage was still half retracted and would not budge. Many Manchesters did not survive such a predicament but this one did, to execute what was later described as a controlled crash across wind on the grass runways at Dunholme. George Black, severely chastened by his first experience of flying, clambered out of the wreckage determined never to take to the air again. He hasn't.

Once the flight had left Dunholme was closed for runway construction. The station site was also extended and additional hangars erected in time for its reopening in May 1943 as a sub-station of 52 Base at Scampton. On 31st May 44 Squadron moved in from Coningsby and finally Dunholme had become an operational bomber station.

44's first operation from Dunholme was against Düsseldorf on 11th June. Three nights later the squadron lost two aircraft in a raid on Oberhausen. Three more aircraft were to fail to return from raids on Ruhr targets in the weeks to come.

After the Ruhr, the emphasis switched to Berlin and 44 was to suffer badly in the series of raids over the winter of 1943–44. It mounted 246 sorties in 20 raids, losing 16 aircraft and 103 men killed, the highest losses in 5 Group.

Its worst night was on 23rd/24th November in what was largely regarded as one of the most successful attacks of the war on the German capital. Three of the twelve aircraft sent from Dunholme that night failed to return. Just one man from the 21 on board survived and one of the aircraft and its seven-man crew were never found. Two others were to be lost on four other raids. On one night, 30th/31st January 1944, there happened one of those oddities of war: the pilot of one Lancaster died while his six-man crew all escaped by parachute; in the second the pilot was blown to safety but all his crewmates died when his Lancaster was hit by flak over the city.

Berlin wasn't the only target that winter and aircraft from 44 were constantly in action against a variety of other targets. Several failed to return to Lincolnshire. Amongst them was KM-B, which went down in the North Sea 60 miles off the Lincolnshire coast on its way back from Leipzig in the early hours of 21st October 1943.

When the attacks were called off on Berlin there was to be little respite for 44 Squadron. Two of its aircraft were shot down on the Nuremberg raid and another damaged. Two aircraft were lost in the confusion during the attack on a Wehrmacht tank park at Mailly-le-Camp east of Paris in May 1944. One of them was a veteran with the squadron. KM-K had completed 13 raids on Berlin and had also spent a period on loan with 617 Squadron, with which it flew wearing its 44 Squadron codes. The second aircraft lost was from 619 Squadron, which had arrived at Dunholme the month before. It, too, was a Berlin veteran and was carrying an eight-man crew, two of whom had been awarded Distinguished Flying Medals only days before.

619's move to Dunholme came after the main runway was extended by some 300 yards to allow larger bomb loads to be carried. The runway had a distinct gradient on it and, until the extension, Lancasters' bomb loads were limited.

619 arrived at Dunholme after a brief stay at Coningsby. It was under the command of Wing Commander J. R. Maling, who was killed when his Lancaster was shot down in a raid on Stuttgart in late July 1944.

One of the aircraft at Dunholme at this time was ED611, 44 Squadron's *Uncle Joe*. It had been delivered to the squadron as KM-U before the move to Dunholme. It quickly became known as *Uncle Joe* and soon sported a picture of the Russian leader on its nose. It flew with 44 throughout 1943 and had completed 45 operations with the squadron before being reassigned to 463 Squadron at Waddington, with which it was to go on to chalk up 117 operations before being written off at Carnaby following an attack on Pölitz in February 1945. Ironically, *Uncle Joe's* 75th trip was to Revigny. Another 44 Squadron veteran at Dunholme was ND578, KM-Y-Yorker. It was delivered in February 1944 in time for a Berlin raid and went on to complete 121 sorties with the squadron by the end of the war, by which time 44 Squadron was at Spilsby.

As a two-squadron airfield, Dunholme became very busy during the summer of 1944, when Bomber Command operations reached a new peak. There were clearly problems with the Dunholme circuit, which overlapped that of nearby Scampton. This wasn't the only place in Lincolnshire where this happened, but a cluster of other airfields nearby began to make life difficult for the Dunholme crews.

The reorganisation of Bomber Command in Lincolnshire in the early autumn of 1944 saw the whole of 52 Base, including Dunholme, being transferred to 1 Group at 15 Base. 619 Squadron moved to Strubby and 44 to Spilsby. Their place at Dunholme was taken by 170 Squadron, which arrived on 22nd October a week after being formed at Kelstern.

By this time a joint circuit had been set up with Scampton but it was clearly suiting nobody as holding times increased for aircraft from both

TC-E of 170 Squadron on a daylight operation from Dunholme Lodge in the autumn of 1944.

airfields so a decision was made to close Dunholme for flying purposes. This happened on 29th November 1944, 170 Squadron moving to Hemswell. Dunholme assumed a non-operational role and spent the remaining months of the war as a centre for glider modification and development.

After the war the airfield was used to house the Polish Record Office and as the home for the three Polish Resettlement Corps. Dunholme Lodge closed in 1947 only to be reopened nine years later as a Bloodhound missile base, protecting the nearby V-bomber stations at Scampton and Waddington. It finally closed in 1966 but there are still numerous reminders around the Welton and Dunholme areas of the airfield which served Bomber Command so well. The original Naafi building forms part of the village school in Welton.

11
EAST KIRKBY

The crumbling wartime airfields of Lincolnshire have become something of a magnet for the men who served in the county half a century and more ago. They have been returning, in ever increasing numbers over the past decade, as the urge to remember grows ever stronger.

The truth is that there is little for them to see. On most airfields where runways once crossed the rich Lincolnshire farmland, crops now grow. And what does remain of the airfield buildings has decayed almost beyond recognition. There is, however, one notable exception. East Kirkby was a wartime airfield, a Bomber Command Base station, and later served as the home for units of the USAF. But then, like many of its neighbours, it closed and its buildings were taken over by chicken and potato farmers.

Among those farmers were the Panton brothers, Fred and Harold, born and raised in East Kirkby. Their elder brother, Christopher, had been killed flying in Halifaxes from North Yorkshire during the war and, after visiting his grave in Germany, they set about providing a permanent memorial to him and the 55,000 Bomber Command men who never returned from operations over Europe. The result is the Lincolnshire Aviation Heritage Centre, essentially a recreation of wartime RAF East Kirkby, even down to its very own Lancaster bomber, now with restored Merlin engines and capable of taxiing along what remains of the airfield's runways.

The actions of the Pantons have been applauded universally. Not only have they succeeded beyond their wildest dreams in providing that living memorial to their brother, they have also preserved a unique part of Lincolnshire's past, one which is arguably more significant than many mainstream definitions of what constitutes 'history'. East Kirkby is living corroboration of what this book is all about: that half a century ago Lincolnshire played a leading, some would say vital, role in helping defeat Nazi Germany.

Fred and Harold Panton with their Lancaster, which has been restored as 57 Squadron's Just Jane, in a wartime hangar at East Kirkby. (Grimsby Evening Telegraph)

East Kirkby itself lies at the point where Lincolnshire Wold meets Lincolnshire Fen, just south of one of the most beautiful areas of the county. A site near the village was first used by the RAF in 1940 when a decoy airfield, complete with wooden Whitley bombers, was created to fool the Luftwaffe. It worked, too, as the Germans bombed the 'airfield' a number of times, much to the amusement of the small RAF contingent there, whose job it was to move the dummies round to maintain the illusion.

In 1942, however, steps were made to provide the real thing. The Air Ministry, looking for homes for its expanding bomber fleet, requisitioned some 800 acres of farmland and work began on building the airfield. Over the next year teams of construction workers laid 4,800 yards of runway and erected three T2 hangars, a watchtower and more than 60 ancillary buildings. The airfield was to prove a source of amazement to the local population in this very rural corner of Lincolnshire, where life went on much as it had in the days of the Old Queen. The RAF brought the trappings of the 20th century with them, including the first flushing lavatories many local people had ever seen.

East Kirkby was allocated to 5 Group which, in turn, selected it as the home for 57 Squadron, then flying Lancasters from the grass strips at

Scampton, where it had lost some of its best crews to 617 Squadron.

57 was to remain at East Kirkby until the end of the war, losing some 80 aircraft while operating from the Lincolnshire airfield. Later, it was to help create a new squadron, 630, with which it shared East Kirkby until the end of the war.

The first station commanding officer was Group Captain R. T. Taffe, a cheerful and much respected character, and he was there on 27th August 1943 as the squadron, which had hours before been involved in a raid on Nuremberg, flew in from Scampton. If the arrival of the RAF came as a shock for the people of East Kirkby, East Kirkby came as something of a shock to the airmen of 57 Squadron. Since their arrival in 5 Group almost a year earlier, they had been used to the splendid pre-war facilities of Scampton. Now they were faced with what amounted to life in the raw. Flush toilets notwithstanding, East Kirkby, with its single pub that doubled as the village slaughterhouse, was a jolt to the system.

The newcomers were not given much time to brood at what they saw as their misfortune. Three nights after arriving 14 crews from 57 Squadron were among 660 aircraft which attacked the twin German towns of München Gladbach and Rheydt. All the East Kirkby aircraft returned safely. The squadron was stood down for a raid the following night on Berlin but they were 'on' for an all-Lancaster attack on the German capital three nights later when one 57 Squadron aircraft failed to return. Later that month a German intruder aircraft shot down a Lancaster approaching the airfield after a raid on Hanover. Five of the crew died.

The squadron was rapidly expanding and was able to send 21 aircraft at a time on the increasing number of attacks on German cities. More than 2,000 personnel were now stationed at East Kirkby and sometimes the facilities did not keep match with the growth. The station Medical Officer is on record complaining that, although he had two wards in his 'hospital,' there was only one bed in each. Add to that the problems he was encountering with dust from the bare concrete floors, and it is easy to see he had justifiable grounds for complaint.

In November 1943 57 Squadron's B-Flight was detached to form a new squadron, 630, which was to share East Kirkby with 57 for the remainder of the war. 630's first commanding officer was Squadron Leader Malcolm Crocker DFC, an experienced pilot who had been at Scampton with 57 and had been its B-Flight commander. Crocker was an American, one of a number in Bomber Command, and he was to complete his tour of 30 operations within a week of taking up his new posting. Soon after, he left the squadron to be replaced by Wing Commander Rollinson. Neither man, however, was to survive for long in what was Bomber Command's worst winter of the war. Rollinson died over Berlin with his crew on the night of 28/29th January while Crocker, awarded a bar to his DFC, was killed leading another bomber squadron.

The Berlin raids were hard on East Kirkby. In the five raids that January, 57 Squadron lost six aircraft and 630 Squadron three. In all, in just one month, 52 men were killed and 13 became prisoners of war. But there was much worse to come for East Kirkby.

Five aircraft from the two squadrons were shot down in the last great raid of the Battle of Berlin, though remarkably 16 men from the three 630 Squadron aircraft shot down survived, one, Sergeant D. M. Morrison, evading capture to make it back to England. 630 was to lose three more of the 16 Lancasters it sent on the Nuremberg raid on 30th/31st March, while 57 Squadron lost one on a night Bomber Command saw 96 of its 779 heavies shot down.

All this was capped in the most horrendous way on 21st June that year when 11 aircraft from East Kirkby were lost in a single night. It was a 5 Group attack on the synthetic oil plant at Wesseling. The marking system went wrong, the weather conditions were wrongly predicted, the night-fighters were out in force and the result was the loss of 37 Lancasters, including six from 57 Squadron and four from 630, with a fifth crashing in England. The crew of one 57 Squadron Lancaster was picked up in the North Sea by an air-sea rescue launch operating out of Yarmouth.

By this time East Kirkby had grown following its elevation to Base station status, with responsibility for the airfields at Spilsby and Strubby. Four additional hangars were erected to handle the servicing requirements of the satellite squadrons and the station headquarters staff was expanded to cope with the additional administration.

630 Squadron lost another commanding officer in July when Wing Commander Bill Deas was killed in a disastrous raid for 5 Group on the night of 7/8th July on a V-bomb storage dump at St Leu d'Esserent. His was one of 29 aircraft lost by 5 Group when the force was intercepted by German night fighters. Wing Commander Deas, who was on his 69th operation, is buried with his crew near Versailles.

The squadron was to lose eleven aircraft that month, including four in an attack on the railway junction at Revigny. There were, however, some remarkable escapes. Sergeant Albert de Bruin, a 630 mid-upper gunner, was one of three members of his crew to bale out over Revigny and parachuted into a forested area east of Paris. Eventually he was picked up by a resistance group and he remained with them until the area was liberated by American troops some weeks later.

Les Barnes had parachuted to safety when his Lancaster was shot down in a raid over Stuttgart in February 1944. He also evaded capture and finally made it back to East Kirkby almost ten months after he left, by which time no one could remember him! Remembered or not, 630 Squadron records showed he still had another 25 trips to do to complete his tour!

Flying Officer Steve Nunns had the distinction of bringing his Lancaster back from a raid on Kaiserslauten single handed. En route the aircraft had caught fire and, unable to extinguish the blaze in the port inner engine, he ordered his crew to bale out over France. Nunns waited until they were clear, engaged the auto pilot and prepared to jump himself when he noticed the fire appeared to be going out. He went to the navigator's table, plotted a route home and returned to the cockpit to head back for England. After a long and lonely journey back over the North Sea he arrived over East Kirkby where he was ordered out to sea again to dump his bomb load before he was finally allowed to land. Remarkably the whole crew, who had dropped close to the Allied lines in France, made it back to East Kirkby within a week.

Both squadrons were in the thick of the action throughout the winter and final spring of the war. 630's S-Sugar was shot down in the devastating 5 Group attack on the historic city of Würzburg at the end of March. It was the last aircraft lost on operations from the squadron. 57's final casualties were the crew of one of the nine 5 Group Lancasters lost in an attack on the synthetic oil plant at Bohlen three nights later.

But the drama was not yet quite over for East Kirkby and its two Lancaster squadrons. On the afternoon of 17th April 1945 they were being prepared for a Group attack on railway yards at Cham in south-east Germany when disaster struck. A fire broke out in 57 Squadron's N-Nan while it was being bombed-up (one report speaks of a photo flash detonating prematurely, another of a fuel leak) and the result was devastating. As the station fire tender arrived two 1,000lb bombs detonated, killing two men instantly. As more rescue workers arrived further bombs began to explode, killing two more men and setting on fire three nearby Lancasters. Further explosions rocked the station as more bombs exploded and the flames spread to other aircraft.

There were some astonishing acts of bravery – later recognised with the award of a number of medals – as ground crew and firemen fought to rescue the injured and prevent further damage. When the fires were

Avro Lancaster LM517 of 57 Squadron at East Kirkby soon after the war ended. (M Hodgson via Peter Green)

finally brought under control and the last of the bombs accounted for, it was discovered that six Lancasters had been totally destroyed and a further 14 damaged, almost the entire strength of 57 Squadron. The damage across the airfield was extensive and it was to be another week before East Kirkby was operational again, just in time for the final operations of the war.

East Kirkby was to remain open until 1958, used initially by the RAF to prepare units for operations in the Far East and later by the United States Air Force. Now, thanks to the efforts of the Panton brothers, it is a living memorial to all the men who served in Lincolnshire with Bomber Command.

12
ELSHAM WOLDS

Blink and you just might miss what was once the largest bomber airfield in 1 Group, Bomber Command. Today the airfield known as Elsham Wolds is pierced by the A15 as it runs north to the Humber Bridge. The dual carriageway runs through an industrial estate right on top of the Lincolnshire Wolds. Modern buildings carrying the logos of national and international companies flash by. The only hint of the site's past is the large black arched-roof building in the centre of the estate. It is a J-type hangar, one of the last visible reminders of an airfield which was once home to two squadrons of Lancaster bombers and the base station in a network of airfields which spread across north Lincolnshire.

Elsham Wolds was among the first of the wave of wartime airfields to be built in Lincolnshire and, remarkably, it was to be the home of one squadron, 103, for almost four years of war. It was also to become the home of probably the most famous Lancaster of all the 8,000-plus built, ED888 which served as M-Mother (later adapted to *Mother-of-Them-All*) with 103 Squadron and Mike-Squared with Elsham's second squadron, 576. It was delivered to Elsham on 20th April 1943 and by the time it was finally retired early in 1945, ED888 had a record 140 operations to its credit.

Construction work at Elsham began in the autumn of 1940 and in early June the following year the advance party of the station staff arrived. With them was 33 year old Group Captain Hugh Constantine, the station's first commanding officer and a young airman who was to play an important role in the development of Elsham Wolds and 1 Group itself. 103 Squadron was due to arrive in less than two weeks to take up residence yet there was no running water, no electricity in the accommodation sites, roads were unlaid and many buildings only partly finished. Constantine, later to be knighted and become an air chief marshal, wasted no time in setting about the contractors. He was

Flying Control at RAF Elsham Wolds near the end of the war. This building later became a house and was only demolished in recent years to make way for industrial development.

a big man (he played rugby for the RAF and Leicester and was a fitness fanatic) and he wasn't used to taking 'no' for an answer.

Constantine was later to endear himself with everyone who served at Elsham by leading from the front. He was an enthusiastic pilot, who flew his share of operations and never distanced himself from the men and women who served under him. He and his wife lived in a cottage in nearby Elsham village where they liked nothing better than to entertain the young men who flew the station's bombers.

By the time 103 arrived from Newton in Nottinghamshire most of the work was complete and Elsham Wolds was ready to go to war, although it was the early autumn before all the accommodation was complete, until then many of the ground crew had to make do with bell tents pitched in a corner of the airfield. The first of 103's Wellingtons arrived at their new Lincolnshire home on 14th July 1941 and within three days were in action with six aircraft being detailed for an attack on Bremen, although two had to turn back with mechanical problems. The fact that their new station had paved runways meant that bomb and fuel loads could be increased and the squadron quickly made the most of their new facilities.

These were the days when crews planned their own method of attack, their own route to and from the target. It was a far cry from the disciplined, co-ordinated raids which were to come, but required enormous skill and courage from the crews of the Wellington bombers.

Between July 1941 and April 1945 over 1,000 young men were to die on operations from Elsham Wolds. The first were Sergeant J. S. Bucknole and his crew, who were killed in a daylight attack on the German pocket battleship *Gneisenau*, while undergoing repairs in dock at Brest.

Losses continued to mount through that first summer, four Wellingtons failing to return on one particularly bad night in early September. The crew of one escaped by parachute in the area between Caistor and Market Rasen when fog prevented them landing, while another crew survived after being shot down en route for Berlin, the pilot, Squadron Leader Tony Ingram, 103's longest serving airman, later being entertained to lunch by the night fighter crew who accounted for his Wellington.

The second crew to survive that night were to have another lucky escape in November when their Wellington suffered severe icing problems on its way home from Mannheim. With one engine misfiring, it was attacked by the anti-aircraft defences around Harwich (always reckoned by aircrew to be amongst the most dangerous in Europe!) and then hit a balloon cable over Immingham which sliced into the port wing root before, fortunately, snapping. The pilot, Pilot Officer Ken Wallis, managed to crash-land his aircraft close to the airfield.

Among the young men who joined 103 as replacements that autumn was Flight Lieutenant David Holford, a remarkable pilot who was to be awarded a DSO and DFC by the time he was 21. Soon afterwards he became the youngest wing commander in the RAF and was appointed commanding officer of 100 Squadron at Waltham where he was killed soon afterwards flying a Lancaster on his third tour of operations.

103 was able to put up a record 16 aircraft by the end of the year for a raid on Wilhelmshaven, despite a bitterly cold winter at Elsham where a constant battle was being fought against the elements to keep the squadron operational. It also provided 19 of the 1,047 aircraft which took off for the first 1,000-bomber raid of the war on Cologne on the night of 30th May 1942. With them were a further eleven Wellingtons which had been flown in to Elsham from 22 Operational Training Unit at Wellesbourne Mountford. One 103 Squadron aircraft was lost and a second was diverted to nearby Kirmington on its return, where it

crashed on take off the following day, killing four of the crew.

In the summer of 1942, 103 Squadron became the first – and, as it turned out, only – squadron in 1 Group to operate the four-engined Halifax, which was already in service further north with 4 Group. Training was placed in the hands of the station's own 103 Squadron Heavy Conversion Unit, which was commanded by Squadron Leader Holford, and one by one crews were instructed on the Halifax MkIIs, which began arriving in increasing numbers at Elsham. Three crashes, one over the North Sea, a second at Ludborough and a third near the airfield with 13 men on board, did little to endear the Halifax to 103 Squadron and it was generally treated with some trepidation by crews new to four-engined flying.

Operations with the new aircraft began on 1st August and over the next few weeks the squadron was to carry out 15 raids with Halifaxes, losing twelve aircraft, a loss rate of almost nine per cent. Morale touched rock bottom and only began to rise in late October when it was announced the squadron would be the first in 1 Group to receive Lancasters, now widely in use with 5 Group further south in Lincolnshire. By 21st November 103 was able to send six Lancasters on a mining trip to the Bay of Biscay and the following night provided twelve Lancasters for a raid on Stuttgart. They all returned safely and morale began to soar again at Elsham Wolds.

103 suffered its first Lancaster loss in a raid on Duisburg shortly before Christmas; it was to lose another 134 before the war ended. It was over Duisburg in May 1943 that 103 set a new Bomber Command record, its 27 Lancasters dropping 113 tons of high explosive and incendiaries. One of the aircraft on that raid was M-Mother, the second of its 140 trips over Occupied Europe.

One unnamed airman had what must go down as one of the luckiest escapes of the war in a training accident at Elsham that spring. He was one of nine men in V-Victor of 103's B-Flight which got into difficulties during a fighter affiliation exercise and the pilot (who was killed trying to land the aircraft) ordered everyone else on board to bale out. One of the passengers on the aircraft grabbed a parachute on which the harness proved to be far too big for him. When he jumped at 6,000 feet it slipped from his shoulders but, as he struggled, his foot caught in the webbing and he spent the remainder of the descent hanging upside down hoping that his foot wouldn't slip any further. He eventually landed in a field and escaped with nothing more serious than mild concussion.

Compared with some of the other squadrons in 1 Group still flying

Wellingtons, 103 in its high-flying Lancasters escaped the worst of the early rounds over the Ruhr but, in a relatively low-key attack on Oberhausen in mid-June, it lost two Lancasters and, with them, 14 men. Three other aircraft aborted on the same raid. Two more went down on a raid ten days later on that old Bomber Command 'favourite', Gelsenkirchen, although this time eight of the men on board survived. Another two were lost a month later in a raid on Essen, this coming in addition to the five Lancasters 103 lost in the series of raids on Hamburg at the end of July, a month which cost Elsham a total of nine Lancasters. With losses like that, it didn't take a mathematical genius to work out the chances of surviving a tour of 30 operations were very slim indeed.

August saw the start of what became known as the Battle of Berlin with the first of a series of major raids on the German capital over the winter months, raids which cost Elsham 31 Lancasters through enemy action or accidents. 103 Squadron went right through the battle, posting a Bomber Command record of sending 30 aircraft on a single raid in November. Heavy though 103's losses were, they were the lowest in 1 Group.

The autumn of 1943 saw major changes at Elsham, with the formation of a second squadron, 576, from 103's C-Flight. The airfield became crowded as never before and, within a few months, up to 40 Lancasters a night were operating from Elsham.

The creation of the Base system also brought more personnel and more work onto the airfield. Three new T2 hangars were erected and from this point on Elsham became the major servicing centre for squadrons at Kirmington and North Killingholme, as well as its resident squadrons.

Inevitably, more aircraft meant more losses. Three 103 Squadron crews failed to return from a raid on Hanover. The last of the series of raids on Berlin cost 576 Squadron two aircraft and 103 one. A second 103 Squadron aircraft, M-Mother (the replacement for ED888 which, by this time, had been transferred to 576 Squadron) was badly damaged by flak and by a night fighter's cannon. The rear gunner was killed and the aircraft was riddled with holes and short of fuel. The pilot, Flight Sergeant Fred Browning, had to use his knees to force the control column forward to prevent the Lancaster stalling as it limped back across the hostile skies of northern Europe. Coned by searchlights, the crew escaped by firing the recognition signals they had seen a night fighter use when it was caught earlier in the raid. Finally they made it back to England where Browning put the Lancaster down at Dunsford,

LM227 of 576 Squadron with members of her aircrew and ground crew. This aircraft, coded I-Squared, went on to complete 100 operations with the squadron, flying from Elsham and later Fiskerton. This picture probably dates from September 1944. (Author's collection)

only for the brakes to fail. The Lancaster slewed off the runway and crashed into the wreckage of a Flying Fortress which had come to grief in a similar manner two days earlier. Four of the crew were awarded DFCs and one a DFM.

Three of the 32 Lancasters sent from Elsham on the Nuremberg raid failed to return. Seven were lost in a single night in the attack on German tank concentrations at Mailly-le-Camp in May and another seven in the twin raids on the railway junction at Revigny in what was the busiest and bloodiest summer of the war at Elsham Wolds.

In the late spring Air Commodore Constantine left Elsham to take up a post as Senior Air Staff Officer at Group HQ and was replaced by Air Commodore R. Ivelaw-Chapman, who had gone to Elsham after a staff posting during which he had taken part in the planning for the coming invasion.

A few days after taking up his new job, the air commodore flew as second pilot in a 576 Squadron Lancaster in a raid on an ammunition dump in northern France. It was a successful attack, but Ivelaw-Chapman's aircraft was shot down and he became a prisoner of war.

S-Sugar of 103 Squadron pictured in March, 1945 with six of her crew at Elsham.
They were to complete 10 operations from Elsham before the war ended. (Mrs A. Selby)

There were real fears that part of the invasion plans could be compromised but Ivelaw-Chapman, holder of the DFC and AFC, kept his secrets to himself and, fortunately, the Germans failed to appreciate the importance of a man they assumed to be just another 'kriegie.'

Elsham's squadrons played a leading role in the furious bombing campaign waged over France in the summer of 1944, in one raid sending 42 Lancasters to attack a V1 site. Bomber Command, however, had not forgotten what it perceived as its main objective, the levelling of vast areas of Germany, and in July eight aircraft, four from each squadron, were lost in a single night over Stuttgart.

In the autumn Elsham reverted to a one-squadron station once again when 576 moved to Fiskerton following the Group reorganisation in Lincolnshire, but it was to be joined by another squadron in the closing stages of the war when 100 moved from Waltham in April 1945. Interestingly, when 576 was preparing to move out, one of the aircraft on its strength was ED888, then with 131 bomb symbols on its nose. It was decided to leave the old girl behind and she completed her final nine trips back with 103 Squadron before being designated 'Cat B', the death sentence for a tired old Lancaster (even though it was less than

Bang on target. This was the scene from Flt Lt Marsden's Lancaster of 103 Squadron in a raid on the Pauillac refinery on the French coast on 4th August 1944. (Author's collection)

two years since she had been built in Manchester). ED888 was finally flown out of Elsham to the maintenance unit at Tollerton in Nottinghamshire by Flight Lieutenant John Henry, one of three Australian brothers who all served on 103 Squadron and who, on one famous occasion, flew together on a raid on Cologne. Before ED888 was broken up, Henry managed to purloin the bomb release cable which was later mounted and is now in the possession of the Elsham Wolds Association.

After the war there was a gradual wind-down at Elsham. 103 Squadron reformed as 57 Squadron and moved to Scampton with 100 Squadron and the airfield was used for a time by Albemarle glider tugs. But the toll of four years of constant use was beginning to tell and the station was finally closed at the end of 1946.

13
FALDINGWORTH

The first 'military aircraft' seen at what was to become RAF Faldingworth were half a dozen wooden Whitley bombers scattered across open fields in the spring of 1940. Faldingworth, which lies just off the Market Rasen-Lincoln road, was then officially the Toft Grange decoy site, one of a series across Lincolnshire intended to persuade the Germans the RAF was much stronger than it really was. Toft Grange was to keep its dummy aircraft for over two years, by which time the airfield contractors had moved in to build yet another Lincolnshire bomber airfield.

The first commanding officer at Faldingworth was Group Captain Neil Mason, and when he arrived to take up his post on 24th July 1943 a sorry place it looked. The runways had been laid and one of the T2 hangars together with some scattered buildings erected. The rest looked like a building site, and was to stay that way for some weeks.

Faldingworth had opened as a satellite of RAF Lindholme in South Yorkshire, 1 Group's Heavy Conversion Base HQ, and within ten days 1667 Heavy Conversion Unit moved in from Lindholme with its mixed bag of Lancasters and Halifaxes. The Halifaxes were used for the first part of the course, with student crews then passing on to Lancasters – the aircraft they would use on squadrons – in the later period of their time at Faldingworth. The first conversion course began in mid-August and over the next few months the instructors of 1667 were working flat out to provide the replacement crews 1 Group needed. The training itself could be hazardous and Faldingworth suffered its first fatality at the end of September when a Lancaster crashed on landing, killing the navigator.

By November Faldingworth had become an all-Halifax HCU when the Lancaster flight moved to Hemswell as C-Flight of the new 1 Group Lancaster Finishing School. Crews at Faldingworth now trained solely on the three flights of Halifaxes before progressing to Hemswell to complete their training on Lancasters.

In the meantime, 300 Squadron was still operating its Wellington Mk Xs from Ingham. The Wellington had been withdrawn from front line service as a bomber, but was still used for minelaying operations. Ingham was unsuitable for Lancasters because it was alone among 1 Group bomber airfields in still having grass runways. So 1667 moved out to the new airfield at Sandtoft and Faldingworth, by now transferred to the control of 14 Base at Ludford Magna, prepared to become a bomber airfield at last.

Three experienced crews from 300 Squadron had moved to Ludford to train on Lancasters and in February 1944 they arrived at Faldingworth to begin passing on their new-found knowledge to the Polish crews as they arrived from Ingham. They brought their Wellingtons with them, and rather than leave them idle while training progressed, the crews were expected to take their turn on minelaying operations, the very first from Faldingworth being staged on 3rd/4th March when three aircraft dropped mines on the approach to the U-boat base at Lorient. All three returned safely, including that flown by Warrant Officer Blachowicz, who was on his 50th operation with 300 Squadron.

Faldingworth now housed a complement of 821 RAF and WAAF personnel, 598 of whom were Polish. 300 Squadron itself was still almost entirely Polish and was anxious to preserve its national identity, something which made losses all the harder to bear.

300 used its Lancasters in anger for the first time on the night of 18/19th April in a successful 1 Group attack on marshalling yards at Rouen in northern France, an attack which was part of the build-up for the Allied landings on Normandy.

The squadron was in action again a week later when twelve aircraft took part in a Main Force attack on Karlsruhe. Nineteen of the 637 Lancasters and Halifaxes sent were lost, including two from Faldingworth. The squadron records speak of the loss of two complete Polish crews as a 'severe set-back'. There were to be many more in the months ahead for the Poles at Faldingworth.

An attack on Dortmund a month later cost the squadron two more of its Lancasters and the lives of eleven men. One of these aircraft suffered an engine failure on take-off, a wing tip clipping the top of the airfield firing range and the heavily-laden bomber cartwheeling into the ground. Miraculously, four of the crew were pulled from the wreckage alive. Four nights later another aircraft was lost in an attack on Gelsenkirchen, while French targets following the invasion were to cost

A message for Hitler is chalked in Polish on the side of this 4,000lb bomb which is being fused ready for delivery by 300 Squadron from Faldingworth. (N. Franklin via Peter Green)

Faldingworth two more Lancasters and their crews.

Four more crews were lost in July but the two aircraft lost in a raid on Stuttgart went down with all-British crews, an indication of the gradual but inevitable transformation of the squadron. The station records at this time show that an increasing number of personnel at Faldingworth were non-Polish.

Throughout Bomber Command the Poles of 300 Squadron were highly respected for their bravery and airmanship. They were to win 106 British gallantry medals in addition to those awarded by the Polish government-in-exile. Typical of their determination were the actions of Warrant Officer Stepien and his crew in a daylight attack on Calais and the gun batteries at Cap Griz Nez. They made one run through the barrage of anti-aircraft fire only to discover their bombs had failed to be released. Undeterred, they went round again, only for the same thing to happen. It was only after a third unsuccessful run across the target that Stepien reluctantly turned for home where it was found an electrical fault had prevented the aircraft dropping its bombs.

Throughout its time at Faldingworth 300 remained a two-flight squadron and was able to contribute up to 15 aircraft a time for the heavy raids of the autumn and winter. It was during this period the

Last landing for a veteran Pole. A Lancaster of 300 Squadron near the airfield at Faldingworth after a wheels-up landing. Note the Polish insignia on the nose, together with the circular gas patch unique to 1 Group aircraft. (J. Croft-Bednarski)

Poles at Faldingworth were watching with growing dismay the events unfolding in eastern Europe, including the lack of support shown for the fighters in the Warsaw ghetto and the decision taken at Yalta to divide Poland.

Nevertheless, the Poles of 300 Squadron went to Dresden, and to Chemnitz, and to all the other targets they were ordered to attack in those closing months of the war. They continued dropping bombs on Germans until their final mission of the war, the attack on Berchtesgaden when Flight Lieutenant Witkowski's Lancaster was hit by flak and two of his crew injured.

300 Squadron was eventually disbanded at Faldingworth in October 1946 and was followed by a second Polish squadron, 305, which disbanded the following year. Unlike some of its neighbours, the airfield was retained by the RAF and used by a maintenance unit for many years, storing and supplying munitions to other operational stations in Lincolnshire. Part of the airfield was then acquired by the British Manufacturing and Research Company, based at Grantham, to develop and test guns and ammunition through its subsidiary, Astra Engineering. This business ended in the mid-1990s and Faldingworth was added to the list of deserted wartime airfields in Lincolnshire.

14
FISKERTON

There was an unusual silence across the airfield at RAF Fiskerton on the morning of 18th August 1943. It was still a relatively new place and not all the 36 dispersal pans were yet stained with oil and hydraulic fluid from resting Lancaster bombers.

Its sole occupant, 49 Squadron of Bomber Command's 5 Group, was still only a two-flight squadron but on that beautiful summer's morning Fiskerton seemed almost empty. The night before, 49 Squadron had taken part in what was to prove one of the most significant bombing raids of the war and a third of the Lancaster bombers it had despatched had failed to return.

Bomber Command's attack on the secret German rocket establishment at Peenemunde had cost the RAF 40 aircraft. But, although the attack by the 560 aircraft which had reached the target had not been as successful as at first thought, sufficient damage was done to delay the launching of the first V2 missiles by a vital two months.

The raid marked a turning point in the bombing war: it was essentially a precision attack by Bomber Command, which had hitherto used sledgehammer raids on most of its targets; it was carried out in full moonlight to aid this precision; and, for the first time on a Main Force attack, it used the Master Bomber technique, which was to become such an essential feature of tactics in the final 21 months of war.

All that was of little consequence that morning at Fiskerton. The night before the squadron had provided twelve of the 117 Lancasters which 5 Group had contributed to the raid. One had turned back with a mechanical defect. The other eleven had all dropped their bombs but, as they turned for home, they were caught by the German night fighters which earlier in the raid had been lured south to Berlin by a spoof attack by Mosquitos. In bright moonlight, the Luftwaffe had fallen on the retreating bombers like wolves on a flock of sheep. 5

Group, which was in the third and final wave of the attack, suffered badly. Seventeen of its Lancasters were shot down and 111 men killed, compared with just three lost by 1 Group, which provided almost the same number of aircraft yet bombed earlier in the attack. What made it worse for Fiskerton was that all the losses were amongst experienced crews. Squadron Leader R. G. Todd-White and his crew, whose Lancaster was brought down in the Baltic, were on the second operation of their second tour; Pilot Officer T. E. Toplin had already won the DFC as his crew amassed 23 ops before that night, yet all that experience couldn't save them when they were caught by a night fighter over Denmark. All 14 men died in both those aircraft, as did those in the third 49 Squadron Lancaster to go down, again over Denmark, piloted by Flying Officer H. J. Randall, who was on his eighth operation.

The only survivors from the ill-fated Fiskerton Lancasters were five men in the fourth aircraft to be lost, which was caught soon after they left the target by a night fighter using the new upward-firing cannon. The pilot, Sergeant Charles Robinson, was blown clear when the aircraft exploded, his parachute being forced open by the explosion of the aircraft's fuel tanks.

The briefing at Fiskerton the night before had mirrored that carried out throughout Bomber Command: Peenemunde was a target which must be destroyed, and, if that meant going back again the following night, or the night after that, then so be it. It was a sobering message for the 600-plus crews being briefed across eastern England, who were all too aware of the dangers of flying in full moonlight over northern Germany. In his excellent book, *The Peenemunde Raid*, historian Martin Middlebrook records the feelings of many men who flew to the previously unheard-of spot on the Baltic coast. One was Sergeant J. E. Hudson of 49 Squadron, who said that most of those at the briefing at Fiskerton expected losses to be heavy. 'When the target was known, we just gave a philosophical shrug and envied those crews who were on leave,' he wrote. His fears were correct. The Peenemunde attack proved to be the worst night of the war for Fiskerton, one of the cluster of bomber airfields built within sight of Lincoln Cathedral.

Work had started on the site, which lay between the villages of Fiskerton and Reepham five miles east of Lincoln, in early 1942. A variety of contractors were used to construct what was a typical Lincolnshire bomber airfield. There were three runways, laid in an A-pattern, and three hangars, two close to the technical site on the south-eastern side of the airfield and a third in the opposite corner. Living accommodation was in the ubiquitous Nissen huts and was dispersed around the camp. A minor road which once linked the villages of Reepham and Fiskerton had to be closed and local traffic was diverted through nearby Cherry Willingham.

The airfield was ready for occupation in November 1942 when the first station personnel moved in. It was two months before its first aircraft, the Lancasters of 49 Squadron, arrived from Scampton. It was not an entirely popular move for the men serving with the squadron. Scampton was a comfortable pre-war airfield, with excellent facilities, and here they were being moved into cold Nissen huts on the edge of the Fens in a Lincolnshire winter. For those of us who have spent our lives in Lincolnshire, it was a wholly understandable feeling.

The squadron had been in action over Berlin on the two nights before the move to Fiskerton where, for the first time, it was able to operate from hardened runways.

It was quickly in action from its new home and took part in two Berlin raids that January, one of its aircraft, Lancaster ED444, failing to return from the second raid. Another early casualty was a Lancaster which crashed on its approach into Fiskerton on its way back from a raid on Hamburg in the early hours of 31st January. 49 Squadron was also called upon to play its part in the extensive mining campaign then being waged on ports from the Baltic to the Spanish coast. One of these, a mining trip to Lorient in February, ended in disaster for one Fiskerton Lancaster when it hit a balloon cable off Plymouth and crashed into the sea.

During the spring 49 Squadron played its part in the heavy attacks on the Ruhr valley and paid the price. Four Lancasters were lost in raids on Texel, Duisburg, Düsseldorf and Bochum. It was the night after the Bochum raid, on 14th June 1943, when the Fiskerton squadron was badly mauled in an accurate but costly attack on Oberhausen. Seventeen of the 197 Lancasters sent that night were shot down, three of them from Fiskerton. Only five of the 22 men on board those aircraft survived.

Fiskerton was then one of only a handful of Lancaster bases in Bomber Command and 49 Squadron was operating with 19 relatively new aircraft. However, its serviceability record suffered in comparison with neighbouring Scampton and Waddington simply because the facilities for its ground crews were so rudimentary. This was one of the problems its commanding officer, Wing Commander Leonard Slee, was determined to put right. More equipment and better facilities were eventually provided and 49's ability to put up most of its aircraft for attacks increased dramatically. It was this kind of approach which made Wing Commander Slee a popular and respected senior officer and those who served at Fiskerton at the time attribute much of the good morale on the station to his leadership.

It was during this period that 5 Group was experimenting with innovative methods of bombing which its AOC, Air Vice-Marshal the Hon Ralph Cochrane, believed would prove a more effective way of using the power of Bomber Command. It involved a timed run to the target from a fixed point and was first used on the night of 20th/21st June against the Zeppelin factory at Friedrichshafen on the shores of Lake Constance. The technique required pin-point navigation and proved to be very effective that night when the factory, which was being used to make air defence radar, was badly hit. It also featured the first use of a 'controller', a system later developed into that of the Master Bomber, who was Wing Commander Slee of 49 Squadron, with Wing Commander Gomm of 467 Squadron, then at Bottesford, as deputy.

It was a small target which needed marking accurately by the four Pathfinder aircraft from 97 Squadron, before the 60 Lancasters from 5 Group made their time-and-distance bombing run. All but one of the Lancasters found the target and widespread damage was caused. Six aircraft were slightly damaged by flak and the German night fighters, which had expected to intercept the bombers on the long haul back across southern Germany and France, were foiled when the Lancasters continued flying south, eventually landing after a flight of ten hours in Algeria in what was to become the first of the 'shuttle attacks' on long-distance targets. Wing Commander Slee, in the meantime, had had to relinquish control of the raid for a short period to his deputy after an engine caught fire and threatened to spread to the rest of the starboard wing. The fire, however, was extinguished and Slee later made it to Maison Blanche in Algeria on just three engines.

It was this same time-and-distance technique 5 Group was to use months later in the attack on Peenemunde, albeit with limited success. 49 Squadron had been amongst those trained in the new technique on the bombing range at Wainfleet. To simulate the run in to the target, aircraft were instructed to find the Grimsby-Peterborough railway line south of Louth and then fly in a straight line over Willoughby to the range target. First attempts were, according to Martin Middlebrook, a complete shambles and it was only when Cochrane flew a Lancaster over this route and dropped his bombs within 30 yards of the target that the 5 Group crews began to stir themselves.

After Peenemunde, 49 Squadron, like most Bomber Command units, found itself pitched against the target few crews relished – Berlin. The attacks on the German capital during the winter of 1943–44 cost Bomber Command dearly, but 49 Squadron was to fare better than any other in the months to come. It mounted no fewer than 20 raids on the 'Big City', flying a total of 273 sorties, losing just seven aircraft. Its loss rate of 2.6 per cent was the lowest in the whole of Bomber Command. That statistic, however, was little compensation for the loss of 58 men from the squadron, only 18 of whom managed to escape from their Lancasters.

The first loss came on the night of 3rd/4th September 1943 when JB126 of 49 Squadron was hit by flak after leaving the target. The pilot, Flying Officer Coates, managed to nurse his aircraft back across Germany and Holland before finally ditching in the North Sea. He and another crew member were drowned when the aircraft broke up and sank rapidly. Five men made it into the aircraft's dinghy but only two, Sergeants Underwood and Nelson, were alive when an air-sea rescue launch found them.

The crew of another Fiskerton Lancaster were more fortunate on the raid of 23rd/24th November. They just made it back to Lincolnshire, crash-landing on the beach at Chapel St Leonards and able to walk to safety. Two nights later a Lancaster on its way home from Berlin crashed two miles short of Fiskerton. Only the two gunners survived. Two aircraft were lost on one raid, on 2nd/3rd January 1944, while the attack on 26/27th November also cost 49 Squadron two Lancasters, one being shot down close to Berlin and the second crashing in flames on its final approach into Fiskerton early in the morning of 27th November.

One of those lost was Lancaster J-Jig, flown by Warrant Officer Bob Petty and his crew. On the night of 2nd December 1943 they were on their bomb run over Berlin when they were attacked by a night fighter. The rear turret had lost power during the long flight from Lincolnshire, but Petty and his crew opted to carry on, even though the loss of the turret provided them with ample grounds to turn for home.

During the attack, the fighter, identified by the crew as a Me110, was engaged by the mid-upper gunner, Sgt Owen Roberts. As he returned fire, one of his two .303 machine guns jammed, leaving just one gun to deter the Messerschmitt. Their luck was in for Roberts' fire set one of the night fighter's engines ablaze and it dived away. They were attacked a second time and, again, Roberts drove away a Me110. Their luck finally ran out as they crossed Berlin. An 88mm anti-aircraft shell hit the starboard wing and immediately the pilot ordered his crew to abandon the aircraft. Six of the eight men on board (J-Jig was carrying a second pilot to give him experience before his own crew became operational) escaped. Among those who survived were Owen Roberts and the Lancaster's skipper.

In the meantime, there had been a few changes at Fiskerton itself. 49 Squadron moved out for five weeks to Dunholme Lodge early in the autumn of 1943 while runway repairs were carried out. It was from Dunholme that 49 flew operationally against a variety of targets, including Hanover, Mannheim, Munich, Kassel and Leipzig, raids which underlined the growing power and efficiency of Bomber Command.

Fiskerton had also been selected as one of the first two airfields in Lincolnshire to be fitted with the new fog dispersal device, FIDO (it stood for Fog Investigation Dispersal Organisation). Installation work had begun in August but had been held up by the boggy conditions of the airfield and by flying operations. The pace of work, particularly the complex operations carried out by Strong-Arc Welding of Lincoln, quickened when 49 Squadron moved to Dunholme, and the installation was ready for the first trial burns on 27th October. FIDO operated by raw petrol being ignited along a system of pipes either side of the runway, the heat dispersing the fog over the immediate area. There were, however, problems for crews attempting to land between the lines of flames. The heat caused an updraught and the glare from the flames impaired visibility.

Both problems were eventually overcome but, on that first occasion, one Lancaster had seven attempts at landing before it finally got down.

The first night-landing trials were carried out the following month and the glow in the sky was so spectacular that Lincoln Fire Brigade was inundated with calls and turned out all its appliances to what was reported as a major fire at Fiskerton airfield.

The FIDO installation at Fiskerton was very successful. It was used on a number of occasions in 1944 and 1945 to land aircraft in conditions which would have been otherwise impossible, including heavy snow. The cost in petrol was enormous. In one burn in December 1944 it consumed 188,000 gallons of petrol.

49 squadron returned to Fiskerton on 24th October 1943 and had almost two weeks' respite before it was in action again, this time over Düsseldorf.

Early in the new year it was joined by 1514 BAT Flight, which arrived with its Oxfords from Coningsby. It was to spend the next year

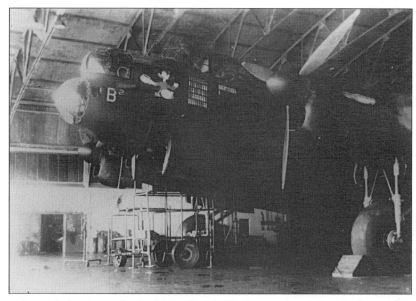

B-Squared of 576, proudly displaying Donald Duck artwork and 61 operation symbols on her fuselage. (Ron Durran via Peter Green)

at Fiskerton.

In the autumn of 1944 there was a major change when Fiskerton was transferred from 5 to 1 group. It was again a sub-station of Scampton, which had been renumbered 15 Base. 49 Squadron was to remain with 5 Group and moved to Fulbeck, near Grantham. Its place at Fiskerton was taken by 576 Squadron, which had been operating in tandem with 103 Squadron at Elsham Wolds for the past year. Interestingly, one thing 576 left behind at Elsham was its veteran Lancaster ED888, known to all at the airfield as *Mother of Them All*. It was returned to 103 Squadron and went on to complete 140 operations.

576 briefly shared Fiskerton with the newly-reformed 150 Squadron, which spent a month there before moving to Hemswell in November 1944.

576 was put to work as soon as it arrived at Fiskerton. Its aircraft arrived at the airfield in the morning and within a few hours were being prepared for a raid that night on Cologne.

Over the next few months its aircraft were involved in numerous attacks on German targets, including at least two raids on Essen, and several daylight attacks. The squadron was also involved in the Manna

I-Item of 576 Squadron after its 100th operation, an Operation Manna food drop over Holland in May 1945. With her are Flt Lt Stuart Simpson and crew plus Item's ground crew. (R. Walkington via Peter Green)

food drops for Dutch civilians and in repatriating Allied prisoners of war. It suffered its final loss of the war on VE Day when Lancaster NN806, which carried the identification letters UL-M2, crashed on take off from Fiskerton.

In the final days of the war 576 had been joined at Fiskerton by 625 Squadron, which moved out of Kelstern in April 1945. Both squadrons disbanded there and by November the airfield had been placed in the hands of a Maintenance Unit.

The airfield was to remain in Air Ministry hands until the early 1960s when most of the land was sold off to local farmers. One part of the airfield did, however, remain operational. In 1960 one of the Royal Observer Corps' first purpose-built Protected Group Control centres was opened at Fiskerton. The project was funded by the Home Office as part of the civil defence programme and Fiskerton was to play a key part in the work of the ROC in Lincolnshire until the Corps was formally 'stood down' in July 1991. Four years later a memorial to all those who served there with both 49 and 576 Squadrons was dedicated. It stands, fittingly, alongside one of the old runways.

15
FULBECK

Fulbeck was unique amongst Lincolnshire airfields in that it was used operationally by both the US 9th Army Air Force and RAF Bomber Command. The Americans used it as part of their airborne assault on Normandy and to support airborne operations in Holland, while two Lancaster squadrons of 5 Group were to fly from Fulbeck for the last six months of the war.

The airfield had first come into use in 1940 when Cranwell was looking for relief landing grounds for its large number of training aircraft. As a result a large, relatively flat site was surveyed three miles west of the village of Fulbeck at the southern end of the Lincolnshire Cliff.

Some temporary buildings were erected and runways laid out on the grassy fields. It was a good site for Cranwell, being relatively close and yet well away from the growing number of operational airfields further north in Lincolnshire.

There is some evidence that it was used extensively, particularly in 1941 as training demands grew almost by the week at Cranwell. There are a number of recorded crashes on the airfield site at Fulbeck, all involving Oxfords or Avro Tutors from Cranwell. In one incident, one Oxford is reported to have landed on top of another on the main runway.

By the end of 1941 agreement had been reached to build a full-scale airfield at Fulbeck for 5 Group of Bomber Command and all flying ceased in February 1942 as the contractors moved in. Three concrete runways were laid and three T2 hangars erected, two others being built some time later for the storage of gliders.

As soon as the runways were down RAF Fulbeck, now an official satellite of Syerston in Nottinghamshire, received its first unit, 1485 (Bomber) Gunnery Flight, which moved in from Dunholme Lodge with a mixed bag of aircraft, including several Manchesters, Wellingtons and least one Whitley.

By December 1942 Fulbeck was deemed to be ready to accept night flying and with no operational squadrons as yet pencilled in, it was allocated once again to Cranwell for night flying training for crews attached to its Service Flying Training School.

In the late spring of 1943, 1506 Beam Approach Training Flight arrived from Waddington with its Airspeed Oxfords and was to remain at Fulbeck until it moved to Skellingthorpe, along with 1485 Gunnery Flight. During its time at Fulbeck 1506 briefly operated two Lancasters borrowed from 1660 Heavy Conversion Unit at Swinderby. These were quickly returned as they were needed for training purposes and were replaced by five unloved Manchesters.

Cranwell's training aircraft had moved north to use Caistor for night flying, but returned briefly in September 1943 after one was shot down by a Luftwaffe intruder looking for richer pickings among the north Lincolnshire bomber airfields. While all this had been going on, Fulbeck, along with three other airfields in south Lincolnshire, had been allocated to the 9th USAAF, looking for bases for its huge fleet of transport aircraft, which were to play such an important role in the Allies' invasion plans.

Fulbeck was allocated to the 53rd Troop Carrier Wing, which numbered it Station 488, and in early October an advance party arrived to be followed a few days later by the four squadrons of the 434th Troop Carrier Group, which flew its C47s directly in from the United States. Under the command of Colonel Fred Stevens, the 434th were quickly into the task of training for paratroop drops and towing Horsa gliders, 32 of which had earlier been brought to Fulbeck and assembled by an RAF maintenance unit.

The 434th were to remain at Fulbeck until March 1944 when they moved to Aldermaston, and were replaced by the 442nd, which again operated four squadrons of C47s. They, too, quickly got down to the serious business of training and on D-Day were allocated the task of dropping the US Airborne's 507 Parachute Infantry Regiment plus its headquarters company, which had earlier been camped on the John Players sports ground in Nottingham.

Forty-five C47s were involved in the drop. Led by the Group's commanding officer, Colonel Charles Smith, they began dropping the paratroops at 2.40 am on 6th June close to the Normandy village of Ste Mère-Eglise. The aircraft were ordered to drop the paras from 700 feet, a height which left the aircraft at the mercy of light flak and small arms fire. Several aircraft crossed the drop zone a number of times to make sure the troops were to be delivered to the right spot. Three C47s were shot down, one after it dropped its stick, and a further 28 returned to Fulbeck with flak damage.

There were some frantic scenes at the airfield that day as the damaged aircraft were patched up and replacements prepared for the following day's operation when some 56 C47s left Fulbeck on a resupply mission over Normandy.

The Americans remained at Fulbeck for only another five days and the airfield was to be all but empty for much of the summer of 1944. 1660 HCU, based at Swinderby, used the runways for practice landings and by the end of August the 9th USAAF returned, this time in the shape of the 440th Troop Carrier Group. It had moved north from its home base at Exeter to prepare for Operation Comet, returning briefly to Exeter when this was cancelled and then moving back north again for the Market Garden operation.

At least 90 C47s used Fulbeck to transport elements of the 376 Parachute Field Artillery of the American 101st Airborne to drop zones in Holland. Unlike its neighbours at Barkston Heath, Folkingham and North Witham, it was not involved in the British drop at Arnhem.

Further glider-borne resupply missions were carried out before the 440th returned to Exeter on 24th September where it was engaged in ferrying supplies to France. A week later the airfield had been relinquished by the Americans and handed back to 5 Group, which was to lose no time in finding new tenants for it.

The availability of Fulbeck coincided with the reorganisation of 1 and 5 Groups in Lincolnshire and the airfield, with its five hangars, was seen as ideal for two Lancaster squadrons. It became part of 56 Base (which had its headquarters at Syerston) and on 10th October 49 Squadron arrived from Fiskerton, flying its first operation from there against Nuremberg in an all-5 Group attack on 19th October.

Two weeks later it was joined by 189 Squadron, which had been formed in mid-October at Bardney, inheriting most of its Lancasters from 9 Squadron. One of these was EE136 *Spirit of Russia*, which had completed some 97 operations with 9 Squadron before being transferred. *Spirit of Russia* took off from Bardney at 2.16 pm on its 98th operational, and 189's first, on 1st November for a daylight attack on the refinery at Homberg. It returned four hours later and the following day moved with the rest of the squadron the twelve miles or so to Fulbeck. *Spirit of Russia* was to fly a further 16 operations from Fulbeck before being retired after a raid on Karlsruhe on 2nd/3rd February 1945.

Both squadrons had an eventful few months at Fulbeck. They

operated together for the first time in an early evening attack on the Rheania-Ossag refinery at Harburg in northern Germany, 49 Squadron losing one of its Lancasters. Another Lancaster from 49 Squadron was lost when it crashed at Dry Doddington after take-off on 26th November before a raid on Munich. Over the same target on 17th December one 49 Squadron Lancaster received battle damage in a tangle with a night fighter. Its crew managed to reach the south coast, the pilot landing the aircraft on Worthing beach where it later blew up. Each squadron was to lose an aircraft in an attack on the Wintershall synthetic oil plant at Lutzendorf in March.

A third unit arrived in early February 1945, the Automatic Gun Laying Training Flight which had been formed at Binbrook and moved to Fulbeck where it carried out trials with 49 Squadron.

The run-down began at Fulbeck on 8th April when 189 Squadron returned to Bardney where it was disbanded, one of the shortest-lived of all Bomber Command squadrons.

49 Squadron, which had been joined briefly by the Bomber Command Film Unit, left Fulbeck itself on 22nd April. It was normal (though not official) practice for squadrons to perform a station 'beat-up' to mark their departure, flying low over the airfield as a final salute. 49's departure from Fulbeck in this fashion was to have disastrous consequences. Lancaster PB463, coded EA-I, was stunting over the airfield when a wing tip hit a building in the technical site. The aircraft cartwheeled into the ground, killing the seven men on board along with eight members of the ground staff who had assembled to watch the display. Another 20 men were seriously injured and of those, four were later to die in hospital. It was a tragic finale to Fulbeck's war.

The station was later handed over to Maintenance Comand and was used for disposal sales of air surplus stores. In the 1950s it housed the Air Historical Branch's aircraft collection, many of which are now in the RAF Museum. Fulbeck was to end its military life as it began, as a relief landing ground for Cranwell.

16
GOXHILL

In the far north-eastern corner of Lincolnshire lies the village of Goxhill. The RFC had a relief landing ground near the village during the First World War and that may have been one of the reasons why the Air Ministry decided to survey land around Goxhill in 1940 as it looked to expand its chain of airfields across Lincolnshire. The surveyors settled on a site east of the village and, early in 1941, the contractors moved in to start work on what was intended as another bomber airfield. By mid-summer the runways were down and some of the technical sites complete and RAF Goxhill officially opened.

Events, however, had overtaken Goxhill and, barely before the concrete had time to dry, it was evident it would never be suitable for bomber operations. As the crow flies, Goxhill lies just three miles from Hull, the target for much of the Luftwaffe's attentions in 1941 and 1942. The extensive defences around the city included balloons, many of which were moored on barges in the Humber, effectively blocking the flight path for heavy aircraft into Goxhill.

The Air Ministry was left with a problem. Goxhill had been allocated to 1 Group of Bomber Command, but the only use they could make of it was to move the group's Target Towing Flight in from Binbrook for a month while expansion went on there. It was used again briefly by the Spitfires of 616 Squadron, then stationed at Kirton Lindsey, and by 15 (P) Advanced Flying Unit as the search went on for a permanent role for Goxhill.

Around this time an advance party of the American 8th Army Air Force arrived in Britain to begin the search for airfields to accommodate the bombers and fighters it was planning to transfer in readiness for operations over Europe. Apart from operational airfields, training facilities were needed, particularly for fighter pilots who needed to adapt to European conditions before going into action. Goxhill fitted the bill.

The first American aircraft arrived on 9th July 1942, big P38 Lightning fighters, which had flown across the Atlantic, staging through Nova Scotia, Greenland, Iceland and Scotland. The P38s were from the 71st Fighter Squadron of the 1st Fighter Group and their eventual destination was to be North Africa where many of the inexperienced American pilots found the battle-hardened Germans in their nimble Me109Gs far too good for them. But the Americans learned fast and Goxhill was to be part of the learning process for them.

Goxhill became the first airfield in England to be officially handed over to the Americans and a special ceremony was planned for mid-August, with Air Marshal Sir Charles Portal handing over to General Dwight D. Eisenhower. The airfield was carefully spruced up for the ceremony, with both RAF and USAAF units brought in as honour guards. Unfortunately, this was the time when the Luftwaffe decided to make its first, and only, attack of the war on Goxhill. A single aircraft dropped just one bomb and, as luck would have it, it fell without

Over here. How most people remember American fly-boys. Air crew and ground crew pose beside one of the field's Mustangs, which is standing on pierced steel matting, one of the innovations the Americans brought to the muddy airfields of Linconshire. (Via Ron Parker)

British bikes and a North American Mustang at Goxhill in 1944 with three cheerful members of the ground crew. (Via Ron Parker)

exploding at the point where the two largest runways intersected.

An RAF bomb disposal team called in from Digby were told they had just three and a half hours to make the bomb safe before the arrival of the first VIPs. The officer in charge, Squadron Leader A. Haraar, found a large hole but no sign of the bomb in the eight-foot deep crater. It had disappeared into the soft Lincolnshire clay.

There was no hope of finding the bomb and defusing it before the ceremony so Haraar roped off the area and Goxhill's third runway was used to land the VIPs' aircraft. Eisenhower was told of the bombing and immediately went to see Haraar and, after being briefed, urged him and his team to exercise all caution. After the ceremony, work began in the search for the bomb. A week later there was still no sign of it and Haraar estimated it was at least 30 feet down and possibly still sinking. With pressure on the station commander to press ahead with training, it was decided to fill in the hole and trust Haraar's advice that if the bomb did go off, it was so deep it could do little damage. The bomb, in fact, remained there until 1947 when it was finally recovered and made safe.

Low level over Goxhill. Three visiting Havocs pictured over the airfield. (Via Peter Green)

American units were by now passing through Goxhill with increasing regularity, flying ex-RAF Spitfires, P38s, P39 Airacobras and, by 1943, 'Jugs', P47 Thunderbolts. Many of the units were destined for the 8th AAF airfields in East Anglia and during their time at Goxhill, they flew as often as possible to familiarise themselves with the kind of conditions they were likely to meet once operational. One unit, the 52nd Fighter Group, did get some limited operational experience in its time at Goxhill, flying some 83 defensive sorties over the North Sea with RAF Spitfires from Kirton. These were the only recorded operational flights of the war from Goxhill.

Many of the 8th AAF's top-scoring fighter pilots got their first taste of European flying from Goxhill, including Colonel Arman Peterson, who commanded the 78th Fighter Group and later became the first man to shoot down a jet fighter, an Me262. Another was Texan Glenn Duncan, who was to claim 21 German aircraft while flying with the 353rd Fighter Group from East Anglia. Sadly, no record can be found that Clark Gable, then a captain in the Eighth Air Force, ever flew from Goxhill, despite persistent local rumours that he did.

By the late summer of 1943 there was a major change at Goxhill which, until then, had handled incoming fighter units in transit. Now Goxhill got its own fighter group, the 496th, with two training squadrons, the 554th and 555th, which flew P38s and the new P51 Mustang. The 496th operated in much the same way as an RAF operational training unit and was formed at Goxhill on Christmas Day 1943, with Colonel Harry Magee, a no-nonsense baseball-loving officer,

Above. A dance at the camp – most of the girls are believed to be WAAFs from nearby North Killingholme. Below. A baseball match in progress at Goxhill in 1944.

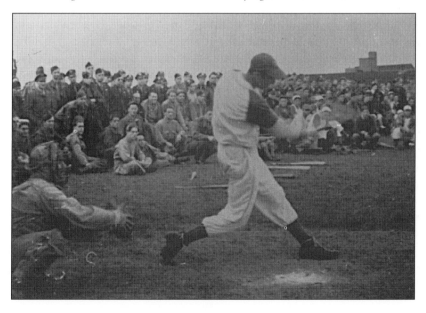

127

who quickly had his new unit up and running. He is a man still fondly remembered by many of the older inhabitants of the Goxhill area.

The Americans made a big impact on the isolated community in which they found themselves. They were looked on with some curiosity by people who, until then, had regarded anyone from as far afield as Hull as an outsider. The Americans, however, quickly won them over with their engaging manner, their relaxed attitude to life and, above all, their generosity. The PX at Goxhill was a place of wonderment for those invited to visit the airfield; the quantity and quality of the food served at their frequent parties was truly awe-inspiring.

A large American Red Cross Club for the personnel at Goxhill, and a small US Army detachment at nearby Immingham, was opened in a former drapery store in the centre of Grimsby and catered for thousands of young men before it finally closed in 1945. The Americans made such good use of the trains into Grimsby from New Holland that the platforms at the nearest station to the airfield, Thornton Abbey, were specially extended to cope with the extra number of passengers.

Like all other training airfields, Goxhill had to endure its share of accidents. Some 23 men were killed and 53 aircraft lost through training accidents, including three Spitfires in a single collision in October 1942. Among the 53 losses was a P38 flown by Second Lieutenant Lane A. Ferrara, who had just taken off from Goxhill on 26th May 1944 when an engine caught fire; the big fighter stalled and plummeted into the ground, killing the young pilot instantly. In 1983 a group of local aviation enthusiasts recovered part of the aircraft, including a propeller blade which has now been incorporated into a memorial to all those who served there during the war.

The Americans finally left Goxhill early in 1945 and on 20th January that year RAF Kirton Lindsey assumed control of the airfield and flying ended. After the war it was transferred to Maintenance Command, which used it to store bombs for many years before it became a Home Office supply depot, storing, among other things, 'Green Goddess' fire appliances. This post-war usage plus the efforts of local landowners and enthusiasts, has ensured that it remains one of the best-preserved of all Lincolnshire's wartime airfields and plans are now well advanced to create an aviation heritage centre at Goxhill.

17
HEMSWELL

When Britain declared war on Germany on 3rd September 1939 RAF Hemswell was the only airfield in north Lincolnshire ready to take part in the coming conflict. It was one of the string of airfields built in the county in the mid-1930s as part of the first stage of the Air Expansion Scheme and had opened in December 1936, initially as a bomber station within 3 Group, transferring to 5 Group nine months later. Its two resident squadrons when it opened were 61 and 144 and they were to remain at Hemswell until 1941, flying Hampdens on some of the earliest and costliest raids of the war.

Today, from a distance at least, Hemswell looks little different to the time when its Hampdens mounted their first operational sortie on 26th September 1939. The four large C-type hangars, built in the familiar arc pattern, are still there, as are most of the brick-built ancillary and technical sites, all clustered together in the style evolved long before airfield dispersal was thought necessary.

The station commanding officer at the outbreak of war was Group Captain Edgar Rice, one of the select band of senior officers with the Military Cross, won in the trenches of Flanders 25 years earlier. It was Rice who was later to command 1 Group, of which Hemswell became an integral part, and it was his association with Hemswell which led to the development and installation of better defensive armament for Lancaster bombers. Rice was at Hemswell at 6.40 am on 29th September 1939 when twelve Hampdens of 144 Squadron took off on what was to be the airfield's first offensive operation of the war. It also proved to be the most disastrous.

Two formations of six aircraft were to attack German warships as they made for Wilhelmshaven after night exercises off Heligoland. The first wave, led by Wing Commander J. C. Cunningham, had just taken off when one of its aircraft had to return to Hemswell with engine trouble. Just as it prepared to land, the second formation, led by

The Hemswell watch office with the large hangars in the background, pictured in 1979. (Scunthorpe Evening Telegraph)

Squadron Leader W. H. Lindsay, was leaving. All the aircraft were armed with four 500lb bombs and they proceeded in two independent formations across the North Sea, Lindsay's aircraft taking a more direct route, while Cunningham's flew north before turning back towards Heligoland. It was this which proved to be fatal for his five Hampdens.

Lindsay's aircraft came across two German destroyers south of Heligoland and three of them went in to attack, the destroyers dodging their bombs and damaging one of their attackers. The second element of three aircraft came under intense anti-aircraft fire over Heligoland itself and wisely headed for home. In the meantime Cunningham's five Hampdens arrived in the same area 20 minutes after Lindsay's aircraft had stirred the hornets' nest, just as 20 Me109s arrived from the fighter airfield at Jever in north Germany. The result was a massacre. All five Hampdens were shot down within minutes, but not before the gunners had accounted for two of the fighters. Five men, one from each of the Hemswell aircraft, survived and were picked up by German patrol boats. The ease with which the Messerschmitts were able to destroy the Hampdens led to urgent modifications on other aircraft then in operational service at Hemswell, Scampton and Waddington.

It was Hampdens from Hemswell, this time from 61 Squadron, which were among the first British aircraft to drop bombs on German soil when they raided the seaplane base at Hörnum on the island of Sylt in March 1940 in retaliation for an attack by the Luftwaffe on the Orkneys two nights earlier. This time all the Hampdens returned to Hemswell.

One of the primary roles of the Hampdens then flying out of Lincolnshire was minelaying – 'gardening' in RAF parlance. Air Vice Marshal Arthur Harris (later Air Chief Marshal Sir Arthur Harris) was the AOC of 5 Group and was an enthusiastic advocate of using his aircraft to mine key areas around the German coast. As a result the three Lincolnshire airfields were each allocated areas for a period of intense minelaying in April 1940, Hemswell's being the Kiel approaches, where 48 mines were to be dropped, and Warnemunde (twelve mines).

It was the first of many such operations carried out in the war by bombers based in Lincolnshire and proved very successful, post-war research showing that at least six major ships were mined in the area allocated to the 5 Group aircraft during April that year. It was not, however, without its dangers, particularly when the Germans began using flak ships, often old hulks armed with a fearsome array of AA weapons. The Hemswell squadrons were to lose more than a dozen aircraft on mining operations and numerous other aircraft returned with visible reminders of the Germans' attempt to stop the sowing of magnetic mines in the approaches to their major ports.

In July 15 Hampdens from Hemswell were involved in one of the most daring attacks of the war when they raided Wilhelmshaven in an attempt to cripple the *Tirpitz* and *Admiral Scheer*. Six aircraft, three from each squadron, were detailed to attack *Tirpitz* and three, two of them from 61 Squadron, to attack *Admiral Scheer*. The remainder of the aircraft were to carry out diversionary raids around what was then the most heavily defended target in Germany.

The crews pressed home their attacks with astonishing bravery but without success. Four aircraft were shot down and most of the survivors damaged (the ground crew of one counted 150 holes in the aircraft the following day) yet none of the modified sea mines dropped by the attackers appear to have damaged the German warships, which were to remain thorns in the side of the British for most of the war.

Hemswell's Hampdens were in constant use through the winter of 1940 and the spring and early summer of 1941 on bombing raids over Germany, a task for which the Hampden was barely adequate. Its lack of range led to many losses as fuel ran out and crews were forced to abandon their aircraft over the North Sea or simply disappeared without trace.

144 Squadron appeared to suffer more than most and twelve of the 27 Hampdens abandoned by their crews over England for this reason were from the squadron. In one extraordinary incident in February 1941 Sergeant Dainty and his crew baled out over Kirton Lindsey, just north of Hemswell, rather than try to land after a raid on Hanover. Their Hampden flew on for another 70 miles before finally crashing at Bircham Newton in Norfolk.

The Hampdens finally flew out of Hemswell in July 1941 as the station passed to its new 'owners', 1 Group, which brought in two Polish squadrons, 300 and 301, from Swinderby, itself transferring to 5 Group. Both squadrons had been formed a year previously and had initially operated Battles before converting to Wellingtons in the autumn of 1940. The two squadrons operated with great success from Hemswell in those early days, quickly building a reputation for themselves as fearless and skilful airmen. Both squadrons were entirely

Early days at Hemswell. A posed publicity picture of Poles of 300 Squadron, probably in the summer of 1941.

Polish when they moved to Hemswell, the majority of the aircrew having served in the Polish Air Force before being forced to flee to England when their country was overrun. Later, as casualties mounted, other nationalities had to be introduced as reinforcements and eventually 301 was disbanded through lack of Polish air crew.

They took part in numerous attacks that first year, largely on dock installations in both France and Germany, along with dropping sea mines, a task the aggressive Poles often found irksome.

Their first station commander was Air Commodore Arthur Wray, another ex-Army officer whose pronounced limp and Military Cross were reminders of his service in France in the First World War. He believed in leading from the front and had already won a DFC before arriving at Hemswell, where he was to be awarded a bar to the medal for his part in the Poles' operations in 1941. He later moved to Binbrook as station commander and won an Air Force Cross at the age of 45.

The fortunes of the Polish squadrons were naturally followed with great interest by the Polish government-in-exile and, in the spring of 1942, General Sikorski, the commander in chief of Polish forces, visited the airfield to present bravery awards.

Soon after this Hemswell assumed control of the new airfield at Ingham and 300 Squadron was dispersed there in May, its place taken at Hemswell by a third Polish squadron, 305, which had been operating out of Lindholme in South Yorkshire.

All three squadrons were to play a key role in Bomber Command raids on Germany that year, including the two 1,000-bomber raids on Cologne on 30th/31st May and Essen the following night.

At the end of January 1943, 300 Squadron returned to Hemswell where, two months later, it was brought fully up to strength when 301 Squadron was disbanded and its personnel transferred. Both squadrons were then moved to Ingham while runway construction work began at Hemswell, the beginning of another chapter in the airfield's history.

While the construction work was going on, the airfield was used briefly as the 1 Group Operational Crew Pool, where aircrew were sent prior to posting to operational squadrons. By the end of the year, however, it was ready to commence its new role as home of the 1 Group Lancaster Finishing School, which had been formed at Lindholme and had previously operated from there and the airfield at Faldingworth. Its purpose was to introduce crews fresh from Heavy Conversion Units to the Lancaster, the bomber they would fly operationally. Crews spent on average twelve days at the LFS,

IQ-B Baker of 150 Squadron at Hemswell in 1944. The nose art shows Captain Reilly Ffoul from the Daily Mirror cartoon Just Jane. It bore the name We Dood It Too, in recognition of an earlier mount of the crew, named We Dood It. (Vernon Wilkes)

depending on weather conditions, during which time they were expected to familiarise themselves with the aircraft and cram in as much flying as possible.

The throughput at Hemswell that year was enormous. In May 136 crews were trained, in June it reached a peak of 150. The training, however, was not without its risk and a number of crews and their experienced instructors were lost in crashes.

Hemswell's No 1 hangar was also pressed into use as a fitting bay for the new Rose turret devised for 1 Group's Lancasters by Lincolnshire engineer Alfred Rose, who lived nearby at Fillingham Castle. The new turrets, which mounted .5 guns instead of the standard .303s in Fraser-Nash turrets, had been developed in conjunction with 'Bomber' Harris, who was a personal friend of Rose, and were built at Rose's factory in Gainsborough, which in peace-time had made tea machinery for plantations in India and Ceylon. The turrets were taken by road to Hemswell and there fitted in Lancasters flown in from nearby operational airfields.

By the autumn Lancasters had become so plentiful that they began filtering through to the HCUs, bringing to an end the need for the Lancaster Finishing School. The LFS wound up at the end of November and was replaced by two operational Lancaster squadrons, 150 and 170. At the same time as the arrival of the squadrons, Hemswell became a sub-station of the new 15 Base station at Scampton.

The newcomers operated together for the first time on the night of 4/5th December when they took part in a raid on Karlsruhe, all the Lancasters returning safely.

During the early spring Hemswell became the setting for what is believed to be the only colour film taken of RAF Bomber Command. The film, which is now available on video, shows brilliantly the working of a heavy bomber station with some dramatic footage shot in what appears to be a Lancaster over Germany. Not all was what it seemed, however. The story goes that the station commander at the time, Group Captain Sellick, was a film enthusiast who added some realism to the producer's efforts by having an elderly Lancaster virtually cut in half and used as a film prop inside one of the station's hangars. Realistic or not, the finished film provides an invaluable insight into what life was like in Bomber Command.

The final months of the war proved costly, eight crews failing to return from operations in March alone. The final casualties occurred in April when Flight Sergeant Thorpe and his crew, flying 170's *R-Roger*, disappeared in a raid on Germany. No trace of their aircraft was ever found.

On 9/10th April both squadrons were involved in a highly successful raid on Kiel (described, quite beautifully, in the station records as a 'wizard prang'!) when the battleship *Admiral Scheer* capsized and the *Admiral Hipper* and *Emden* were both badly damaged. Several crews from Hemswell claimed to have dropped the bombs which did the damage.

Hemswell, with its excellent facilities, was to remain as an operational airfield after the war when it was used by several squadrons flying Lancasters, Mosquitos, Lincolns and finally Canberras. It was then used briefly as a site for intercontinental ballistic missiles before closing in 1963, for a short time reopening as part of the 7 School of Recruit Training. Today the giant hangars remain as EU grain storage silos. Some of the wartime buildings are also still used for commercial purposes, while the airfield regularly hosts one of the largest antiques fairs in the region.

18
HIBALDSTOW AND CAISTOR

One of the most extraordinary flights of the Second World War was made from Hibaldstow in the spring of 1945, then the home of a detachment of 53 Operational Training Unit at Kirton Lindsey. It involved a young woman mechanic and a veteran Mk Vb Spitfire which, by some strange quirk of fate, is still flying in Lincolnshire as part of the Battle of Britain Memorial Flight.

After an engine service it was customary for instructors to run up the engines on the ground and then carry out a short air test. It was necessary during engine runs for a member of the ground staff to either lay across the tail or sit on it to prevent it rising and the Spitfire ground-looping.

ACW2 Margaret Horton was a mechanic who had been at Hibaldstow, near Brigg, for around a year. On this particular day in April 1945 (some accounts put the incident in February, but, in an interview with the author some years ago, Margaret clearly remembered it taking place in April) she had finished work on Spitfire AB910, which carried the squadron codes MV-T, when the pilot, Flight Lieutenant Cox, began his engine test. She climbed onto the tail and remained there while he taxied the aircraft around the airfield to the end of the main runway. 'On some Spitfire airfields, when the winds were above a certain force, we were given the order "Tails" and we had to climb on while they were moving round the perimeter track to prevent the aircraft tipping on its nose,' explained Margaret. 'On reaching the take-off point, the pilot stopped while the mechanic slid

Margaret Horton pictured some time after the war sitting on the tail of Spitfire AB910.
(Campbell Gunston)

off. That was the theory but I think my pilot had not heard the final order and took off straight away with me still in place.'

She clung on grimly as Flight Lieutenant Cox climbed to 800 feet, banked and did a circuit of the airfield, unaware of his passenger a few feet behind him.

'I felt sure I had reached my end when I found myself in the air,' said Margaret. 'I was then possessed with the idea that I would be saved if I had faith and so it happened. I landed quite unshaken.'

The incident was observed from the ground by a number of the staff at Hibaldstow, including Flight Lieutenant Tony Cooper, then an instructor with 53 OTU. He was sitting in the cockpit of one of four Spitfires waiting to take off as Cox came in to land. Cooper first noticed a strange shape on the tail of the Spitfire and, as it came closer, realised it was one of the ground crew clinging on for dear life.

Later, Margaret Horton was to receive a severe reprimand for her unofficial flight, even though she had been following instructions by riding on the tail of the Spitfire. She was also made to account for the gloves she lost on her brief flight!

The particular aircraft she rode on had seen action over Dieppe and had one Do217 bomber to its credit, plus a half share in a Fw190, before being pensioned off to 53 OTU and a training airfield in north Lincolnshire.

Hibaldstow had been among the first wartime airfields built in the north of the county. It was on an ideal site, alongside the A15 on well-drained farmland between the Lincolnshire Cliff and the river Ancholme. It was originally intended for Bomber Command, hence the three A-pattern concrete runways, unique amongst fighter airfields in Lincolnshire. It opened early in 1941 and its first occupants were 255 Squadron, which arrived from Kirton with their Defiants at the end of May. They were a night fighter squadron and immediately began converting to Beaufighters on their arrival at Hibaldstow. 255 was to remain at Hibaldstow for much of the summer, working up on its new aircraft before moving to Coltishall. Several night fighter sorties were flown from Hibaldstow during the summer of 1941, some by a section of 29 Squadron, which had recently moved from Wellingore, south of Lincoln, to West Malling in Kent.

Hibaldstow was a popular airfield with those who served there right from the start. There was a refreshing lack of 'bull' and, although the accommodation was spartan (some ground crew lived in tents until beds were found for them in one of the dozen Blister-type hangars erected on the airfield), they found a warm welcome in the pubs in

Hibaldstow and nearby Redbourne.

Fighter Command's only VC holder, Eric Nicholson, arrived at Hibaldstow in the early autumn of 1941 to take command of a night fighter experimental unit. 1459 Flight was operating twin-engined Douglas Havocs fitted with a Turbinlite in the nose. The idea was for the radar operator in the Havoc to locate an enemy aircraft, which would then be illuminated with the Turbinlite and attacked by an accompanying single-seat fighter. The flight was joined at Hibaldstow by 253 Squadron, which moved from Scotland with its Hurricanes, and trials got under way. It took extraordinary skill on the part of both pilots to effect a 'kill', but one was finally achieved in the spring of 1942.

Nicholson, who won his VC after shooting down a Me110 in his blazing Hurricane during the Battle of Britain, was still recovering from his injuries during his time at Hibaldstow, where he commanded 1459 Flight for six months prior to his posting to the Far East. 1459 Flight became 538 Squadron and was joined at Hibaldstow by a second Turbinlite squadron, 532, in September 1941. But the days of illuminating aircraft were numbered thanks to advances in radar and 253 Squadron left with its Hurricanes in November and both Havoc squadrons were disbanded. Hibaldstow's operational days were over.

At nearby Kirton, 53 Operational Training Unit was at full stretch, providing instruction for new fighter pilots and refresher courses for old hands. The paved runways at Hibaldstow were a godsend to a unit which was operating from dawn until dusk. By May 1943 Hibaldstow had officially become a relief landing ground for Kirton and soon afterwards an official satellite of its pre-war neighbour.

A section of 53 OTU was detached to Hibaldstow and continued providing flying training until the end of the war. By 1947 the airfield had closed and most of the buildings, including the twelve Blister and one Bellman hangars, dismantled.

By Lincolnshire standards the airfield a few miles away across the Ancholme valley at Caistor was very small indeed. It had four short grass runways, a single Blister hangar and precious little else. Its brief life was spent as a support airfield for training units stationed around the county. The site, just west of Caistor alongside the road to North Kelsey, lies in the lee of the Wolds making the airfield suitable only for light aircraft.

It was first used in 1940 as a relief landing ground for the fighter units at Kirton, with six Defiants from 264 Squadron spending a month there. A concrete perimeter track was laid to improve facilities but

Some of the men and women of 53 OTU at Hibaldstow in the winter of 1944. (Via Pat Horton)

Caistor's operational life was to be very brief and, by early 1942, the airfield was placed in the hands of 15 (P) Advanced Flying Unit, which was then using the newly-built airfield at Kirmington.

After a spell of hosting circuit-and-bump flights, Caistor closed completely until April 1943 when it was used by the RAF College Service Flying Training School at Cranwell for night flying. This was curtailed when one of the Miles Masters operating from Caistor was shot down by a German intruder. Cranwell continued to use Caistor for some daylight training and limited use of the airfield was made prior to D-Day by an American Army unit.

Caistor did have one unusual visitor in September 1943 when a Lancaster being used by 166 Squadron at Kirmington for conversion training got into difficulties and crash-landed on the grass strip.

All flying ended in the autumn of 1944 when the last Cranwell units moved to Coleby Grange. Caistor was home briefly to 233 Maintenance Unit but the airfield closed completely when the war ended and the land was returned to agriculture. It was to be reopened in the late 1950s to house three Thor ballistic missiles, closing again when the missiles were removed in 1963. The site is now used by Cherry Valley Farms as part of their major duck-rearing business in the Caistor area.

19
INGHAM

It is hard to believe there ever was a wartime bomber airfield at Ingham. It is not that there are no visible reminders: the brick wall of the gun-butts, a scattering of concrete huts, a storage building that looks like it began life as a hangar, a strip of perimeter track and at least two well-preserved Nissen huts.

It is just that Ingham is so close to its mighty neighbour, Scampton. Was it possible that airfields were planned so that they were only separated by half a dozen fields? It seems they were, though in this case the size and quality of Scampton contrasted sharply with the primitive nature of Ingham.

The site at Ingham lies on top of the Lincolnshire Cliff, bounded on the east by the A15 and on the west by the B1398. It was one of a number surveyed by the Air Ministry in the late 1930s and construction began soon after the war started. The facilities were rudimentary, the airfield being deemed ready for use in March 1940. There was still no real pressure on airfield space in Lincolnshire and it was 1942 before Ingham became operational. In the meantime, the facilities were upgraded, with the construction of a concrete perimeter track and the erection of additional buildings, including more accommodation huts.

Ingham opened for business in mid-May 1942 when the Wellingtons of 300 (Masovian) Squadron began to arrive from Hemswell, of which Ingham was now an official satellite. The squadron had been formed within 1 Group in 1940 from Polish aircrew who had escaped from both the Germans and, it later transpired, the Russians. Few could speak English, still fewer could understand the strange ways of the Royal Air Force. What wasn't in doubt was their airmanship, courage or determination to take the war back to the Germans.

Despite its lack of amenities, the Poles were relatively happy at Ingham. They enjoyed the rural life it offered, bartering for food with

A badly damaged Wellington IV of 300 Squadron, BH-V, after a heavy landing at Martlesham Heath following a raid from Ingham either late 1942 or early 1943. (R Jones via Peter Green)

local farmers, and supplementing their diet with some of the native wildlife. They liked, too, the WAAF girls stationed with them at Ingham and were decidedly unhappy when they were replaced by some of the 1,500 Polish women recruited into the force.

300 Squadron moved back to Hemswell at the end of January 1943 to be replaced by the only RAF bomber squadron which was destined to use Ingham, 199, formed two months earlier at Blyton. It flew operational sorties on 50 occasions from Ingham, almost half of them minelaying. They lost a number of aircraft in operations during this period, including two in an attack on Essen in March from which only one man survived. Flying Officer Kitson was captured after his Wellington was shot down by an Me110 night fighter and spent the rest of the war in Stalag Luft 3 where he discovered he had been promoted to flight lieutenant. He was more fortunate than another 199 member, Sergeant Austin, whose Wellington was lost in a raid on Dortmund in May. Austin was one of three men who survived but he was killed a month later, shot by German guards while trying to escape. In June 1943, 100 Squadron was transferred to 3 Group and Ingham was reoccupied by the Poles, this time both 300 and 305 Squadrons moving from Hemswell, where flying had stopped for runway laying.

The Poles were quickly in action again and on the night of 21st/22nd

June lost three aircraft, two of them from 300 Squadron, in a raid on Krefeld. Thirteen men were killed, two became prisoners of war and another evaded capture and made his way back to Britain. Two nights later, 300 lost two more Wellingtons over Wuppertal and with them ten more men, two of whom became prisoners. Losses like these were hard on any squadron, but were particularly bad for the Polish squadrons as the number of Polish replacements coming through the system was beginning to run dry.

Early in September, Ingham was reduced to a one squadron station again when 305 was taken off operations and transferred to what was to become the 2nd Tactical Air Force.

Less than a month later eight Wellingtons from 300 Squadron took off for a raid on Hanover. They were joined by a further 19 Wellingtons from 432 Squadron at Skipton-on-Swale in North Yorkshire. All returned safely in what was to be the final bombing operation of the war in Europe for the veteran Wimpey. From then on 300 Squadron concentrated on minelaying operations for the remainder of its stay at Ingham.

Early in the new year several crews were transferred to Ludford Magna where they began converting to Lancasters in preparation for the squadron's move to Faldingworth in March. Ingham's offensive war was over. For the next six months it was home to 1687 Bomber Defence Training Flight, which flew a number of elderly Spitfires and Hurricanes on fighter affiliation exercises with the Lancasters from the 1 Group Lancaster Finishing School at Hemswell. This included both day and night flying and kept the unit extremely busy. One pilot, Flight Lieutenant Reg Todd, completed over 200 affiliation flights, which lasted anywhere from 30 minutes to two hours, during the few months he spent at Ingham.

1687 BDTF moved in the early autumn of 1944 across fields to Scampton, now a 1 Group airfield, leaving the Night Bomber Training School, which had moved in during the spring, as the only occupants. They used the handful of Wellingtons left behind by 300 Squadron until they, too, moved to Worksop early in 1945.

Various other non-operational units used the buildings at Ingham, including the Polish Air Force Film Unit, before the airfield officially closed at the end of 1946.

20
KELSTERN

Kelstern is about as high as you can get in Lincolnshire without actually flying. At 420 feet above sea level, it is one of the highest points on the Lincolnshire Wolds, which is probably one of the reasons why the site was first surveyed for an airfield in February 1942. There had been a landing ground half a mile away during the First World War but the site then under consideration was meant for something much bigger.

Kelstern became very much the archetypal Lincolnshire bomber airfield. It was built in little more than a year, it housed a single Lancaster squadron and, once the war was over, gently disappeared once again into the rich farmland on which it had been built.

It was never a comfortable posting for the men and women who served there with 625 Squadron of 1 Group, Bomber Command. It was, at times, a bleak and windswept place. The North Sea was a dozen miles away and when the wind was set in the north-east it could be as cold a place as you could find in Britain. Its accommodation sites were utilitarian, concrete huts or corrugated iron and brick Nissen huts which did little to protect the occupants from the elements. Yet Kelstern and the camaraderie of 625 Squadron seemed to exert some kind of magic over those who served and survived there.

Although it was one of the very first of the wartime airfields to be returned to agriculture, Kelstern saw the unveiling of the first post-war airfield memorial in Lincolnshire and the 625 Squadron veterans still assemble early in May each year to pay homage to the crews of the 66 Lancasters lost from the airfield in the 18 months it was operational. Those who served at Kelstern remember it for its qualities, not the hardship they endured in the Lincolnshire winters. It was a well-run, efficient station but one where, nevertheless, there was an air of informality, a lack of the 'bull' that plagued some airfields. It was also a relatively lucky station. 625 was to take part in 187 raids while flying from Kelstern. Its loss rate of 1.9 per cent was well below the 1 Group average.

The contractors were still putting the finishing touches (some who served there claim it never was really finished) to Kelstern when it was officially opened in August 1943 by Air Commodore Arthur 'Hoppy' Wray, the commanding officer of 12 Base of 1 Group, of which Kelstern was part. Also present was Group Captain R. H. Donkin, who had been appointed the first commanding officer of Kelstern. He was an enormously popular man, whose leadership contributed much towards the spirit which was to pervade Kelstern over the next year and a half. He remained at the station until March 1945 when he was posted to Andover. The station records note the universal dismay at his departure. Not the same could be said of every station commanding officer in Lincolnshire at that time.

It was Air Commodore Wray, a First World War RFC pilot who had overall control of three airfields within 12 Base, who landed the first Lancaster on the new runways on 7th October. A week later 625 Squadron, which had been formed from C-Flight of 100 Squadron at nearby RAF Grimsby, finally touched down. Kelstern was officially in business.

625 Squadron aircraft began flying on 13th October 1943, its crews engaged on a series of 'Bullseye' navigational sorties around Britain. Five days later they were finally on operations, nine aircraft taking off to join 351 other Lancasters in a raid on Hanover. Eighteen of the attacking force were shot down but all the Kelstern aircraft returned safely. 625 suffered its first casualty on the night of 3rd/4th November, one of the twelve aircraft it contributed to a Main Force attack on Düsseldorf.

The new squadron at Kelstern was quickly pitched, along with most other Lancaster squadrons in the county, into the Battle of Berlin, which opened on 18/19th November. Kelstern's first casualties in the battle came in the second of the great raids on the German capital, on 26/27th November when Lancaster ED809, 625's T-Tommy, was shot down near Apeldoorn in Holland. The pilot, Flying Officer R. McSorley, and his crew were all killed. There were no losses in the next Berlin raid but on 16/17th December the squadron's Gunnery Leader, Flight Lieutenant W. D. Crimmins, was lost along with six other men when their aircraft crashed in Germany.

This was a particularly bad night for Bomber Command, and 1 Group in particular. Twenty-five aircraft were lost and another 36 crashed on their return as thick fog shrouded many of the airfields in

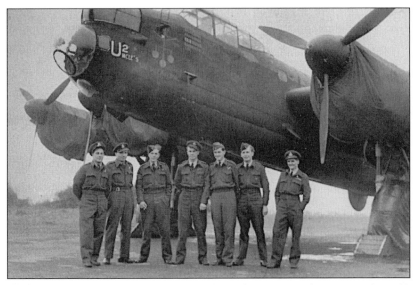

625 Squadron U-Uncle, which sported a pawnbroker's sign on the nose together with the message: 'We Take Anything'. Pictured with her are her crew P/O Wharton (flight engineer), Sgt Gus Hallgren (navigator), F/O Faloon (bomb aimer), F/Lt Tom Greenslade (pilot), F/Sgt Reay (wireless operator), P/O Serienko (rear gunner), and P/O Fuoco (mid-upper gunner). (Gus Hallgren)

eastern England. An American pilot on an exchange with the RAF was killed when his 625 Squadron Lancaster crashed near Kelstern. Two other members of the crew also died, the survivors being taken to hospital in nearby Louth. A second Lancaster overshot the airfield and crashed in farmland nearby, the crew all escaping injury. A third Kelstern Lancaster, U-Uncle, landed on three engines at Blyton with a wounded navigator on board.

625 lost single aircraft in Berlin raids on 23rd/24th December and 15/16th February. But the squadron's worst nights were yet to come. Bomber Command sent 823 aircraft to Leipzig on the night of 19/20th February 1944, losing 78 of them, including three Lancasters from Kelstern. The station's casualties included one of the squadron's two flight commanders, Squadron Leader Barry Douetil, who was to spend the rest of the war as a prisoner of war. And on 24/25th March three of the 72 aircraft lost in the final raid in the Battle of Berlin were from Kelstern.

There were some moments of good fortune for the men and Lancasters of 625 Squadron. In one of the Berlin raids a Lancaster flown by Sergeant Doyle was hit over the target by incendiary bombs dropped from another of the attacking force. The rudder controls were seriously damaged but Doyle and his crew used their ingenuity to carry out running repairs with an intercom lead and eventually made their way back to the home base.

The men at Kelstern, and particularly the ground crews, were proud of the high serviceability of aircraft they achieved in that hard Lincolnshire winter. They made every effort to keep the station operational even under the most severe conditions. In February almost two feet of snow fell one night at Kelstern and everyone on the station worked for 48 hours to clear the runways. They were proud to record they achieved operational readiness 48 hours earlier than their neighbours at Binbrook, who hadn't helped their cause by clearing the wrong runway!

The early months of 1944 were the period of heaviest losses for the squadron. Two Lancasters were lost over Stuttgart on 15th March 1944, another three nights later in a raid on Frankfurt. Kelstern lost one Lancaster on the ill-fated Nuremberg raid, with two more seriously damaged.

All the casualties did not occur over occupied Europe. A 625 Squadron Lancaster and its crew were lost after a mid-air collision over Waddington (something which was bound to happen in the crowded skies of Lincolnshire) while another was shot down by a German intruder after returning from a raid on marshalling yards in northern France in early May. The build-up to the invasion saw 625 Squadron in almost nightly attacks on targets in France. One of these, on the night of 3rd May was directed against German tanks massed at the old French training area of Mailly-le-Camp, south-east of Paris. It was a meticulously planned raid involving 346 Lancasters from 1 and 5 Group, but went terribly wrong. The first wave of 5 Group Lancasters bombed accurately but then a communications breakdown led to the second wave, all from 1 Group, being left orbiting beacons of flares while the German night fighters raced to the scene. Twenty-eight of the 173 1 Group Lancasters were shot down, three of them from Kelstern. (For a fuller account of the Mailly-le-Camp raid see the chapter on RAF Coningsby.)

June 1944 saw the Kelstern squadron deliver a new record of 1,202 tons of bombs to targets in France as part of the build-up and support of the Normandy invasion. Casualties were sometimes disproportionate to the target attacked: 625 Squadron losing three of the 19 Lancasters it sent to attack a rail junction at Acheres; three weeks later

The ground crew of JB122, H-Harry of 625 Squadron at Kelstern. (Tony Castle)

it lost another three in a similar raid on Vierzon. The irony of these losses was that before the disaster at Mailly, attacks on French targets counted as only a third of an operation towards an operational tour.

The operations went on almost without pause that summer. In July 625 dropped 1,200 tons of bombs for the loss of two aircraft (both over Germany). In August three aircraft were lost as some 1,249 tons were dropped on German and French targets. Thirteen of the raids mounted in that time were against V1 sites in France.

In September 625 was expanded into a three-flight squadron and was able to send 31 aircraft on the first of the two 1,000-bomber raids mounted in a single day against the city of Duisburg.

The first of these raids took off at first light and one of the Kelstern aircraft, Q-Queenie, immediately got into difficulties. An engine caught fire and, laden down by a full bomb load, it was clear the Lancaster was doomed. Minutes after take off the pilot, Flying Officer Hannah, ordered his crew to jump for their lives. Hannah remained at the controls and managed to lift the aircraft clear of the village of Fulstow before it crashed into a field at Little Grimsby, near Louth. One of the crew died when his parachute failed to open but the other five survived and, in the spring of 1995, three of Q-Queenie's crew returned to Little Grimsby where a plaque recording Flying Officer Hannah's act of bravery was unveiled in the village church.

148

The day after the Duisburg raid, 625's C-Flight was detached to form the nucleus of a newly reformed 170 Squadron and then moved to Dunholme Lodge, near Lincoln.

There was much celebrating in the Kelstern messes that Christmas but it ended abruptly at 11 am on Boxing Day when the squadron was ordered to provide all available aircraft for an attack two hours later on German armour at St Vith in Belgium. Incredibly, by 1.05 pm the 15th aircraft loaded with fuel and 14,000 lbs of bombs was preparing to take off. 625 was later congratulated by Group HQ at Bawtry for its magnificent effort in providing so many aircraft at such short notice.

It was to be another hard winter for 625 Squadron. The bombing campaign was reaching its peak while Lincolnshire was hit by some of the severest weather on record. In mid-January 1945 a blizzard left Kelstern cut off for three days by snow drifts up to twelve feet deep. It made for miserable conditions on the airfield as men shivered in damp and draughty huts. Once the snow cleared operations were resumed and 625 found itself involved in deep penetration attacks on eastern Germany, including the raids on Dresden and Chemnitz.

There was an interesting experiment carried out at Kelstern around this time. Although the Lancaster had been in service for less than three years, its replacement, the aptly-named Lincoln, was already at advanced prototype stage and due to enter squadron service in 1945. The problem was that it was a larger aircraft than its predecessor, for which facilities on most bomber airfields had been tailored. In particular there was no way the Lincoln could be coaxed into the standard T2 hangars, then used for most of the major servicing in Bomber Command, in the conventional way. Kelstern was selected as the trial site for a novel way of overcoming the problem.

Tram tracks taken up in nearby Grimsby were laid across the apron and into one of the airfield's hangars. A specially-made trolley arrived at Kelstern and this was duly mounted on the track. One of the Lincoln prototypes was flown in, gently mounted onto the trolley and then dragged sideways into the hangar. It worked, but it was obvious that if the Lincoln went into widespread use on airfields where only T2 hangars were available, then a great deal of time and money would have to be spent carrying out the necessary adaptations.

In the event the Lincoln did not come into service until the summer of 1945, by which time many of the airfields with the smaller hangars were being closed. Traces of the apron and tracks still remain, however, at Kelstern.

In the meantime, the war was still going on. On 3rd April 625 sent 25

A proud moment for F/O Alf Castle of 625 Squadron and his family as they stand outside Buckingham Palace after he received a DFM (awarded before he was promoted) following the completion of his tour at Kelstern. His family now live in Southern Australia. (Tony Castle)

aircraft to attack what was then believed to be military barracks at Nordhausen. The 'barracks' turned out to be the concentration camp from which the Nazis drew their slave labour for work on rocket research being conducted in nearby tunnels. Two of the 247 aircraft sent were lost. One of them was flown by Flight Sergeant Collier of 625 Squadron. He and his crew were the last casualties of the war at RAF Kelstern. Two days after the Lancasters returned orders came through that the squadron was to move to Scampton.

By 9th April Kelstern was empty. Its Lancasters had flown out, its ground crews had left by road. The war still had a month to run but the airfield perched on top of the Lincolnshire Wolds would play no further part in it.

It was officially closed in October 1945 and by the following year the land was returned to agriculture and work began on demolishing the buildings and tearing up the runways, dispersals and perimeter tracks. Today very little survives. A few bricks here, a slab of concrete there. And, of course, that roadside memorial.

21
KIRMINGTON

The names on the destination board are different now ... Palma, Tenerife, Alicante. Fifty years or more ago they would have read Essen, Hamburg and Berlin. Humberside International Airport, a somewhat grandiose title for a doing-nicely-thank-you regional airport, began life as RAF Kirmington, a heavy bomber station in No 1 Group, home for all its brief life to 166 Squadron.

The site at Kirmington was just what the Air Ministry surveyors had been looking for when they moved into the area towards the end of 1940. It was a large, flat site, sitting just south of the village of Kirmington between the main Grimsby-Scunthorpe road and the main rail line which ran across north Lincolnshire. It took just a year to build but then, once work was complete, the contractors were called back in again to move some of the accommodation sites. There were real fears about Luftwaffe intruder attacks and it was felt prudent to detach the living quarters from the technical sites which surrounded the airfield and this meant moving them into nearby Brocklesby Park, owned then, as now, by the Earls of Yarborough.

This dispersed nature of the camp was to cause many problems in the years to come, not the least of which was the number of serious road accidents involving personnel travelling between the airfield and their Nissen huts hidden away in the Brocklesby trees.

The A18 road was diverted through the nearby village of Croxton to allow the main runway to be extended almost into Kirmington itself, the road being used by local traffic which was halted when flying was taking place by the simple means of a wood-and-wire barrier which was dragged across the road. Danger, however, was never far away on the numerous other dark country roads for the unwary. In a booklet issued to all new personnel at Kirmington, the first station commander, Group Captain Graham, described the dispersed nature of the airfield

151

The easy way to clean engines. A-Flight engine mechanics Dave Price and Tommy Guest of 166 Squadron hose down a Lancaster's port inner Merlin with petrol pumped up from a 40-gallon drum. (N. Ellis)

as 'one of the discomforts we all have to endure'.

RAF Kirmington was opened in January 1942 but it was to be another nine months before it became operational. In the meantime further work was carried out and the 150 foot wide runways were used by the Oxfords and Ansons of 21 Group Flying Training Command.

In October of that year Kirmington officially became a satellite of nearby Elsham Wolds and its first occupants arrived, 150 Squadron, one of the original 1 Group units, with its Wellingtons from Snaith in South Yorkshire. Six weeks later it was on its way again, this time to Blida in North Africa where it was to serve with the Desert Air Force before eventually returning to 1 Group in north Lincolnshire in 1944. One echelon of the squadron remained at Kirmington where it was joined by another echelon from 142 Squadron, then at Waltham, to reform 166 Squadron, which had last seen action in the First World War.

Initially, 166 operated as a two-flight squadron, much of its earlier 'trade' being in mining operations in the North Sea and Bay of Biscay. But bombing was to be its main occupation and by early 1943, 166 was playing its full part in the growing campaign aimed at Germany's industrial heart.

That year saw what became known as the Battle of the Ruhr and 166 was involved in most of the major raids during the spring and early summer. The squadron lost two crews on the night of 29/30th March in an attack in appalling conditions on Bochum when 40 of the 149 Bomber Command Wellingtons turned back because of icing problems. One of the Kirmington aircraft, H-Harry, was shot down by a night fighter and the second, X-Xray, crashed in Holland, probably due to flak damage. There were no survivors from either crew.

A few nights later two more were lost, one due to severe icing. The crew of the second Wellington all managed to bale out after their aircraft was hit by anti-aircraft fire and spent the rest of the war as 'kriegies'.

Towards the end of April, 166 was involved in a raid on Mannheim and one Wellington again suffered severe icing problems, this time as it returned across the North Sea. With one engine out, the aircraft was forced to ditch. Only four of the five-man crew made it into the dinghy and one of those died a few hours later. The three survivors were to spend the next five days in their tiny dinghy before they were eventually spotted by an RAF fighter pilot and a launch directed to pick them up.

A raid on Dortmund early in May claimed two more Kirmington Wellingtons and their crews, seven of whom were Canadians. Another all-Canadian crew went missing when Bochum was the target again on 13th May. It later transpired their aircraft had ditched in the Zuider Zee and four of the six on board, one of whom was a new pilot, were picked up.

There was worse to come for Kirmington on the night of 23rd/24th May in one of the heaviest raids so far on the Ruhr. Dortmund was the target for 826 bombers, 150 of them Wellingtons, six of which were lost including three from 166 Squadron. There were no survivors. An attack on Essen a few nights later claimed another aircraft and its crew from 166 and further aircraft were lost in raids on Krefeld and Gelsen-kirchen.

In July attention switched to Hamburg and 166 was to lose four Wellingtons in the series of raids which almost destroyed Germany's second city. The first three attacks were unqualified successes for Bomber Command. The RAF used 'window' (thin strips of aluminium which, when scattered from aircraft, effectively blinded German ground radar) for the first time and this, combined with the hot and dry conditions and the widespread use of incendiaries, led to the virtual destruction of the ancient Hanseatic city. A fourth raid, however, ended in near disaster with the bombing force running into a fearsome thunderstorm, which scattered the attackers far and wide.

Only a handful of the 787 aircraft got through to Hamburg and one of those was C-Charlie of 166 Squadron. The Wellington's crew was to endure a terrifying ordeal as their aircraft was flung about in the storm and became so badly iced, it fell from 14,000 to 3,000 feet before the pilot, Sergeant Marks, regained control. It was only when the aircraft was back at Kirmington that the crew realised a wheel had been torn away during the dive. With the flaps buckled and no brakes, Marks gently put C-Charlie down on the grass at Kirmington, the battered Wellington finally coming to rest in an adjoining field. It was during the debriefing which followed that the crew heard for the first time that a recall message had been broadcast. Sergeant Marks earned the DFM he received for his efforts that night.

Big changes were in the wind at Kirmington. In September, Lancasters began arriving to replace the squadron's Wellingtons. They were mostly 'second-hand' machines, previously used by 103 Squadron at Elsham, but were nonetheless welcomed by the Wellington crews, fed up of watching Lancasters flying many thousands of feet above them on raids. The squadron size was also increased to three flights and then Kirmington itself became a sub-station of 13 Base at Elsham.

166 flew its Lancasters operationally for the first time in a raid on Hanover towards the end of September and was now ready to play its full part in the winter offensive against the biggest target of them all – Berlin. It took part in 16 raids on the German capital, losing 17 Lancasters in battle and two more in crashes. Although it missed three of the raids, its losses of 109 men killed and 25 taken prisoner were the highest in 1 Group.

The first of those losses came on the night of 23rd/24th November, five of the crew surviving. In the same raid, another 166 Squadron Lancaster was attacked by a night fighter and raked by machine gun and cannon fire. Both turrets were damaged and the rear gunner, Sergeant George Meadows, badly wounded when he was hit in the back, the bullet being deflected by the wiring in his electrically-heated suit and coming out in his groin. The aircraft was attacked again and this time both the wireless operator and navigator were wounded. Despite his injuries, Meadows, one of the many Canadians to serve with 166, remained in his turret, kept up a running commentary for the pilot and helped beat off eight further attacks. He was later awarded the Conspicuous Gallantry Medal, his citation speaking of '.. skill, courage and fortitude of the highest order.'

Two nights later two more 166 Squadron aircraft failed to return, again five crew from one surviving. The next raid on 2nd/3rd December claimed another Lancaster and six men while a second aircraft, piloted by Flying Officer Foran, was attacked over Brandenburg by a Me110, cannon shells from which severed the oxygen supply to the rear gunner, who was to die on the return flight to Lincolnshire.

On the night of 16/17th December 166 lost another Lancaster, the aircraft crashing near Hanover. Tragically, two more crashed back in Lincolnshire when they encountered thick fog, one hitting high ground near Caistor and the second crashing near Barton-on-Humber.

Berlin wasn't the only target in this, the busiest winter so far for Bomber Command. On 21st December 166 went to Mannheim as part of a diversionary force for a major raid on Frankfurt, one of its Lancasters returning with a badly-wounded rear gunner.

The squadron's aircrew were winning their share of DFCs and DFMs during this long, hard winter, but medals were also being won at Kirmington for acts of bravery on the ground. A George Medal went to a member of the station's medical staff, Flying Officer Dhenin, for rescuing two men from an aircraft which crash-landed near the airfield and caught fire. One of the riggers received a similar award in March 1944 when he tackled incendiaries which accidentally fell from a Lancaster being bombed up for a raid on Berlin. His actions saved this and three other aircraft at nearby dispersals. That night, however, four of the Lancasters despatched to Berlin failed to return, only five of the 28 men on board surviving.

Two nights later another Lancaster failed to return from a raid on Essen and then, on the night of 30th/31st March, four more went down on the ill-fated Nuremberg raid, a fifth being badly damaged. Three of the crews lost were amongst the most experienced at Kirmington, with 47 operations between them. The raid cost 166 the lives of 19 men, with 13 more becoming prisoners, including the mid-upper gunner of the damaged Lancaster, who baled out after the aircraft was attacked by a night fighter. In the space of six nights 166 Squadron had lost 45 per cent of its operational strength.

There was an incident at Kirmington in April 1944 which demonstrated to all on the airfield, and those living in nearby villages, the awful, destructive power of a Lancaster's bomb load. 166 had been ordered to provide 23 Lancasters for an all-1 Group attack on marshalling yards at Aulnoye in France and 17 were already airborne when the 18th, F-Fox, blew a tyre, slewed across the runway and, as its undercarriage collapsed, caught fire. The crew had just scrambled clear when the bomb load began exploding, nine of the 14 1,000lb bombs detonating within a few minutes. The explosions blew a 50 foot wide crater in the runway and reputedly smashed every window within a mile radius of the airfield. There were no casualties but, with the main runway closed, the remaining aircraft were grounded and those heading for Aulnoye were ordered to land back at nearby airfields.

The station commanding officer, Group Captain Graham, was determined, however, that this situation would not last long. By six o'clock the following morning he had 100 men at work shovelling some 500 tons of soil into the 15 foot deep crater. In the meantime, work began on repairing damage to the airfield buildings, including fitting new doors to one of Kirmington's T2 hangars, which had been buckled by the force of the blast. By 10 am the main runway was declared 'usable', but it was to be another ten days before the airfield was declared operational again. The following month, however, it had to close again when subsidence forced further repair work on the main runway. The slight dip that remained in the runway (and is still there today) became known as Gibbons' Gulley after the unfortunate pilot of F-Fox. Pilot Officer Gibbons was to be shot down two months later, his Lancaster being one of four lost by 166 Squadron in an attack on railway yards at Revigny in France. He survived along with five of his crew and successfully evaded capture, returning to Kirmington in September to complete his tour of 30 operations.

Attacks on French targets both before and after the invasion were to cost 166 dearly. Three Lancasters were shot down in the Mailly-le-Camp raid and a total of five in the two Revigny attacks.

Kirmington got a new commanding officer in May when Group Captain Carter took over. He had a hard act to follow. His predecessor, Group Captain Graham, had personally searched a burning Lancaster for survivors soon after it crash-landed on its return from Brunswick. Carter soon showed he, too, was made of the right stuff by accompanying Flying Officer Hutchinson and his crew on a hazardous daylight operation which saw them complete their tour.

There was little respite for 166 that summer, the squadron losing eight aircraft in attacks on French and German targets. Two Lancasters were shot down in a raid on a V1 site at Agenville on 31st August. The wireless operator in one of them was Flying Officer Donald Pleasance, who survived to become a prisoner of war and later one of Britain's most successful post-war actors.

166 lost a total of 114 Lancasters and 39 Wellingtons during its time at Kirmington. In spite of this, it was noted for the longevity of some of

Kirmington on the afternoon of 16th June 1944, before an attack on a synthetic oil refinery plant at Sterkrade in the Ruhr, with Ivon Warmington (standing) and John Clark, pilot and navigator of I-Item. (J. F. Clark)

its aircraft. Four Lancasters which served with 166 completed 100 operations but, tellingly, only one spent its entire operational career at Kirmington. ME746, known as Roger Squared, first flew on a raid on Cologne on 20th/21st April 1944 and completed its 100th the following March in a raid on Kassel. It was finally credited with 124 operational sorties in all and remained with the squadron until it was disbanded at Kirmington in the autumn of 1945. Roger Squared was scrapped the following year.

In October 1944 a second squadron, 153, was formed at Kirmington. It acquired 21 'used' Lancasters from 166 Squadron and flew briefly in operations from the airfield before moving to Scampton.

The winter and early spring of 1944-45 saw 166 in almost constant action and there were few periods when there were no empty dispersals at Kirmington following raids on Germany. Two were shot down in an attack on Cologne in December, three in a raid on Ludwigshafen, two more over Dortmund and three in a raid on Nuremberg. Training, too, brought its tragedies. In mid-October 1944 a 166 Squadron Lancaster took off with three spare gunners on board for a fighter affiliation exercise with a Hurricane from Ingham. The aircraft collided over Hemswell and all ten men on board the Lancaster were killed.

Not every sortie resulted in bombs being dropped. Before a raid on Stuttgart in February 1944 crews were warned that bombing had to be accurate because of the proximity of a prisoner of war camp. One Kirmington crew arrived late over the target and could not spot the markers, so chose to bring their bombs home rather than risk the lives of the prisoners.

Kirmington's final target of the war was Hitler's Bavarian mountain retreat at Berchtesgaden, the squadron also completing a number of Manna and Exodus operations, dropping food over Holland and flying home prisoners, mainly from Belgium, before the war ended.

Following the disbandment of 166, the airfield was used for a number of major Air Ministry disposal sales before finally closing. The A18 was reopened, most of the buildings disappeared and much of the land reverted to agriculture. But the runways remained and, in the early 1970s, the airfield was acquired by the old Lindsey County Council and opened in March 1974 as Lincolnshire (Kirmington) Airport. A week later ownership passed to the new Humberside County Council, and after an uncertain beginning, it developed rapidly into a successful regional airport.

Today, a plaque inside the airport terminal and a memorial in nearby Kirmington village remind visitors of the airport's history.

166 Squadron's I-Item, named the Imp Rides Again!, bombed up in readiness for an attack on Kiel on the night of 23rd July 1944. (J. F. Clark)

22

KIRTON LINDSEY

The three big brick-built C1 hangars still stand like sentinels on the Lincolnshire Cliff, plainly visible to all who use the old Roman road which bisects north Lincolnshire and heads these days for the Humber Bridge. Today, however, the military personnel who assemble on Kirton Lindsey's parade ground are soldiers, not airmen, and those who fly from this former fighter airfield do so in modern gliders, not the Spitfires and Hurricanes which once operated from its grass runways.

It was the mid-1930s when the site, just south of the small town from which it takes its name, was identified as being suitable for an airfield. The air expansion programme was then being set in motion and Kirton was earmarked as a fighter airfield, providing cover for much of South Yorkshire, the Humber ports and shipping in the North Sea.

The airfield officially opened on 10th May 1940 and had as its satellites Coleby Grange, south of Lincoln, and Hibaldstow, just three miles away. 222 Squadron, whose pilots included Douglas Bader, were moved north with their Spitfires from Duxford and were joined by the Hurricanes of 253 Squadron from Kenley. Bader was later to recall his time at Kirton as the period of 'fun' for the squadron.

The newly-arrived fighters were given the task of patrolling the Humber area and were warned to stay above a height of 14,000 feet over the estuary; anything lower 'belonged' to the anti-aircraft batteries and if they strayed below this height they were liable to be regarded as hostile and fired on. It was a warning which was to be repeated to bomber squadrons based in Lincolnshire and Yorkshire, whose crews came to regard the Humber batteries as second only in hostility to those around Essen.

Many of the patrols in that first summer were flown at night, providing good experience for the young pilots, experience which was to stand them in good stead in the hard battles ahead. From Kirton, 222 was sent south to cover the Dunkirk evacuation, being replaced briefly by 65 Squadron. When 222 returned, Bader sheered off his under-carriage in a hairy landing at Kirton and was lucky to climb out with only a few bruises.

The Kirton fighters had their first brush over home territory with the Luftwaffe when Pilot Officer Morant's 222 Squadron Spitfire inter-cepted a He111 off the east coast. The Heinkel managed to escape.

Fighter squadrons, unlike their bomber cousins, rarely remained at one airfield long enough to put down roots. And so it was at Kirton, an airfield far enough north to be used as both a transit station and for the regrouping of squadrons which had been in the thick of the Battle of Britain.

So quickly was the war situation deteriorating that Fighter Command was already planning for the evacuation of eastern England, with airfields further north and west being earmarked as 'rearward' stations. Kirton's was Ringway in Cheshire (now Manchester Airport), and in mid-July a section of 253's Hurricanes was sent there to test the facilities. Soon after this the entire squadron was sent to Turnhouse in Scotland, an airfield later to become Edinburgh Airport, to provide cover for the Firth of Forth. Its place at Kirton was taken by Defiants of 264 Squadron, which brought its 19 aircraft from Fowlmere to begin patrols over the Humber. On 15th August they claimed their first (and Kirton's first) victim, a Do17 shot down over the North Sea.

Next to arrive at Kirton was 74 (Tiger) Squadron, which moved in from Hornchurch with its Spitfires, staying only three weeks before moving south again to Coltishall. The Defiants of 264 were also posted into the front line at Hornchurch with the intention of adding the firepower of their Fraser-Nash turrets to the air battles raging over the south-east, but they were quickly to find the Defiant was hopelessly outmatched by the Me109. It had no forward-facing armament and could only use its turret to engage aircraft on either beam or astern. The turret alone weighed three-quarters of a ton and a month earlier 141 Squadron had almost been shot out of the sky in its first brush with the Luftwaffe. The use of 264 Squadron in these circumstances demon-strated the desperate straits Fighter Command was in at this crucial stage of the Battle of Britain. Just eight days later 264 Squadron flew its surviving aircraft back to Kirton Lindsey. The Defiant was never used again as a day fighter.

222 Squadron (now minus Bader, who had left to command 247 Squadron), moved to Hornchurch at the end of August, with 74 Squadron going to Coltishall, their places being taken by 616 and 307 (Polish) Squadron, which was formed at Kirton and began working up on Defiants. The Poles, however, found the welcome they received at Kirton puzzling. The station commander, anxious to impress the newcomers, had what he thought was a Polish flag made for them. Unfortunately, it consisted of a Prussian black eagle on a white background, not the more familiar Polish white eagle on a red background!

While 264 Squadron moved out to the small airfield at Caistor, 616 with its Spitfires was assigned to the new Duxford Wing formed at the airfield near Cambridge by Kirton old boy Douglas Bader. The squadron's aircraft would leave Lincolnshire at first light, refuel at Duxford and then take part in whatever operation the Wing was engaged in before returning to Kirton at dusk.

Other squadrons to operate from Kirton during this hectic autumn of 1940 included 85, 255 and 71 (Eagle) Squadron, the latter being the first of three all-American units formed in Fighter Command. They arrived with their MkII Hurricanes from Church Fenton in Yorkshire and spent four months in Lincolnshire before moving to Martlesham Heath. In May 1941 the second Eagle squadron, 121, was formed at Kirton and became operational two months later, moving to Kent later in the year. The third, 133, was formed at Kirton in January 1942.

The American squadrons were initially led by experienced RAF officers. 121's first commanding officer was Squadron Leader Peter Powell and its first flight commanders were Hugh Kennard and Royce Wilkinson. Kennard later became the squadron's commanding officer and led it on sweeps across the Channel following its relocation to North Weald. He was to recall the efforts which were made at Kirton to make the squadron feel at home. Intelligence officers for the squadrons were mostly well-heeled RAF officers and one of them, Michael Duff Assheton-Smith, who was a godson of the Queen, took to inviting them to his estate in North Wales. Another attempted to make his new colleagues feel less home-sick by ordering five-gallon tins of peanut butter from Harrods. All three Eagle squadrons were transferred to the US 8th Air Force in September 1942.

The comings and goings went on at Kirton. 65 Squadron spent six months there in 1941 along with 452, the first Australian squadron in Fighter Command. Its flight commanders included the legendary Irishman Paddy Finucane and it was to fly fighter sweeps across

The fledgling RAF Regiment ready for action at Kirton Lindsey in February 1942. The men had all just been drafted into the regiment and their task was to guard the airfield with whatever means they had. In Kirton's case it was an array of home-made armoured vehicles. (Via Pat Horton)

northern France from Kirton. As in the days of the Duxford Wing, the Kirton Spitfires would leave at the crack of dawn, refuel in the south-east and then join other 12 Group squadrons on large-scale 'Circus' operations over France.

They were not the only Kirton units to see action around this time. 255 Squadron was operating its Defiants in a night fighter role during the widespread Luftwaffe raids on England's northern cities and ports. In May 1941 two Ju88s were shot down near Kirton and later that month the squadron claimed six German bombers shot down in one of the heavy raids on Hull. Soon after this the squadron moved across the fields to set up home at nearby Hibaldstow.

Among the numerous squadrons formed at Kirton during this period was 136, which was later to cover itself in glory in the Far East where it became the RAF's top-scoring fighter squadron. It was known to all as the Woodpecker Squadron, a name dating back to its time at Kirton where a certain bawdy song about a woodpecker was adopted as their own by 136 Squadron pilots during one particularly riotous evening in the Queen's Head public house. The name stuck and eventually a woodpecker appeared on the squadron's crest.

There was one tragic incident during 136's stay when nine

163

Hurricanes took off for practice formation flying. Two of the aircraft collided and one of the pilots, New Zealander Theo Hewland, was killed when his aircraft crashed near Redbourne Lodge. Despite this, those who served with 136 remember their time at Kirton as a happy one and particularly recall how virtually the whole town turned out to wave them off when they left, bound for India.

Among the next occupants were 486 (New Zealand) Squadron, and two Polish units, 303 and 306, both flying Spitfires. While 303 were in residence, four Spitfires were scrambled to intercept a pair of Ju88s and both were shot down near Horncastle. The following day the Polish pilots drove to the crash sites and recovered the Iron Crosses worn by the unfortunate bomber crews and claimed them as squadron souvenirs.

The Americans returned in midsummer, this time their aircraft sporting the stars-and-bars of the United States Army Air Force, the air party of the 94th Fighter Squadron flying in with their P38s after a transatlantic crossing. They had been earmarked for the American base at nearby Goxhill, but it was already bursting at the seams, and Kirton was used for seven weeks to acclimatise the Americans to European conditions. They were followed by a second USAAF unit, the 91st, which spent nine weeks there before leaving for North Africa with its P39 Airacobras.

Another squadron to leave Kirton for North Africa was 43, which

The equipment section of 53 OTU at Kirton in June 1943. (Via Pat Horton)

had arrived with its Hurricanes from Tangmere and spent two months in north Lincolnshire before embarking for the Mediterranean. The Poles, in the meantime, were still flying from Kirton and 303 was used to help provide air cover for the Dieppe raid.

Kirton's days as an operational station were numbered and, following its further use by additional Polish squadrons, 12 Group transferred the station to Flying Training Command. In May 1943 it became the home of 53 Operational Training Unit, which had previously been at Llandow in South Wales. It brought with it over 100 aircraft, including at least 80 well-used Spitfires, together with 20 Miles Masters and a few Martinets.

Despite its non-operational role, Kirton had never been busier, with flying going on almost around the clock. Mary Richardson, then a corporal clerk at Kirton, remembers it became so noisy that one day two nuns arrived at the camp from a nearby convent to ask if the station could please keep the noise down during their morning prayers!

Mrs Richardson, then Corporal Mary Mitchell, also recalled the eccentric commanding officer at the time, Group Captain Hawtry, a cousin of the actor best remembered as part of the Carry On team. In the summer of 1944 Hawtry was much taken by the progress of the invasion and he ordered everyone to assemble in one of the hangars to follow events while the hapless Mary Mitchell, who was his private clerk, had to relay news via a WAAF runner from notes she took down from the radio in his office.

When Allied pilots began operating from forward airfields in France, Hawtry thought it time his own trainee pilots should learn to rough it a little and moved them out of their comfortable barracks into bell tents erected around the airfield. He also thought it would teach good co-ordination if they all learned to skate and had a special rink set up in one of the buildings near the guardhouse.

53 OTU operated four flights, one flying from Hibaldstow, and was staffed usually by experienced pilots resting from front line service. One was as young as 19! The OTU was to remain at Kirton until the war ended, being disbanded a week after VE Day. Kirton continued as an RAF training airfield until it was taken over by the army in 1965, and it is still used today as the headquarters of No 16 Light Air Defence Regiment, which used its Rapier missiles so effectively in the Falklands War.

23
LUDFORD MAGNA

There is precious little left today to indicate that RAF Ludford Magna was once the home of one of the key squadrons in the whole of Bomber Command.

From the autumn of 1943 until the final days of the war, 101 Squadron operated its special ABC Lancasters from the hastily-built wartime airfield, which stands at almost the highest point in the county, just off the Market Rasen-Louth road. These aircraft flew on almost every Main Force raid, whether or not their parent 1 Group was involved, providing rudimentary electronic counter measures to try to reduce the effectiveness of the Luftwaffe night fighters and their control system.

Later in the war the same task was to be provided on a much wider scale by the specially-created 100 Group but, in the autumn of 1943, 101 Squadron, with its specially-adapted Lancasters and German-speaking eighth crew member, were all Bomber Command had. ABC, officially known as Airborne Cigar, Lancasters were fitted with receiving and transmitting equipment through which a German-speaking operator could locate night fighter frequencies and then jam them with noise picked up by a microphone mounted in one of the aircraft's engines.

Not all 101's Lancasters were ABC equipped and even those that were, were still required to carry and deliver a bomb load (this was generally 1,000 lb less than the non-ABC aircraft to compensate for the weight of the additional equipment and operator). The ABC aircraft were expected to operate even when the remainder of the squadron and 1 Group itself were stood down with the result that 101 Squadron flew more operations during the latter stages of the war than just about any other RAF unit.

ABC was a closely-guarded secret for the whole of the war, even though the Germans must certainly have known of its existence from examining the wreckage of the many 101 Squadron aircraft scattered across northern Europe. In the meantime, even those working at Ludford were not told about it.

Ludford Magna opened as a new station in June 1943 when 101 Squadron flew in with its Lancasters from Holme-on-Spalding Moor, near Market Weighton, Yorkshire. Ludford was a big airfield, destined to become even bigger before the year was out, and had been built hurriedly at a total cost of some £800,000 on land formerly farmed by the Hilldred family. First to arrive were the ground crews, who came by road from East Yorkshire. They found a station still being built. Few of the accommodation sites were ready and some 'erks' found themselves billeted in makeshift homes like the station cinema, where they would live for their first six months at Ludford.

Despite its height (at 430 feet above sea level, it was the highest in Lincolnshire), it was notorious for its muddy conditions. Mudford Magna was the popular name and its first commanding officer, Group Captain Bobby Blucke, described the place as 'a joke in very bad taste played by the Air Ministry at our expense'.

The geography of the site meant that the airfield was one of the few in eastern England with its main runway running north to south and this was to provide a perpetual problem for Lancaster crews who frequently had to land in cross-wind conditions, not something to be taken lightly on this exposed hilltop airfield.

101's arrival on 15th June 1943 followed a raid the night before on Bochum, from which one of the squadron's aircraft failed to return. The first loss it suffered from its new Lincolnshire home was Lancaster ED656, flown by a Canadian, Pilot Officer Thornton, who died with his crew over Mülheim a week after the move to Ludford. The Battle of the Ruhr was now at its height and 101 lost single aircraft on the next two raids and two on the third, an attack on Gelsenkirchen.

A raid on Hanover on the night of 23rd/24th September 1943 brought with it a bravery award unique to 101 Squadron – two Conspicuous Gallantry Medals being won by the pilot and flight engineer of one of the squadron's aircraft. Warrant Officer Arthur Walker and Flight Sergeant Stan Meyer were in a Lancaster coned by searchlights on its approach to the target. It was immediately attacked by a fighter which caused serious damage to the Lancaster, setting one of the engines on fire. Walker dived to evade the fighter and extinguish the flames but, in the meantime, a second fire had started in the fuselage. Meyer, 'displaying great gallantry' according to the citation, managed to beat the flames out before being overcome by fumes. He was dragged clear by other members of the crew and, after the pilot

Familiar accompaniments to life at Ludford – a bicycle and a bucket for fresh water. (Redfearn collection)

had continued on to the target and dropped his bombs, stood beside the pilot all the way back to Ludford where they managed to land the badly damaged Lancaster. A third CGM, the second highest award to a Victoria Cross, was to go to another 101 Squadron flight engineer, Sergeant Jeffrey Wheeler, who helped nurse another damaged Lancaster back to Ludford in March 1945 despite serious injuries caused by shrapnel.

The introduction of ABC in the early autumn of 1943 was treated with some suspicion by 101 crews, particularly after the first two aircraft to be fitted with the device were lost on operations. There was a fear that the Germans could home in on the transmissions from the Lancasters, which were operating in pairs, spaced out in the stream. The fears were unfounded; it was just the Grim Reaper at work.

101 was to fly the second highest number of sorties in the series of Berlin raids and to lose 22 aircraft and, with them, the lives of 133 airmen. But the squadron's worst night of the war came on 30th/31st March 1944 when it provided 26 ABC-equipped Lancasters for a force of 795 bombers which attacked the southern German city of Nuremberg. It was a horrendous night for Bomber Command which lost 96 aircraft, seven of them from Ludford Magna, almost a third of

The station band performs at the Christmas dinner, 1943. (Redfearn collection)

the entire squadron.

In his book on the Nuremberg raid, historian Martin Middlebrook recalls the thoughts of one of the survivors the following day: 'We were an experienced crew and accustomed to losing the odd one or two aircraft. But, with nearly a third of the squadron gone, this was a big kick in the guts for us all. We waited up until mid-day before going to our huts, stunned, shocked and silent, each crew wrapped in his own mental anguish.'

101 was to go through a virtual repeat of this tragedy six weeks later when five Lancasters were lost in the disastrous attack on German tank formations at Mailly-le-Camp, west of Paris. Forty-two Lancasters were lost that night, 28 of them from 1 Group squadrons. One Ludford rear gunner had one of the most remarkable escapes of the war in this raid. Sergeant Jack Worsford's aircraft was literally blown in half by a burst of cannon fire from a night fighter and, trapped in the spinning tail section of the aircraft without his parachute, he had no chance of escaping. But, instead of falling directly, the tail unit spun like a sycamore seed until it struck a line of high tension cables and bounced into nearby trees. Worsford was able to climb out of the remains of his

Post-op char and wad for a 101 Squadron crew at Ludford Magna, 1944. (Redfearn collection)

turret uninjured, his only problem being to explain to his German captors how he came to fall 5,000 feet without a parachute.

Wing Commander Robert Alexander was the commanding officer of 101 at the time of both Nuremberg and Mailly and many years later still recalled the sense of loss at Ludford after both raids. 'Everyone had their private grief, I suppose,' he told the author. 'But we just had to carry on with the job we had been given.' The village of Ludford Magna is now twinned with a French village close to Mailly-le-Camp, a village where 14 men, the crews of two Lancasters from 101 Squadron, are buried.

There was a special role for 101's ABC Lancasters in the early hours of D-Day, 24 crews flying a predetermined box pattern for some seven hours, disrupting any attempts by Luftwaffe night fighters to get among the bombers and transport aircraft dropping paratroops behind the invasion beaches.

Ludford, in the meantime, had become the headquarters of 14 Base within 1 Group, with responsibility for the major servicing and administration for the neighbouring airfields of Wickenby and

Faldingworth. It meant an increase in the station's population and the construction of three additional T2 hangars.

Apart from ABC, there were other innovations at Ludford Magna. It became the first airfield in 1 Group to be equipped with FIDO, the petrol-burning fog dispersal equipment developed in 1943 to combat the threat of fog on bomber airfields. Ludford was chosen because of its ABC role but it proved to be an unhappy choice. Work had begun in the late summer of 1943, carried out by Monk Construction and Strong-Arc Welding of Lincoln, but airfield flooding led to such long delays that some of the contractors were moved to Fiskerton, where FIDO was proving much easier to install.

The equipment was finally ready in January 1944 and was used operationally for the first time on 10th March when a number of 50 Squadron Lancasters were diverted from Skellingthorpe where visibility was particularly bad. Trials were hampered by the windy conditions at Ludford and it was quickly discovered that the airfield suffered from the wrong sort of fog: FIDO had been designed for the radiation fog found on most Lincolnshire airfields but Ludford's 'fog' was, as often as not, low cloud. The north-south runway also meant that when FIDO was lit, the heat was blown away from the runway by the prevailing wind.

Nevertheless, it did have some limited successes. In late August, 14 aircraft from 619 Squadron at Dunholme Lodge landed successfully at Ludford and, in November, it was used to land 24 101 Squadron aircraft after a raid on Düren. Two Lancasters which had been on a night training exercise also used the flames to get down safely. The visibility at Ludford that night was so bad that FIDO had to be left on so that ground crews could find the Lancasters and tow them back to their dispersals.

Not all landings were successful. On the night of 21st December 1944 a 617 Squadron Lancaster, which had been diverted from Woodhall Spa and was running low on fuel, crashed while attempting to land at Ludford.

Another innovation first introduced at Ludford was the Rose turret, which replaced the traditional Fraser-Nash rear turret fitted to the squadron's Lancasters. The turret was fitted with two .5-inch heavy machine guns in place of the standard four .303s. It was also larger, which meant the gunner could keep his parachute on, visibility was better and it was warmer thanks to changes in the slipstream.

101 Squadron remained at Ludford until the war ended. It lost over 100 aircraft while flying from the airfield yet remarkably two of the

T-Tommy of 101 Squadron at a sunny dispersal in the summer of 1944. (Redfearn collection)

aircraft on its strength there, DV302 H-Harry and DV245 S-Sugar, were to complete over 100 operations. S-Sugar, better known to all on the squadron as *The Saint*, failed to return from a daylight attack on Bremen on 23rd March 1945 on its 122nd operation. H-Harry survived the war with 121 operational symbols painted on its fuselage.

101 Squadron remained at Ludford throughout the summer of 1945 before it finally closed for flying. The runways were retained by the Air Ministry and the airfield was reactivated briefly as a base for Thor missiles in the late 1950s. Today only a few scattered buildings and part of the perimeter track remain to remind motorists heading for Louth and the Lincolnshire seaside towns of the proud wartime record of RAF Ludford Magna.

24
MANBY AND THE RANGES

Today, if you live in the rich fertile plain of east Lincolnshire or in one of the pretty villages clinging to the edge of the Wolds, you will probably receive your council tax demand from a local authority which has its headquarters in what was one of the key training centres for the wartime Royal Air Force. Manby is now the home of East Lindsey District Council but between 1939 and 1945 was the centre of armament training in the RAF. It was here that air gunners, bomb aimers and armament officers learned their skills.

The airfield site had been one of those chosen for the first phase of the expansion of the RAF in Lincolnshire in the mid-1930s. Work started in 1936 on what was to be a typical airfield of the period, complete with three brick-built C-type hangars and administration buildings, messes and barracks, most of which still exist today. It was also the first Lincolnshire airfield to have a paved runway, a real innovation at the time. Interestingly, when the runway was laid it was immediately camouflaged to look, from the air, like a stream meandering across a Lincolnshire meadow.

During the construction period Manby was also used for the trials of an experimental cross-wind landing screen, a huge steel-framed and fabric-covered affair which stood 50 feet high and was some 1,500 feet long. Experiments were carried out using a variety of aircraft and were completed by the time the station opened in 1938. The screen was dismantled and taken by road to Wiltshire where additional trials were scheduled but were overtaken by the outbreak of war.

Manby opened as the home of the RAF's No 1 Air Armament School in August 1938 and its opening was to have a profound effect on this quiet corner of Lincolnshire. Piped water and electricity were still the exception rather than the rule in east Lincolnshire and the arrival of the

Manby under construction in the late 1930s. The quality of the building work ensured that much of what was built then remains there today. (J. Vinter)

RAF changed for ever the lives of all those in this most rural of communities.

No 1 AAS brought with it a wide variety of aircraft in which to train gunners and bomb aimers. These included Hawker Harts, Furys, Demons and Henleys, Westland Wallaces, Gloster Gauntlets and Fairey Battles. There was even a long-obsolete Boulton Paul Overstrand, a biplane bomber noted only for its power turret which was used for ground training purposes at Manby.

The station's role was further enhanced in July 1940 when the No 2 Ground Armament School was formed there. It looked after the ground training while No 1 AAS had responsibility for the flying element. The ground school was to remain at Manby for 18 months before moving to Lancashire.

The need for airfield defences across Lincolnshire had been demonstrated during the summer of 1940 by a number of nuisance raids by the Luftwaffe. Initially army units had been stationed at airfields but many of these were withdrawn during the late summer of 1940 to strengthen the anti-invasion forces then being assembled, leaving airfield defences in the hands of the RAF. It was this emergency which was to lead initially to the formation of airfield defence squadrons and, from 1942, the RAF Regiment. Manby was one of the airfields where a defence squadron, No 2782, was formed in the summer of 1941, its members manning an assortment of machine guns, 20mm cannons and Bofors.

It was the RAF defenders at Manby who were credited with shooting down a Ju88 on 21st December 1940, the raider crashing near South Cockerington. This raider had been picked up on radar and a night fighter, a Beaufighter from 29 Squadron at Wellingore, vectored onto it. It was about to make an interception when the Manby gunners intervened. The Beaufighter's pilot was Flight Lieutenant Guy Gibson, who would have to wait until the new year before making his first 'kill'.

Even with the department of 2 GAS, Manby remained an extremely busy airfield, its assortment of aircraft, which had now been joined by a detachment of Wellingtons, flying constantly to meet the demands for trained bomb aimers and gunners. It also trained the trainers, providing courses for armament and bombing instructors and a bomber leaders' course. The demands of all these courses led to Manby assuming control of the small airfield at Caistor in December 1942 for use as a relief landing ground. However, it proved to be unsuitable and within three months responsibility for Caistor was transferred to Cranwell.

The status of Manby's No 1 Air Armament School was enhanced when it was reformed as the Empire Central Armament School in the late spring of 1943, under the command of an air commodore. This was the signal for a further major expansion of Manby's role. New training techniques were devised and perfected and there is no doubt that the quality of the training provided, particularly for bombing leaders and instructors and armament instructors, was to have a profound effect throughout Bomber Command.

Two additional paved runways were laid and the aircraft inventory updated. Wellingtons, by now withdrawn from front line service, were widely used and in the final stages of the war they were joined by Hudsons, Blenheims, Lancasters and a single Mosquito. The final wartime change at Manby came at the end of 1944 when the Empire Central Armament School was reformed as the Empire Air Armament School.

The end of the war inevitably brought a winding down of the scale of training at Manby, but the airfield continued to play a significant role until the mid-1970s when it finally closed. It was at Manby in 1949 that the RAF Flying College was formed while, two years later, 25 Group HQ was established at the airfield to oversee the RAF's new all-jet Advanced Flying Schools. It was also to be the home of the RAF

Aircraft of the Empire Air Armament School drawn up as if on parade, Manby 1944. The collection includes Lancaster PB136, a Wellington, Anson, Spitfire, Hurricane, Magisters and Masters. (Peter Green)

Handling Squadron, the role of which was to assess the many new aircraft then about to go into service. In 1962 the RAF Flying College was renamed the College of Air Warfare and remained at Manby until the airfield closed in 1974.

Much of the wartime training at Manby involved the use of the Lincolnshire bombing and gunnery ranges. There were four major ranges, all on the coast, on the Wash at Holbeach and Wainfleet, and further north at Donna Nook and Theddlethorpe. Of these, the latter was set up specifically to service the Air Armament School at Manby.

Theddlethorpe was just six miles from Manby, the range laying three miles north of the seaside town of Mablethorpe. The range itself was on the wide foreshore and had its own permanent staff, whose job it was to service the targets, mark the bombing and report the results back to Manby. Theddlethorpe's role became even more important with the outbreak of war and many of the new techniques developed at Manby were first tested there.

The range was also to be the scene of a number of mishaps involving aircraft from Manby. At least two Battles crashed there in the autumn of 1939 and in August 1942 the four-man crew of a 1 AAS Hampden were killed when their aircraft suffered engine failure. The aircraft lost power as it pulled away from the range and the pilot, Sergeant Dent, lowered the undercarriage while the aircraft was at 500 feet. The Hampden stalled and dived into the sea, the subsequent inquiry blaming 'pilot error' for the crash.

One of the worst incidents of the war at Theddlethorpe also involved aircraft from 1 AAS at Manby. In May 1944 two Blenheims collided

176

over the range, crashing onto the beach and killing all those on board.

The Theddlethorpe range remained in use until the 1970s when it was closed, partly because of the proximity of a new natural gas terminal.

The range at Holbeach was established in the 1920s on mud flats close to the mouth of the river Nene. It originally bore the name of its parent airfield, Sutton Bridge, where fighter squadrons were based during their annual armament practice camps.

The RAF expansion of the late 1930s brought with it a need for more target facilities in south Lincolnshire and in 1937 a second range in the Wash was opened on Wainfleet Sands. During the war Wainfleet became the main bombing range for 5 Group of Bomber Command and was one of the few ranges where high explosive bombs, and not the 20 lb practice bombs usually used, could be dropped. Both Wainfleet and Holbeach survived the war and became major ranges for NATO aircraft.

Lincolnshire's fourth major coastal range was at Donna Nook, a remote spot on the coast a mile and a half from the village of North Somercotes. It was close to the relief landing ground used by both Manby and North Coates (for a fuller description, see the chapter on RAF North Coates). The foreshore off Somercotes Haven had been pressed into use as a range in the late 1920s by aircraft from North Coates and by the late 1930s had become one of the principal ranges for Bomber Command. In 1940 control of Donna Nook passed to 1 Group of Bomber Command and it was used almost exclusively by the group's Wellingtons and Lancasters until the end of the war. It closed after the war but was later reopened following the decision to close Theddlethorpe.

25
METHERINGHAM

'It was a terrible place, cold, bleak, isolated. We faced a two mile walk
to our huts, which were as bad as you would find anywhere in the
RAF. They were draughty, ran with condensation and we had so little
fuel for the single stove that some of the Aussies on the squadron took
to stealing other people's doors to burn. By the time I left there was
hardly a lavatory door left.'

This was how Eric Brown, a flight engineer with 106 Squadron,
remembers his time at Metheringham, an airfield built in the winter of
1942-43 on the flat fenlands ten miles south-east of Lincoln. It was built
for 5 Group of Bomber Command and shared this fertile area of the
county with neighbouring airfields at Bardney, Woodhall Spa,
Coningsby and Digby.

RAF Metheringham officially came into being in mid-October 1943
when the station staff arrived to prepare for its first, and only,
occupants, 106 Squadron. It was a pre-war unit which had begun the
war at Finningley, near Doncaster, where it operated in a training role.
It was quickly transferred to 5 Group and moved to Syerston, near
Newark, where it operated in an offensive role with, first, Hampdens,
then Manchesters and, from the summer of 1943, with Lancasters.

106 moved to its new home on 11th November 1943 and within a
week was operational, 13 aircraft going to Berlin as part of a force of
440 Lancasters. All returned safely to Metheringham. Four nights later
15 squadron aircraft again attacked Berlin and once more returned
safely. Berlin was the target yet again the following night and all
Metheringham's Lancasters made it home. So far, so good for 106.

Their luck ran out on the night of 26th November when 18 aircraft
took part in yet another raid on the German capital, the fourth in eight
nights. One 106 Squadron aircraft, flown by Flight Officer J. Hoboken
DFC, was brought down near Frankfurt and the crew, which unusually
contained five officers, all died. It was the squadron's first operational

loss for a month. A second Lancaster, flown by Pilot Officer R. Neil, turned back over the North Sea with engine trouble and crashed while attempting to land. The only injury was a broken arm, suffered by one of the gunners. A third Lancaster from Metheringham, ED417, was in the circuit after the long flight back from Berlin, when it collided with a Yorkshire-based Halifax looking for a friendly airfield. Only one of the Lancaster's crew survived.

In nine more raids on Berlin, 106 suffered fewer casualties than other Lancaster squadrons in Lincolnshire. It was to lose eight aircraft, half the number of both 44 Squadron at Dunholme and 57 at Scampton and a quarter of the losses of 460 Squadron at Binbrook. Relatively light though the losses were, they still had a profound effect on life at Metheringham. Two aircraft were lost together with 13 lives on New Year's Day 1944, and the sight of the empty dispersals the following morning was one that few who served at the station will forget.

On the Berlin raid of 29/30th December 1943, one of 106's Lancasters, JB583, was hit by flak as it strayed over Bremen on the return flight. The engineer was killed and power lost on two engines, but the pilot, Flying Officer Leggett, managed to nurse his badly damaged aircraft back to Metheringham. Once on the ground, the aircraft was inspected and towed into one of the airfield's three hangars from where, 24 hours later, it emerged with two new engines and its shrapnel scars repaired. It was air-tested and took off later that same day for yet another attack on Berlin. It was a remarkable achievement by the ground crews to ensure that the maximum number of aircraft were available for the assault on Germany.

The Nuremberg raid at the end of March 1944 was particularly hard on 106 Squadron. It provided 17 of the 779 aircraft which were due to attack Nuremberg that night. Four failed to returned to Metheringham, three were shot down by night fighters and a fourth crash-landed at Manston. All 21 men on board those aircraft shot down were killed but the crew of the Lancaster which crash-landed at Manston escaped injury. Theirs, however, was to be a brief reprieve. Flying Officer Penman and his crew were to die five weeks later in an attack on a seaplane base at Brest, the only aircraft lost in the attack.

Among the 106 Squadron crews who made it back to Metheringham from Nuremberg was that of Flying Officer Mifflin. They had been together since their time at 1654 HCU at Wigsley, near Newark, flying first Stirlings and then Lancasters at the 5 Group Lancaster Finishing School before joining 106 in its time at Syerston. They had survived the Battle of Berlin, cheating the Grim Reaper when they got home despite flak damage and a night fighter attack over the Big City on 2nd December 1943.

On the night of 30th April they took off on what was to be the final trip in their tour of 30 operations: a deep penetration attack by 206 5 Group Lancasters plus nine ABC Lancasters from 101 Squadron to Schweinfurt, Germany's centre of ball bearing manufacture.

Mifflin's flight engineer was Norman Jackson, a Londoner who had just celebrated his 25th birthday. He had been with the crew since its days at Wigsley and had already completed his tour after flying as a replacement with another Metheringham crew. He volunteered for the Schweinfurt raid to be with his own crew when they ended their tour: they all planned to go together to a Pathfinder squadron after a spell off operations. It was a particularly memorable day for Jackson, who had received a telegram a few hours before take off that his wife had given birth to their first son.

It was a long haul across Europe to the target in the south-east of Germany and by the time they arrived at Schweinfurt it appeared everyone else had bombed and gone home (it later transpired that strong winds and fierce opposition led to most of the force dropping their bombs some distance from the target). They bombed what they believed to be the aiming point and had just turned for home when the wireless operator, Flight Sergeant Sandelands, picked up an ominous blip on the 'Fishpond' radar, warning of an aircraft approaching from the rear. It was a night fighter and suddenly the Lancaster was raked by cannon fire and, as Jackson looked out, he saw the starboard inner engine burst into flames. He activated the internal extinguisher but the flames were too strong and there was a real danger they would spread to an adjacent fuel tank. The crew had often discussed such an emergency and Jackson had come up with a theoretical solution: now was the time to put it into practice. Grabbing an extinguisher, he released his parachute canopy inside the fuselage and, with the bomb aimer and navigator holding the chords, climbed out through the upper escape hatch into the 200mph slipstream.

Jackson lowered himself onto the starboard wing, took hold of the leading edge air intake and crawled along the wing to the burning engine where he pushed the extinguisher into the cowling and managed to put out the flames. But as he was beginning to edge his way back towards the fuselage, the Lancaster banked sharply as it was attacked again by the night fighter. Shrapnel from the attacker's cannon fire hit Jackson in the leg and he was burnt as the damaged engine burst into flames again. His injuries forced him to release his grip on the wing and he was flung backwards into the slipstream behind the stricken bomber. Inside, his colleagues were playing out Jackson's smouldering parachute before they finally let it slip free. Somehow it opened and Jackson fell quickly, landing heavily in a thicket of bushes. He was found by German civilians the next morning and, despite his injuries, forced to march ten miles to the nearest town where he finally received treatment. He was to spend the next ten months in hospital.

The full story of his bravery was not revealed until the surviving members of his crew – the pilot and rear gunner both died when the Lancaster finally crashed – were released from a prisoner of war camp. On 13th November 1945 Norman Jackson, watched proudly by his wife and 18 month old son Ian, received the Victoria Cross from King George VI at Buckingham Palace.

One of the worst enemies of the Lincolnshire bomber crews was fog and a number of airfields, including Metheringham, were selected for the installation of fog dispersal equipment, universally known as FIDO. Metheringham was in the second group of airfields to receive the equipment, the installation being carried out by A. Monk and Co and the pipe-working and welding by Strong-Arc of Lincoln. Installation started in January 1944 and was completed in time for the first trials in May when a 106 Squadron Lancaster, returning early with engine trouble from a raid on Tours, became the first aircraft to land using FIDO at Metheringham.

The installation itself was supplied by a fuel pipeline which ran from railway sidings near Blankney to holding tanks on the airfield itself. The Metheringham installation was one of the most efficient at any airfield. In one two-hour burn it consumed 26,600 gallons of petrol, compared with 220,000 gallons burnt in one operation at Carnaby in East Yorkshire. Certainly, 106 Squadron crews were impressed with it when they were invited to use it officially for the first time later that year.

Eric Brown recalls his crew were among the first to land with FIDO operational. Following its installation, he remembers Pathe Gazette sending a film crew to Metheringham but they waited in vain for a week for the weather to deteriorate before returning to London. Sure enough, the next day the fog rolled in and FIDO was lit. Flying Officer Arnott's crew, in which Eric Brown was flight engineer, were air-testing their Lancaster when they were warned over the radio they would be landing with the aid of the new device.

'We had been instructed how to get down, but now were faced with reality,' recalled Mr Brown. 'Because of the heat generated, there was a lot of rising air over the runway and it was necessary to fly the Lancaster down instead of the standard practice of cutting the power and dropping gently onto the runway. If you cut the power with FIDO you simply floated.'

Mr Brown, who joined the police force in his native Grimsby after the war, remembers one Lancaster crashing, killed all eight men on board, when attempting to land using FIDO at Metheringham. The aircraft was almost certainly a Lancaster from 83 Squadron at Coningsby. FIDO made an immediate difference for crews at Metheringham; before its installation crews often carried overnight bags in case they were diverted to fog-free airfields.

Eric Brown and his crew (which included three Australians and a gunner on his second tour) flew 16 ops with 106 before joining 97 Squadron at Coningsby. It was an eventful time, including flak damage over Giessen and an abortive raid on Trondheim when, because of a smoke screen over the U-boat base and the prohibition of anything less than accurate bombing of Norwegian targets, the Lancasters had to bring their bombs back to Metheringham. Their last two trips with 106 were both minelaying in the Kattegat and, interestingly, Eric Brown remembers their Lancaster, X-Xray, also carrying armour-piercing

Flying Officer Arnott and his crew pictured at Metheringham in the autumn of 1944. Sgt Eric Brown is on the extreme right of the back row. (Eric Brown)

When 106 was disbanded after the war the squadron held a ceremonial 'funeral', digging this grave in front of one of the hangars at Metheringham. In the background is one of the last Lancasters to serve with 106 Squadron. (Peter Green)

bombs to use if they came across any German shipping.

The only other wartime occupant at Metheringham was 1690 Bomber Defence Training Flight, which moved in from Scampton with its Spitfires and Martinets in the autumn of 1944. Its role was to provide fighter affiliation training for 5 Group squadrons.

106's wartime swansong came on the night of 25/26th April 1945 when it provided 14 of the 107 5 Group Lancasters which bombed the Vallo oil refinery, near Tonsberg in Norway in what was the final bombing operation of the war by Lincolnshire-based Lancasters. Earlier in the day, the bulk of 1 and 5 Groups had raided Berchtesgaden, so it fell to the Lancasters of 106 Squadron to bring the curtain down on Lincolnshire's bomber war.

106 remained at Metheringham until it was disbanded the following February, when the airfield closed. Today memories of Metheringham's wartime role are kept alive by the Friends of Metheringham Airfield, a group of volunteers who man the Airfield Visitors' Centre at Westmoor Farm and preserve what remains of the airfield. An impressive memorial to 106 Squadron stands on a section of the perimeter track while close to the centre is a second memorial, this one to S/Ldr Robertson and his crew. He was 106's 'A' Flight commander when his Lancaster was shot down over Holland in July 1942.

26
NORTH COATES AND DONNA NOOK

No individual Lincolnshire airfield exercised such an influence over its wartime sphere of operations as RAF North Coates (the local spelling is 'Cotes', but the RAF always insisted on an additional 'a', and that is the style we will use).

As North Coates Fitties, the airfield had been operational in the First World War and later reopened, first as an armament practice camp, and later as a permanent station, initially as No 2 Air Armament School then, in 1938, as No 1 Air Observers' School. When the war began this was moved immediately and the airfield was used briefly as a recruit training centre and by the No 1 Ground Defence School until, in February 1940, it passed to Coastal Command. Work began on extending the airfield, including the laying of a 1,400 foot concrete runway, together with a wider grass runway at right angles to it.

The first Coastal Command flying units moved in while this work was going on. First to arrive was 235 Squadron with its Blenheims and it was later joined by 236 and 248 Squadrons, whose role was to provide long range patrols over the North Sea. All three squadrons moved south in April and were replaced by 22 Squadron's Beaufort torpedo bombers, and by 812 Squadron Fleet Air Arm, which was equipped with Swordfish biplanes, used for convoy patrol and minelaying work. While at North Coates, 22 Squadron's Beauforts were converted to carry torpedoes, the engineering work involved being carried out on the airfield, and the squadron was operational by September, when it carried out its first attack in its new role, sinking a merchant ship off the Frisian Islands. The Swordfishes were also kept busy and on one night were used to bomb invasion barges in Dutch ports.

In March 1941, 812 Squadron was replaced by a second FAA

22 Squadron Beauforts at North Coates in the spring of 1941.

squadron, 816, which remained at North Coates until May, the last Fleet Air Arm squadron to serve in Lincolnshire and the last to use biplanes in an operational role. Nine Beauforts from 22 Squadron were detached to St Eval in Cornwall in the spring of 1941 and 42 Squadron arrived to take over anti-shipping operations until they returned. Both units were then replaced by another Beaufort squadron, 86, in the summer of 1941, joined by 407 (RCAF) Squadron, flying Hudsons. 86 remained at North Coates until January 1942.

Together, these squadrons began to set the pattern for North Coates' role in the war, operating 'Rover' offensive anti-shipping sweeps along the Dutch and Belgian coasts. The area selected for these was between Ijmuiden and the Heligoland Bight and on every suitable night this was to be patrolled by a section of four aircraft. The Hudson crews flew one night on, one off, with two more on stand-by or two-hour availability. If they were on the latter, they could leave the base but had to leave a note at the guardroom where they were going. On many nights cinema shows in nearby Grimsby were interrupted by messages instructing 407 Squadron personnel to report back to base immediately. Transport would be waiting in the town's bus station to take them the six miles back to camp.

Among the men stationed there during this period was a young Canadian mechanic by the name of Edmund Hockeridge, later to become one of the most popular singers on both sides of the Atlantic. He was to recall the hardships he and his comrades endured at North Coates, their first British posting. His abiding memory of the place was the cold, not the cold they were used to in Canada, but a deep, penetrating dampness made only bearable by the wonderful generosity of the local people, who welcomed the young Canadians into their

185

homes. During his period at North Coates, he remembered there was no running water on the camp and the men were taken into Grimsby once a week in lorries for a hot shower at the town's public baths.

Most operations were flown at this time from the relief landing ground at Donna Nook. This was a small grass airfield a few miles further down the coast which had been in use since 1936. It had also been used briefly as a relief landing ground for Manby in the early weeks of the war and had then been chosen as a decoy site for North Coates, complete with its own dummy Blenheims and landing lights.

By the winter of 1941/42 Donna Nook was used for offensive operations by the North Coates-based squadrons. Aircraft would be air-tested from North Coates and then landed at Donna Nook. The crews would return in the evening and were faced with a long walk across the airfield from their lorries to the aircraft. There was no luxury of crew buses for Coastal Command!

The Rover offensive proved a fruitful period for the North Coates squadrons. Despite the dangerous nature of their low-level attacks, they were to claim 150,000-tons of shipping sunk or damaged in the months to come.

Early one night in October 1941 three aircraft were sent off in atrocious conditions and spotted a convoy which appeared to be stationary off the island of Borkum. There were 15 ships in all and after an initial attack, the aircraft climbed to radio back news of their 'find' to North Coates. Most of the crews were on stand-down because of the bad weather and there were no available aircraft at Donna Nook. However, the station commander at North Coates, Group Captain Mason, gave permission for all available crews to take what serviceable aircraft there were and attack the convoy.

In the meantime, the first three Hudsons had returned, were rearmed and sent out again on another operation. Several ships were claimed as sunk and all the North Coates aircraft returned safely. A Canadian journalist, who was visiting the airfield at the time, wrote a glowing account of the attack and the part played by what he named Canada's 'Demon Squadron'. The name stuck and 407, which flies with the RCAF today, is still known by this title.

The squadron was involved in one of the worst tragedies of the war on a Lincolnshire airfield on 22nd January 1942. A raid on Borkum had been aborted and Hudsons were returning to Donna Nook with their bombs still on board. At 10.40 pm one of the aircraft crashed on landing and immediately caught fire. The five men on board were killed on impact but then the bomb load exploded, killing another eleven RAF

Trevor Hawkins in front of Hudson H-Harry of 407 Squadron at North Coates in 1941.

ground crew plus two soldiers from the local defence force. A further 16 men were injured, some badly.

Operational losses were also heavy and first 86 Squadron was withdrawn in January 1942 and 407 went a month later. It had only five aircraft captains left and was posted to Thorney Island to reform. North Coates had one further tragedy up its sleeve for the Demon Squadron. Sergeant Bill Goulding and his crew, minus his wireless operator, packed their aircraft with their personal kit and took off. As the aircraft climbed out it seemed to stall and crashed near the airfield, killing all those on board. It appeared the bags loaded on the aircraft had slipped to the rear of the aircraft, holding down the tail and inducing the stall.

Two further Hudson squadrons, 52 and 59, moved in as replacements and began operating for the first time officially as the North Coates Wing. Later in the year two more squadrons, 206 and 224, had spells at the airfield, which was now also hosting the Lysanders of No 6 Anti-Aircraft Co-operation Unit and a Walrus, Ansons and Lysanders of 278 Squadron, which flew in an air-sea rescue role.

Trials began on mixing the weapon loads carried by the North Coates aircraft but the first experiments, involving torpedo-carrying Hampdens of 415 (RCAF) Squadron and radar-equipped Hudsons of 59 Squadron were not successful and Coastal Command decided it needed something more potent with which to attack shipping. The 'something' they had in mind was the Beaufighter, which had already distinguished itself as a night-fighter and was about to do the same as a strike aircraft. Coastal Command came up with the idea of a strike wing of three squadrons of Beaufighters, two armed with cannon and bombs (and later 60lb rockets) to suppress the flak ships while the third carried torpedoes.

143 Squadron arrived at North Coates in August 1942 and was shortly joined by two others, 236 and 254 and together they began evolving tactics first tried off Malta that summer and now adapted for operations in the North Sea.

The first major sortie was on 20th November when the commanding officer of 236 Squadron, Wing Commander H. D. Fraser, led 25 aircraft, nine of which carried torpedoes, in an attack on a convoy off the Dutch coast. It was a shambles. The promised fighter escort failed to show up, three Beaufighters were shot down, seven more damaged and two crashed back at Donna Nook and North Coates. Their only success was to sink a German tug. More training was required and that is what they got that winter, constantly practising the art of concentrated attacks on heavily-defended convoys.

By the spring of 1943 the North Coates Wing was back in business. Wing Commander H. N. G. Wheeler of 143 Squadron, led nine 'Torbeaus' of 254 Squadron, six cannon-equipped Beaufighters of 143 Squadron, and six bomb-carrying aircraft of 236 Squadron in an attack on a convoy off the Hook of Holland. This time they were covered by 22 Spitfires and six Mustangs and, in a devastating four-minute attack, sank a large collier and left two minesweepers and an armed trawler ablaze.

Rockets were added to the firepower of the North Coates Wing that summer and were used for the first time in an attack on a convoy off Scheveningen with only limited success. Two ships were badly damaged but two Beaufighters were lost and four others suffered at the hands of the flak gunners. An attack on a convoy off Texel in August was more successful when a big ore carrier was sunk and four escorts damaged.

There was a feeling within some elements in the RAF that the North Coates Wing was an expensive luxury. In the previous year it had claimed 21 ships sunk, yet aerial mining was responsible for four times that figure. The debate raged on but finally a compromise was struck: the North Coates Wing remained, but lost 143 Squadron, which moved to St Eval. However, all the training was now beginning to pay off. Even with its reduced strength, the wing's aggressive tactics forced the Germans to virtually abandon daylight operations in and out of Rotterdam and on the Ems-Hook route.

143 Squadron was to return early in 1944 to take part in experiments using flares dropped by Wellingtons to illuminate targets at night, moving to Banff in September.

The availability of long-range Mustangs for fighter escorts opened part of the North German coast to the North Coates Wing and in one text-book attack in June, Wing Commander A. Gadd led a force of 19 Beaufighters which sank two merchantmen and an escort vessel.

It was around this time that a young Cockney engine fitter arrived at North Coates. He had been married the year before when he was stationed at Hornchurch and suddenly home seemed a long way away for young Max Bygraves. He made life a bit more enjoyable for himself, and lots of others at North Coates, by starting a camp concert party with a show entitled 'Chock's Away!' which regularly played to full houses in one of the camp's Nissen huts.

As Allied forces moved through Belgium and into Holland, targets for the wing became fewer and the aircraft were used to fly box patrols over the North Sea to combat the threat posed by German midget

British and German war graves, side by side in the village churchyard in North Coates. (Grimsby Evening Telegraph)

submarines. They did this with some success and in March 1945 launched 16 attacks, claiming six submarines sunk.

The final operation of the North Coates Wing came in dramatic fashion in April 1945 when both remaining squadrons flew from Lincolnshire to attack and sink a U-boat and four merchant ships in the Kattegat and a tanker in Kiel bay, where they also claimed an 11,000-ton ship as damaged. They landed in Holland, refuelled and rearmed, and took off again the following day, attacking a destroyer and then sinking five U-boats before returning to North Coates.

Soon afterwards the North Coates Wing was disbanded along with 236 Squadron, 254 Squadron moving to Devon. The airfield was transferred to Maintenance Command and was occupied by 53 Maintenance Unit and 5131 Bomb Disposal Wing which had the task of scrapping Lancaster bombers and clearing the county's airfields of unused bombs.

North Coates was later for a time the home of the first helicopter-borne air-sea rescue unit and had two spells as a base for Bloodhound missiles before finally closing some years ago. Some limited use is still made of its facilities by a local flying club. Donna Nook, in the meantime, closed in 1945 although RAF Donna Nook was to live on at a slightly different site as a Nato bombing range.

27
NORTH KILLINGHOLME

It looked for all the world like a pattern of runways set in a marsh. That was the impression the aircrew of 550 Squadron had as, one by one, they brought their Lancasters in to North Killingholme on a cold, overcast day early in January 1944.

550 had been formed at Waltham the previous month and had already flown a handful of operations before they moved to their new, still unfinished, home at North Killingholme, twelve miles north of Grimsby.

One pilot still remembers the airfield looking like 'something out of Flanders' as the aircraft flew in on 3rd January. Great areas were covered in standing water (the airfield lies only a few hundred yards from the Humber estuary) and work was still going on to provide some basic amenities for the men and women who were to serve there.

North Killingholme had a brief but eventful life. It was operational for just 16 months and housed only one squadron. But in that time 550 became one of the most efficient squadrons in Bomber Command, topping the 1 Group bombing 'league table' on a number of occasions that year. It was 550 which was chosen to put into practice some of the many theories of the group's Air Officer Commanding, Air Commodore Rice, about the maximum load of fuel and bombs a Lancaster could lift. The first squadron commanding officer, Wing Commander Jimmy Bennett, was to recall trials carried out by the squadron when the weight of bombs was so great that the wings of the Lancasters visibly flexed as they lifted off.

550 was also to write its own little bit of history when one of its aircraft, Lancaster LL811 J-Jig – known as Bad Penny II – dropped the very first bombs to mark the opening of the assault on the Normandy

Bad Penny II, the 550 Squadron Lancaster from North Killingholme credited with dropping the first bomb on D-Day.

Five minutes beside the fire in the operations centre for a WAAF officer. (Via Rowland Hardy)

beaches in June 1944. The crew of that aircraft was later awarded a collective Croix de Guerre by the French to mark the role the aircraft played in Overlord and today a plaque marking the feat can be seen in the church which overlooks the site of the airfield.

550 was quickly in action after its move to North Killingholme. Berlin was no stranger to its crews, one Lancaster being lost over the German capital on the squadron's final raid from Waltham, and they soon found themselves back over the Big City from their new home.

One aircraft, O-Oboe, had a lucky escape when it was attacked by a night fighter on the final leg to the target on the night of 30th January. The pilot, Flying Officer Morrison, managed to shake the fighter off and dropped his bombs close to the aiming point. O-Oboe was then set upon by a second night fighter, cannon fire killing both gunners. The navigator misunderstood an order over the intercom and baled out.

Morrison needed all the help he could get from the three remaining members of his crew as he struggled to keep the damaged Lancaster in the air. With no navigational aids, he tried to put the aircraft down at

193

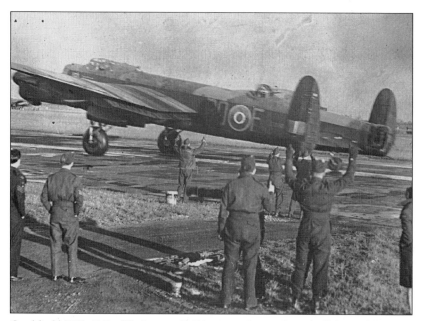

Good luck! 550's F-Freddie is waved off by ground crew for a daylight raid in 1944.

an airfield showing landing lights, only to realise at the last minute it was a Luftwaffe night fighter airfield in Holland. O-Oboe managed to regain height and Morrison headed out across the North Sea, finally landing on the emergency strip at Woodbridge in Suffolk. 550 lost a second Lancaster on the same raid, but the entire crew managed to bale out and spent the remainder of the war as PoWs.

Losses were well below average at this time on 550, possibly because the squadron had a high proportion of experienced crews and they, statistically, had a better chance of surviving. The squadron's efficiency was evident right from the start and within two months of arriving at North Killingholme it recorded the second highest tonnage total in 1 Group, despite operating as only a two-flight squadron. Losses, too, were to remain low for the next few months.

The ill-fated raid on Nuremberg at the end of March 1944 cost 550 two of the 17 Lancasters it sent. One was flown by Sergeant Arthur Jeffries, a young man from Hertfordshire who had a chequered career in the RAF, including spells with both 101 and 100 Squadrons, before joining 550 at Waltham. Two weeks before the attack on Nuremberg he had been recommended for a Conspicuous Gallantry Medal after his

The Christmas card produced by 550 Squadron in 1944, depicting B-Baker – The Phantom of the Ruhr.

25th operation. The award was still being processed when Jeffries and his crew were killed, their Lancaster being hit by flak over Belgium and crashing near Liege. His posthumous CGM, one of only 22 awarded in 1 Group, was later presented to his parents at Buckingham Palace.

On the run-up to the invasion, 550 played its full part in Bomber Command attacks on targets both in France and Germany. In April it topped the 1 Group bombing table, as it did again in May when it also had the least number of aborted operations, a sure sign of a good squadron. 550 returned unscathed from Mailly-le-Camp, when other 1 Group squadrons took a severe mauling, and its losses over northern France during June were among the lowest in Bomber Command.

Operations with 550 were not, however, without incident. One aircraft, flown by Sergeant T. Lloyd, made it back from France with just three crew members on board, the remainder baling out when ordered to do so when their aircraft caught fire. After being attacked by a fighter, the Lancaster went into a steep dive and began to fill with flames. Lloyd regained control and the flight engineer and navigator (who had decided not to jump) used the fire extinguishers and the contents of their drinks flasks to put out the fire and the pilot was able to make it back to Manston.

In an attack on Gelsenkirchen, Flying Officer Clark's Lancaster had two engines disabled by flak over the target. As the aircraft limped

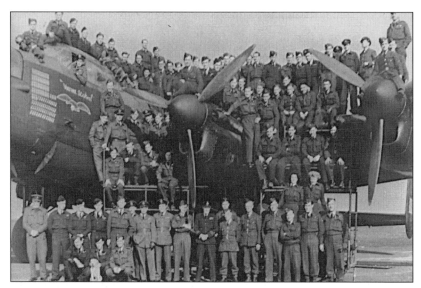

*The whole flight turned out for this photograph to mark the 100th operation of 550's
The Vulture Strikes. (Via Roland Hardy)*

back across the North Sea a third engine failed. Clark brought the
Lancaster back across the coast at 2,000 feet but he was unable to lower
the flaps. Any attempt to reduce power on the remaining engine would
have left the bomber uncontrollable. With the Lancaster now down to
800 feet, Clark held the aircraft steady while the crew baled out one by
one. The automatic pilot would not work and, as he attempted to jump
himself, the Lancaster hit power lines and crashed. The pilot's supreme
act of courage had, however, saved the lives of six fellow airmen.

The hectic summer of 1944 inevitably led to losses at North
Killingholme, among them two squadron commanders. Wing Commander Peter Connolly, who had succeeded Bennett as 550's
commanding officer, was killed on the night of 14/15th July in the
second of the series of raids on marshalling yards at Revigny, one of
three Lancasters lost from North Killingholme in the two nights of 1
Group attacks on the target. He was succeeded by Wing Commander
A. F. Sisley, who was killed in a daylight raid on V2 rocket storage sites
in France at the end of August.

Autumn saw the resumption of deep penetration raids on Germany
and in one of them, a 550 Squadron crew had a remarkable escape. N-
Nan was one of 17 Lancasters from 550 which took part in an attack on

196

North Killingholme's most famous Lancaster, BQ-B, Phantom of the Ruhr, pictured here being bombed up prior to its 100th raid on 5th September, 1944. The armourers on the picture are Jack Lamond and Taffy Davies. (L Browning)

a refinery near Leipzig. Over the target the Lancaster was hit repeatedly by incendiary bombs scattered from another Lancaster above them. One went through the skin near the wing root and ignited. With the mid-upper gunner giving them directions, the flight engineer and navigator used the escape axe to chop a hole in the fuselage and then, leaning out into the slipstream, managed to extinguish the blaze.

N-Nan's tribulations were still far from over. While they were still over the target area there was an enormous crash and the Perspex nose cone of the Lancaster disappeared, sheered off by a 1,000 lb bomb dropped by another aircraft.

It was a long, cold ride back to Killingholme for the crew of N-Nan, which at one time began to fill with snow blown in through the gaping hole in the nose. Back at the airfield, an inspection revealed that part of the tail had been hit by yet another 1,000-pounder and a search revealed 50 unexploded incendiaries still lodged in the fuselage and wings. N-Nan never flew again.

The good fortune which often seemed to accompany 550 saw three of the squadron's Lancasters amass 100-plus operations, although only one, PA995, served exclusively at North Killingholme. Best-known of the trio was EE139, *Phantom of the Ruhr*, which had started its operational career with 100 Squadron at Waltham in the summer of 1943. It was there it received its lurid nose art depicting a skeletal figure scattering bombs. The nose art was the work of its first engineer, who was inspired to do it after watching the film *Phantom of the Opera* at a cinema in Grimsby. It flew 32 operations with 100 Squadron before being one of the aircraft allocated to 550 when it was formed in November 1943. It went on to become one of the real veterans of Bomber Command, completing 121 operations, including 14 raids on Berlin, before being retired at the end of 1944. It later served with 1656 HCU and was scrapped in February 1946.

Not all veterans were treated with reverence by the crews who flew them. One Lancaster, another N-Nan, at North Killingholme had over 80 operations to its credit but was so disliked by all who flew it that few tears were shed when it was ditched by an Australian pilot in the nearby Humber, the story going the rounds that he mistook the reflection of the moon on the surface of the river for Killingholme's main runway. The crew paddled ashore in their dinghy and had to endure much ribaldry back at North Killingholme. When their replacement aircraft arrived they were amused to see 'SS Nan' stencilled on the fuselage.

By the end of 1944, 550 had expanded to a three-flight squadron. During its first twelve months of operations from North Killingholme it had dropped 11,748 tons of bombs, and there was to be no let up in the new year, the squadron achieving an all-time record of 1,534 tons of bombs in March 1945.

550 finished the war with food drops over Holland and flying home prisoners of war from collection points in Belgium. In its time at North Killingholme, it had taken part in 192 bombing raids, flown a total of 3,582 sorties and lost 59 aircraft. The loss rate of 1.6 per cent was one of the lowest in Bomber Command.

The airfield itself closed in October 1945, just 23 months after the main contractors, John Laing and Co, handed it over to the RAF. Today North Killingholme airfield is surrounded by the vast petro-chemical plants which stretch along the south bank of the Humber. The airfield itself is a very large industrial estate, its crumbling runways used for open storage and its remaining hangars for warehousing.

28
SCAMPTON

No single airfield embodies Lincolnshire's aviation history more than RAF Scampton. From its grass runways 617 Squadron lifted off on their epic dambusting raid. Three Victoria Crosses were won by airmen who served there. And its very location, standing astride the main road through the county just three miles north of Lincoln Cathedral, has long made it the most potent symbol of the county's deep affiliation with the Royal Air Force.

The airfield was never really at Scampton at all. It began life in the First World War as a fighter airfield when it was known as Brattleby. When it was reopened in 1936 it was as RAF Scampton. It could, just as well, have been RAF Aisthorpe, for the new airfield was equidistant from the three small villages which stand on the road at the foot of the Lincolnshire Cliff.

Scampton was initially within 3 Group but soon after its opening transferred to 5 Group, in whose control it was to stay until 1944. Its squadrons, 49 and 83, had been equipped with the range of weird and wonderful aircraft then in service with the RAF before receiving the new twin-engined Hampden soon after it came into service in 1938. Within six hours of the declaration of war nine Scampton aircraft, six of them from 83 Squadron, took part in the RAF's first offensive sweep of the war over the Schillig Roads off Wilhelmshaven.

It was something of a fiasco, the aircraft were late taking off, it was dark by the time they reached the target area and most of the crews had never flown a Hampden at night before. They turned for home and, with navigation lights on to help the formation stay together, finally arrived back at Scampton at midnight. Among the pilots on that first sortie were Flying Officers 'Babe' Learoyd and Guy Gibson, both of whom were to win VCs flying from Scampton later in the war. Their second operation, in late December, turned out to be just as unsuccessful, twelve Scampton aircraft failing to find the pocket battleship *Deutschsland*, which had been spotted off southern Norway. One of the 49 Squadron aircraft crashed near Acklington, killing two of the crew. Fuel shortage, always a problem with the Hampden, was the likely cause.

Scampton's Hampdens were also involved in a major mine-laying operation in April 1940 but bombing was their main business and they were in the thick of the action during the Germans' lightning push through Belgium and northern France. It was during this period that a Scampton airman won the highest non-combat award for bravery, the George Cross.

Pilot Officer Donald Parker was just about to lift off in his Hampden L4044 on the evening of 8th June for a raid on German troop concentrations at Amiens when an engine failed, the Hampden slewed across the grass and burst into flames. All four men on board, including Parker, were injured. The navigator and rear gunner managed to scramble clear of the burning aircraft but the wireless operator was unconscious and trapped. Parker, despite his own injuries, went back into the Hampden and dragged the man to safety.

The station's first Victoria Cross was awarded in August to Roderick Learoyd, by now a flight lieutenant, of 49 Squadron, the first VC to be

A 49 Squadron Hampden being bombed up at Scampton in the spring of 1940. (Via Grimsby Evening Telegraph)

won in Bomber Command. Learoyd had been with the squadron since early 1937 and was among the first pilots in the RAF to fly Hampdens when they came into service with 49 Squadron in 1938. He had flown on the squadron's first operational sortie of the war and by 12th August 1940 had already completed 23 operations when Hampdens from Scampton were detailed to attack the Dortmund-Ems canal while six others carried out diversionary raids nearby. Learoyd was the fifth to bomb the target and had already watched two 83 Squadron Hampdens shot down before he went into his bomb run. Several searchlights coned his aircraft and two AA shells tore into the starboard wing but Learoyd held his Hampden steady to allow his bomb-aimer, John Lewis, to bomb the aqueduct north of Münster which was their specific target. Learoyd then nursed the badly damaged Hampden back to England and arrived at Scampton soon after 2 am. The aircraft's hydraulics had been damaged in the attack and, rather than risk a night landing (Scampton then had no fixed flare path), Learoyd decided to circle the airfield for three hours before landing at first light. Apart from his Victoria Cross, a DSO went to Squadron Leader Jamie Pitcairn-Hill of 83 Squadron, who had led the attack, and a bar to the DFC of Flying Officer A. R. Mulligan, the pilot of one of the two shot-down Hampdens. Soon afterwards Learoyd was taken off operations. He later commanded 83 Squadron at Scampton and became commanding officer of Bomber Command's first Lancaster squadron, 44 at Waddington.

Pitcairn-Hill was not so lucky. The son of a Presbyterian minister, he survived a ducking when his Hampden ditched off Skegness in the summer of 1940 but failed to return from an attack on Le Havre a few weeks later.

Scampton's second Victoria Cross was won a month after Learoyd's award, this time by an 18 year old wireless operator who had only been in the RAF for just over a year.

Sergeant John Hannah arrived at Scampton the day before Learoyd won his VC. He had served briefly with 106 Squadron at Thornaby-on-Tees before being posted as a wireless operator/air gunner to 83 Squadron. It was a hectic period for the Scampton squadrons and Hannah flew on a number of day and night raids on North Sea ports where the Germans were believed to be assembling their invasion fleet.

On the night of 15/16th September 83 Squadron sent 15 aircraft to bomb shipping in the harbour at Antwerp, Hannah flying as the WOP/AG in the crew of Pilot Officer Connor, an experienced Canadian pilot. As they approached Antwerp it seemed as though every flak gun around the port opened fire simultaneously as searchlights probed for the attacking Hampdens. Connor and his navigator, Sergeant Hayhurst, could clearly see a mass of barges moored in the harbour. Their first bomb run was unsuccessful as the aircraft drifted too far from the target so Connor decided to go round and try again, this time from 2,000 feet.

Just as the Hampden dropped its bombs, it was hit in the bomb-bay by an anti-aircraft shell, shrapnel damaging the rear of the fuselage and the port wing, where fuel tanks were ruptured. The leaking petrol immediately caught fire and the aft section of the Hampden, containing Hannah and the rear gunner, Sergeant James, was enveloped in flames. James, his turret literally melting around him, baled out. Hannah reported the fire to Connor as 'not too bad' but when Hayhurst, the navigator/bomb aimer, climbed through to the rear of the aircraft, he saw the young wireless operator seemingly engulfed in flames and, judging that the aircraft was doomed, clipped on his parachute and jumped.

Hannah, in the meantime, had succeeded in forcing open the door leading into the mid-section of the fuselage. Noticing that his parachute had begun to smoulder, he grabbed an extinguisher in an attempt to put out the fire as ammunition exploded around him. When the extinguisher ran dry he used his log book to beat out the flames; when that caught fire he used his hands. Although badly burned, he crawled through to the front of the aircraft and then helped navigate the badly damaged Hampden back to Scampton.

Hannah was immediately hospitalised at Rauceby, near Sleaford and it was while he was there that he learned first of his award of the Victoria Cross and then that Pilot Officer Connor, awarded the DFC for his heroics that night, had been killed when his Hampden crashed into the sea on a later operation.

John Hannah was never to fly operationally again. When he had recovered from his injuries, he spent some time as an instructor before finally being discharged on medical grounds in 1942. His health deteriorated and he died in 1947. Twenty years later, his widow presented his Victoria Cross to his old squadron at a special ceremony at Scampton.

By early 1941 Scampton had become one of the largest bomber airfields in the country, its two squadrons operating 52 Hampdens between them, with almost 2,500 service personnel living on or around the airfield, many of them in tents until more accommodation could be found. And it became even more crowded in the autumn with the arrival of the 5 Group Target Towing Flight, which was to remain at Scampton for much of the winter.

In two years of war Scampton squadrons had lost over 150 Hampdens on operations, but its days as a front-line bomber were numbered and in December 1941 its replacement, the Avro Manchester, began arriving at Scampton and 83 Squadron was fully operational by January. Modern though the new aircraft might have been, it was instantly disliked by the 83 Squadron crews who found it unforgiving and a brute to fly after their Hampdens. It was also a mechanical nightmare and sortie after sortie was aborted as a result of problems with its Rolls-Royce Vulture engines and its hydraulic systems. 49 Squadron also converted to Manchesters but, by the early summer, both squadrons were being re-equipped with the four-Merlin engined version of the Manchester, the Lancaster.

83 Squadron moved to Wyton where it became part of the new Pathfinder Force and its place was taken by 57 Squadron, which moved in from Feltwell. A third squadron, 467 (RAAF), was formed at Scampton and moved soon afterwards to Bottesford. 57 Squadron flew its Lancasters in anger for the first time on the night of 12/13th October 1942 in a small-scale 5 Group raid on Wismar. One of its aircraft, piloted by Flight Lieutenant Curry, was mauled by a night fighter and two of the crew badly wounded.

One of the Lancasters at Scampton at the time was R5868, Q-Queenie of 83 Squadron. It was delivered to the squadron at the end of June 1942 and was to complete 136 operations with 83 and later with 467 Squadron as S-Sugar at Bottesford and Waddington before being retired. Miraculously, it survived the breakers and became part of the RAF's Historical Aircraft Collection. It was to return to Scampton in 1959 where it stood as the gate guardian for eleven years before finally being given a place of honour in the new RAF Museum at Hendon, where it is still preserved today.

Not so fortunate were the six Lancasters destroyed in an accident at Scampton in April 1943. The aircraft had been bombed up the previous day for a raid which was then cancelled as thick fog descended on Lincolnshire. By the following day it was noticeable that a number of the aircraft were beginning to show the strain of the weight of bombs and fuel they held, so ground crews were ordered to unload the bombs. According to one of the ground crew involved, the trouble began when a photo flash fell from one the machines. The area was immediately evacuated and he recalls the only casualty was a man who sustained minor injuries when he fell from a fire appliance. The damage was

An 83 Squadron Lancaster during an engine test at Scampton, mid-1942. (Via Grimsby Evening Telegraph)

enormous, however, and would have been more so had the explosion not occurred on the western edge of the airfield.

As Scampton became the 52 Base HQ in the late spring of 1943, it assumed responsibility for the neighbouring airfields at Fiskerton and Dunholme Lodge and it was to the former that 49 Squadron moved. Its place was taken by what was very quickly to become the best known squadron in Bomber Command – 617. It was formed on 21st March 1943 initially to perform just one task, the destruction of the Ruhr dams. Wing Commander Guy Gibson, who had won a DFC at Scampton flying Hampdens earlier in the war, arrived from Coningsby, where he had led 106 Squadron, to take command.

The story of 617's time at Scampton has passed into RAF legend. Just seven weeks after the squadron was formed Gibson led 19 Lancasters on their epic attack on the Möhne, Eder and Sorpe dams, which provided hydro-electric power to much of the Ruhr. Three of the Lancasters had to return because of mechanical problems but the remaining 16, each carrying one of Barnes-Wallis's 'bouncing bombs'

Picture of a hero: Guy Gibson VC.

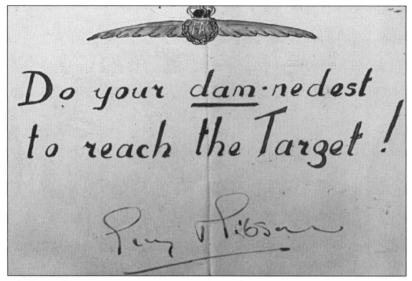

A personal reminder from Guy Gibson. (Lincolnshire Echo)

breached the Möhne and Sorpe dams in spectacular fashion. Eight of 617's Lancasters failed to return.

Thirty-three gallantry awards were made as a result of the raid, including the Victoria Cross to Gibson. Research after the war has shown that the military and commercial value of the raid was far less than the British believed at the time, but there is no doubt that the attack was one of the great morale boosters of the entire war for the people of Britain.

Although 617 Squadron will be forever linked with RAF Scampton, their stay there was brief. They carried out one more raid, an attack on power plants in northern Italy led by their new commanding officer Squadron Leader George Holden, before moving to Coningsby in late August.

During the time 617 was preparing for and carrying out the attack on the dams, life at Scampton went on as usual, with 57 Squadron heavily involved in attacks on the great industrial centres of the Ruhr. It lost several crews, including that of Sergeant Glotham, whose Lancaster lifted off for a raid on Essen on the night of 30th April. En route to the target their aircraft was seen to be attacked but nothing more was heard or seen of ED706 until 1987 when reclamation work on the Zuider Zee uncovered the wreckage of the Lancaster and the bodies of its crew.

Scampton's grass runways were now unsuitable for further heavy bomber operations and, as the concrete runway contractors moved in, the squadrons moved out, 57 moving to East Kirkby the day before 617 left. No more operations were flown from Scampton until 20th October 1944, by which time it had passed into the control of 1 Group and become the home of 153 Squadron. In the interim the airfield was used by a series of training schools and, once the runways were usable, by 1690 Bomber Defence Training Flight.

153 was in action within hours of arriving at Scampton, seven aircraft taking part in a raid on Emmerich. There were to be few quiet periods for 153 for the remainder of the war as the bombing campaign against Germany was resumed in its full fury following the switch to tactical French targets during the summer. In one attack on Cologne a Scampton Lancaster, piloted by Flying Officer 'Whizz' Wheeler had a lucky escape when it was hit by a 1,000lb bomb dropped by another Lancaster. The bomb tore a hole the size of a kitchen table in the starboard wing but Lady Luck was smiling on Wheeler and his crew: the bomb had not fallen far enough to arm itself and when it hit the wing it missed everything vital, including the fuel tank, engine, flaps and ailerons. Wheeler, in the best traditions of Scampton, went on to bomb the target and returned to Lincolnshire to tell the tale.

As the war drew to a close and targets became fewer and fewer, 153 found itself back on 'gardening' duties, dropping sea mines just as the Hampdens did five years earlier. And it proved just as dangerous. On the night of 11th March 1945 five Lancasters, each carrying six 1,500lb mines, left Scampton for the Kattegat. Three were shot down, a fourth disappeared over the North Sea and the fifth landed badly damaged. Morale dropped sharply at Scampton as the squadron was put on stand-by for more mining operations. So sensitive was the squadron's Wing Commander (Flying), Francis Powley, to this that he volunteered to lead the next mining trip, despite a premonition that he would not return. On the following night he led five 153 Squadron Lancasters to lay mines in the Kattegat. Powley's aircraft was shot down by a night fighter and a second 153 Squadron Lancaster failed to return, along with a third Lancaster from a neighbouring 1 Group squadron. The losses seemed only the more pointless with the war in Europe so obviously in its very last stages.

The night after the loss of Wing Commander Powley, 153 Squadron took part in a 1 Group attack on a benzol plant at that old Bomber Command favourite, Gelsenkirchen, in the Ruhr Valley.

One of the aircraft which flew that night was *Vicious Virgin*, the

Lancaster of Flying Officer Bob Purves and his crew. Purves was a Canadian and at the time had a girlfriend, Iris Price, who was a WAAF stationed with him at Scampton. She was curious to know what it was like to fly in operations over Germany and that night she got her chance. As Purves was taxiing out at Scampton to take off, Iris was waiting at the side of the runway on the pretext of waving goodbye to the Lancaster as it took off, a common enough occurrence on any airfield. But, when no one was looking, she ran across to the Lancaster, a door opened and she was dragged inside. Iris Price was to become probably the only WAAF to fly on operations with Bomber Command. Iris, who now lives in Christchurch, New Zealand, recently told the story for the first time and still recalls the feeling of utter terror as she sat in the fuselage of the dark, noisy Lancaster as it began its bomb run at 16,000 feet over one of the most heavily defended areas on earth. She was relieved when she felt the Lancaster rise as its bomb load fell and Purves began to turn for home. However, Iris's problems were only just beginning. Her oxygen line became blocked and she lost consciousness as the aircraft headed back for England. When she was found, the crew thought at first she was dead. Knowing the trouble they would have explaining the presence of a dead WAAF on board when they returned to Scampton, they planned to dump her body in the North Sea. Iris, however, was far from dead and, with her oxygen line cleared, she regained consciousness as the *Vicious Virgin* crossed the Dutch coast.

Back at Scampton her friend Doris Roberts was waiting to pick up Iris as the Lancaster taxied to its dispersal pan and later both women were sworn to secrecy by Purves, who would have faced a court martial if the story of his unauthorised 'passenger' ever leaked out. The crew survived the war and later Flying Officer Purves returned to Canada where he died some 20 years later.

153 Squadron was joined in the final weeks of the war by 625 Squadron, which moved in following the decision to close Kelstern, and both took part in the last major Bomber Command raid of the war.

Scampton went on to become one of the RAF's key airfields in the post-war years. It housed American B29s at the height of the Berlin airlift, Lancasters, Lincolns and, at the start of the jet age, Canberras. In the mid-1950s the airfield underwent a major expansion, including lengthening the main runway, which necessitated diverting the adjacent A15 road, to accommodate the new V-bombers coming into service. The first Vulcans moved in to Scampton at the end of 1958 and, appropriately, they went to 617 Squadron, which was later to be joined

A 153 Squadron crew at Scampton in 1945. Their aircraft was a real Bomber Command veteran, having previously served with 12, 427 and 300 Squadrons. It was scrapped in May 1947. (Tom Tobin)

in what became known as the Scampton Wing by 83 Squadron, the same unit which had flown Hampdens from the airfield 20 years earlier.

In later years Scampton became the home of the Central Flying School and the Red Arrows display team. Now the airfield is closed and its future uncertain. Whatever does happen, links between the village of Scampton and the young men who flew from the airfield which bore its name will never be severed. Half of the picturesque village churchyard is filled with the graves of dozens of young airmen who gave their lives for their country. And buried alongside them are the bodies of eight Luftwaffe aircrew, killed in attacks on Scampton more than half a century ago.

29

SKELLINGTHORPE

Of all Lincolnshire's wartime airfields, none can claim a closer affinity with Lincoln itself than RAF Skellingthorpe.

It was built amid the gravel pits and birch trees three miles west of the city centre in 1941 and today the airfield site is actually within the city boundary. It was named after the nearby village of Skellingthorpe but it was, and always will be, regarded as Lincoln's very own bomber airfield.

Skellingthorpe was a 5 Group heavy bomber station and for much of the war was 'home' to 50 Squadron, which was joined for two spells by 61 Squadron. 50 flew first Hampdens, then Manchesters and finally Lancasters from the airfield. Squadron records show it flew 4,710 Lancaster sorties from Skellingthorpe. It was credited with taking part in more raids than any other heavy Bomber Command squadron and the tonnage of bombs it dropped, around 21,000, was the highest in 5 Group.

50 Squadron had been in action since the early days of the war, flying its Hampdens from Waddington, Lindholme and Swinderby before it was finally given the order to move down the Fosse Way to the new airfield at Skellingthorpe in late November 1941. It was joined the following day by a second squadron from Swinderby, 455 of the Royal Australian Air Force, whose personnel remained in the comfortable pre-war quarters and, for three months, 'commuted' to Skellingthorpe. The move of both squadrons had been accelerated because of the need to lay concrete runways at Swinderby and 455 was to remain at Skellingthorpe until February 1942 when they moved to the new airfield at Wigsley, near Newark.

50, in the meantime, had been in almost constant action with its Hampdens, taking part in raids on Germany and the Low Countries during the first few months at its new home. The Hampden's limitations were still bedevilling the squadron. On the night of 1st

December 1941 Hampden P1202 crashed just two miles from Skellingthorpe after returning from a raid on Hamburg. It had run out of fuel. The same fate led to the loss of another Hampden from Skellingthorpe on 11th January 1942. Sergeant Williams and his crew were returning from an attack on Wilhelmshaven when they became lost and their aircraft ran out of fuel and eventually crashed in Cumberland. Three 50 Squadron men died when their Hampden crashed near York after running out of fuel when it encountered bad weather on the return from a bombing raid on Coblenz. In the same week, another 50 Squadron Hampden was shot down on a daylight minelaying operation off the Frisian Islands.

It wasn't just offensive operations which cost the squadron dearly. A cross-country navigation exercise from Skellingthorpe on 21st January 1942 ended when one of the aircraft involved flew into Kinder Scout in the Peak District, killing all four men on board.

Minelaying operations around Brest led to two other aircraft being lost, along with all eight men on board, while a minelaying operation in Oslo fjord resulted in a 50 Squadron aircraft being brought down by flak. The crew of four are all buried in the Norwegian capital.

The Hampden was clearly obsolete and in April 1942, 50 Squadron began converting to the new Avro Manchester. At first sight, it was a great improvement: it carried a crew of seven, a bigger bomb load, more fuel and much better armament. But the initial enthusiasm at Skellingthorpe quickly waned. Crews found the Manchester grossly underpowered, so much so that its unreliable Rolls-Royce Vulture engines were unable to haul the bomber to 20,000 feet, a height even the elderly Hampdens could operate at quite comfortably.

50 was not alone in its views on the Manchester and within a matter of weeks Avro's chief designer Roy Chadwick came up with a simple solution – extend the wings and add four Merlin engines. The result was the Lancaster, the outstanding bomber aircraft of the war. In the meantime, however, 50, and the other unfortunate squadrons already converted to Manchesters, had to soldier on. 50's first operation was to Paris on 8th April when they scattered leaflets across the city. They were to fly on 33 further operations with the Manchester, only 15 of them bombing raids, before the aircraft was finally withdrawn.

One of those raids came on the night of 30th/31st May when 50 Squadron provided 15 Manchesters for the first 1,000-bomber raid of the war against Cologne. One of the aircraft was flown by Flying Officer Leslie Manser, a 20 year old pilot who had already flown 13 operations in two spells with the squadron.

Flt Lt Leslie Manser, who won a posthumous Victoria Cross as pilot of a Skellingthorpe-based Manchester bomber. (Via Grimsby Evening Telegraph)

Manser's name was not amongst those originally detailed to take part in the raid. Earlier in the day he had flown a 'spare' aircraft into Skellingthorpe from Coningsby and was only included on the battle order after an air test showed that the ex-106 Squadron aircraft, known as D-Dog, was airworthy.

Airworthy it may have been, but D-Dog lived up to its name and Manser found that, fully laden, it was incapable of flying at more than 7,000 feet, 11,000 feet below the height prescribed in the pre-raid briefing.

Despite D-Dog's shortcomings, Manser decided to press on and, after negotiating the city's formidable searchlights and flak, dropped the aircraft's 5,000lbs of incendiary bombs somewhere near the centre of the city. But, just as Manser hauled D-Dog clear of the target, the Manchester was rocked by a direct hit in the bomb bay. Part of the bomb bay doors was blown away and shrapnel peppered the wings and fuselage. The rear gunner was wounded and smoke and flames began to fill the aircraft.

Manser dived through a hail of light flak before levelling out at 800 feet clear of the Cologne defences, but, as D-Dog struggled back up to 2,000 feet, the port engine burst into flames. Manser ordered his second pilot, Sergeant Baveystock, to feather the engine and operate the internal extinguisher. This appeared to work as the flames subsided and then went out altogether.

The Manchester, which was by now over Holland, was hard enough to fly on two engines, on one it was almost impossible and as D-Dog began to lose height it quickly became clear that it was not going to make it back to the emergency airfield at Manston in Kent. Manser ordered his crew to bale out and five of them got away safely, leaving Baveystock and Manser at the controls. As Baveystock clipped on his own parachute he tried to clip Manser's onto the pilot's front harness. But Manser waved him away. 'For God's sake, get out!' he shouted.

Baveystock struggled to the open front hatch and dropped clear. The aircraft was so low that his parachute did not have time to open before he plunged into a dyke filled with water. As he did he saw the Manchester explode in flames in a field close by. Astonishingly, only one of the six men who escaped from the aircraft was captured. The others, including Baveystock and the wounded rear gunner, were picked up near the Belgian village of Bree by the resistance and within weeks were passed through the Comet escape network to Spain and Gibraltar and flown back to England.

On their return they told the full story of Manser's courage in

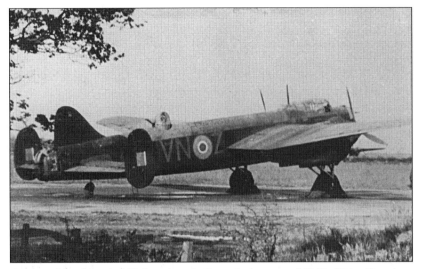

An Avro Manchester of 50 Squadron in the early summer of 1942. (Peter Green)

sacrificing his own life to save those of his crew. On 20th October 1942 Flying Officer Leslie Manser was posthumously awarded the Victoria Cross. It was presented to his widow at a ceremony at Buckingham Palace the following year.

Today, the name of Leslie Manser lives on in Skellingthorpe. In 1981 a new secondary school was opened on land which was once part of Skellingthorpe airfield and Lincolnshire County Council decided to name it the Manser School in memory of a courageous young airman.

50 Squadron struggled on with its Manchesters until June 1942 when the squadron moved out of Skellingthorpe temporarily while concrete runways were laid. They went down the road to Swinderby and it was here that they began converting to the new Lancaster bomber. They were one of the first squadrons to get the new machine and were immediately delighted with it. It was a joy to fly and its four Merlin engines gave it all the power they had dreamt about while struggling for height in their Manchesters.

Skellingthorpe was ready for use again in September and the first aircraft to use the new runways were the conversion flights of 97 and 106 Squadron, which spent three weeks working up on their new Lancasters before changing places with 50 Squadron.

Back at Skellingthorpe, 50 was operational in time to take part in one of the most daring bomber operations of the war, the daylight raid by 94 Lancasters from 5 Group on the Schneider factory at Le Creusot, which was providing guns, tanks, armoured cars and locomotives for the German war machine.

Led by Wing Commander Slee of 49 Squadron, then based at Scampton, the Lancasters flew at low level across France before climbing to between 2,000 and 7,000 feet and dropping their bombs. The raid was timed to allow the aircraft to return under the cover of darkness. The only casualty was a 61 Squadron Lancaster which was brought down by the blast from its own bombs as it attacked the factory's power station.

50 Squadron played its full part in the bombing campaign of the winter of 1942 and the spring of 1943. The squadron also paid its toll in men and machines, losing its first Lancaster on the night of 29/30th July over Saarbrücken. Flight Sergeant Foster and his crew, on their third operation, were to become yet another statistic on the balance sheet of the bombing campaign. More fortunate was another 50 Squadron Lancaster, VN-B, which was badly damaged by flak in a raid on Hamburg on its 26th operation. The wireless operator was killed and both the pilot and navigator wounded, but somehow they got the aircraft back to Harwich where it crash-landed in a field.

The full might of Bomber Command was now turned on the Ruhr and on the night of 5/6th March 50 Squadron contributed 14 Lancasters to the force which raided Essen. It was the start of the Battle of the Ruhr, a long and bloody encounter for both the Germans and the Royal Air Force.

A second raid on Essen on 12/13th March cost 50 Squadron a Lancaster and its seven man crew. Another aircraft from Skellingthorpe was lost following a raid on Duisburg, the damaged Lancaster crashing in the North Sea on its way back from the target. No trace of the crew was ever found.

A raid on Bochum on 12/13th June cost 50 Squadron three Lancasters and with them the lives of 18 aircrew. Three men managed to escape and spent the remainder of the war as prisoners. An attack on Oberhausen the following night left another empty dispersal and seven more empty beds at Skellingthorpe. The loss of Australian pilot Flight Sergeant J. Brock and his crew over Wuppertal rounded off a bad month for 50 Squadron.

Another 50 Squadron Lancaster was shot down in an attack on Gelsenkirchen on the night of 9/10th July while a second aircraft, flown by Sergeant Clifford, ditched in the sea off Bexhill after flak damage led to it losing fuel. The pilot and five of his crew were picked up by an ASR launch. The flight engineer was killed as the aircraft hit the water.

50 Squadron had long regarded itself as one of the premier units in Bomber Command, with some justification. It was also a good squadron to serve on. There was a real *esprit de corps* at Skellingthorpe in those days, a spirit which even the losses over the Ruhr that summer and the war of attrition shortly to be waged over Berlin could do little to dim. The squadron was well-led, it had a good core of experienced airmen and, of course, the delights of Lincoln were close at hand.

Like other squadrons, it had its superstitions. One was the playing of the Andrews Sisters' *The Shrine of St Cecilia* before ops. On one occasion the precious record was broken and a delegation was sent into Lincoln to scour the shops for a replacement.

The squadron was also selected as one of those to take senior war correspondents on a Berlin raid early in December 1943. Two Australian correspondents went with 460 Squadron and both their aircraft failed to returned (see the chapter on Binbrook), while 50 was chosen to carry two Americans, Lowell Bennett and Ed Murrow. Murrow, probably one of the best-known broadcasters of the time, went with Wing Commander Jock Abercrombie, whose Lancaster bombed the target and returned unscathed to Skellingthorpe. Murrow was later to tell his American listeners of his experiences over Berlin.

The city, he said, looked like an orchestral hell, a terrible symphony of light and flares. 'The incendiaries went down like a fistful of rice on black velvet, while the cookies were burning below like sunflowers. It is an unpleasant form of warfare, but to the men of Bomber Command, just a job to be done.'

Lowell, in the meantime, was not so fortunate. His aircraft, flown by Flight Lieutenant Ian Bolton, was caught by night fighters on its way to the target and shot down on its way to Berlin. Six of the seven crew and their American passenger managed to escape by parachute and spent the remainder of the war in a prisoner of war camp.

A month before this incident 50 Squadron was joined at Skellingthorpe by 61 Squadron, which arrived from Syerston with its Lancasters. 61 was another of the original 5 Group squadrons and was returning to its county of adoption after spells at North Luffenham, Woolfox Lodge and Syerston in Nottinghamshire. It appeared to have some divided geographic loyalties: it was known as 'Hull's Own' yet the Lincoln Imp formed part of its squadron crest!

61 Squadron suffered badly over Berlin, losing eleven aircraft and 71 aircrew killed from some 267 sorties. 50, perversely, flew more sorties, 281, but lost fewer aircraft and men, eight and 48. Soon after the squadron arrived at Skellingthorpe two Lancasters and their crews

Staff at the sergeants' mess, Skellingthorpe 1944. (Via Peter Green)

were lost in a single night over Berlin. A third Skellingthorpe Lancaster, this time from 50 Squadron, went down on the same night but six of the crew managed to parachute to safety. A second 50 Squadron Lancaster crashed onto a farmhouse in East Yorkshire on the return flight when it ran out of fuel. Five of the crew died along with the farmer and his wife. A month later there was more tragedy for Skellingthorpe when a 50 Squadron Lancaster ditched in the sea on its way home from Berlin. Six of the crew perished but the seventh, Sergeant H. E. Groves, was finally picked up by destroyer in the aircraft's dinghy suffering from exposure.

61's first stay at Skellingthorpe was brief. In January 1944 it moved to Coningsby to relieve the pressure on air space around Lincoln and operated there until April 1944 when it moved back to Skellingthorpe to make way for the Special Duty – Pathfinder – squadrons which were to provide the marking for 5 Group for the remainder of the war.

50 Squadron had one of its worst nights of the war at the end of March when three of the 15 Lancasters it sent on the Nuremberg raid were shot down, 15 men were killed and seven others taken prisoner. A fourth Lancaster crashed on take off from Skellingthorpe, the crew escaping unscathed, a fifth was badly damaged in a heavy landing at Winthorpe on its return. It represented a loss of in excess of 25 per cent in one night.

Both 50 and 61 were to play their full part in Bomber Command operations over France in the summer of 1944 and the renewed

Skellingthorpe's veteran N-Nuts being bombed up on 11th August 1944 prior to a raid on Bordeaux, its 120th operation. In the cockpit is Flying Officer Norman Hoad.

campaign against Germany in the autumn and winter.

Six weeks after the war ended both 50 and 61 Squadrons left Skellingthorpe for the last time, going to the new airfield at Sturgate, near Gainsborough. Their places were taken by 619 from Strubby and 463 (RAAF) from Waddington. 619 was disbanded shortly afterwards, followed by 463 in September. Skellingthorpe closed for flying in October and a month later the station officially closed and the land was returned to agriculture and later redeveloped as part of Lincoln's expanding Birchwood Estate.

Although virtually all traces of the airfield have now disappeared, there are plenty of reminders of the role played by RAF Skellingthorpe in the bombing campaign. Many of the roads on the estate bear the names of Lincolnshire airfields and there is a magnificent memorial on Birchwood Avenue commemorating all those who gave their lives while serving at Skellingthorpe with 50 and 61 Squadrons. There are also smaller memorials in the church of St Luke and St Martin on the estate, in a local health centre and the estate's public house.

It will be a very long time before the exploits of those who served at RAF Skellingthorpe will be forgotten.

30

SPILSBY

They say that first impressions count. So when the first elements of 207 Squadron of Bomber Command arrived at RAF Spilsby on a pleasantly warm day in September 1943 that first view was to set the tone for what was generally regarded as a happy and well-run airfield within 5 Group of Bomber Command. 207 was to be one of two squadrons to use Spilsby in the 20 months remaining of the Second World War; the second, 44, was to arrive a year later following the transfer of Dunholme Lodge to the neighbouring 1 Group.

RAF Spilsby was built on 630 acres of land two miles east of the market town from which it took its name. A little under five miles to the east lay the North Sea and, pleasant though it must have seemed on that day in September 1943, Spilsby could match anywhere in Lincolnshire for its coldness and bleakness during the two wartime winters to come.

Among the first members of 207 to arrive was a young LACW, Fay Hill, who had served in the squadron's signals section at Langar, near Nottingham, before the move to rural Lincolnshire. Her role in the squadron's advance party was to help set up the signals section (it was located next door to the station HQ) ready for operations to commence as soon as the aircraft moved in.

The place seemed 'absolutely marvellous' to the 19 year old WAAF, who had been trained at Cranwell before joining the squadron at Langar. Everything was new and, unlike many other Lincolnshire airfields which came into use during 1943, most of the building work was finished before it became operational.

The station was spread over a very wide area and bicycles were issued to the newcomers within days of their arrival. The WAAF accommodation site was some distance from the airfield, close to what was then known as Banks' Farm, a place where the young airwomen always found a welcome from the farmer and his family and the source of a constant supply of fresh eggs. The accommodation was in standard Nissen huts where the rule was first in got the beds nearest the single coke stove.

It was mid-October before 207's aircraft arrived, the squadron taking the opportunity to make the move during a ten-day period when no heavy bomber operations were carried out. 207 had been reformed at Waddington three years earlier and was among the first squadrons to use the ill-fated Manchesters before converting to Lancasters in the spring of 1942. Spilsby was to be its final home.

Once at Spilsby, 207 was quickly in action, with Hanover, Leipzig, Kassel and Düsseldorf all appearing on the operations board. But these were just the preliminaries for the main event of the winter of 1943-44, Berlin.

207 mounted its first attack on the Big City on the night of 18/19th November when 16 aircraft were among 440 Lancasters which staged a largely inconclusive attack on the German capital. All the Spilsby aircraft returned, one of them only by dint of the extraordinary courage and airmanship of its pilot, Flight Lieutenant Baker. His aircraft, V-Victor, was in the stream some 25 miles from the target when the nose

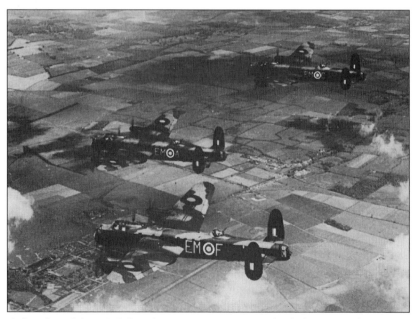

A fine shot of three 207 Squadron Lancasters over England. (Via Grimsby Evening Telegraph)

of the aircraft hit the rudder of a 9 Squadron Lancaster from nearby Bardney. The force of the impact tore away the Perspex nose-cone of V-Victor and the bomb aimer, Sergeant Shimeld, who was in position for the attack (and would not have been wearing his parachute), plunged to his death. The impact tore away part of the rudder of the 9 Squadron Lancaster and killed the rear gunner; the six survivors baled out and the aircraft crashed north of Berlin. Baker, in the meantime, decided to press on to the target despite the damage to V-Victor only to find the bomb release mechanism would not work once over the centre of Berlin.

With the front of the aircraft torn off, an icy blast of air blew into the damaged Lancaster but Baker managed to bring it back to Spilsby where the frostbite he suffered was so severe he was to lose several fingers. He was awarded an immediate Distinguished Flying Cross.

207 was to return to Berlin many times that winter and to leave the wreckage of more than a dozen of its Lancasters scattered across northern Europe. Some crews were luckier than others. On the night of 23rd/24th November 207's H-Harry was attacked by an unseen night fighter which was probably using an upward-firing cannon. Incendiaries in the bomb-bay were ignited and only quick action by the pilot, Pilot Officer Pryor, in dumping the bomb load, saved the aircraft. It later landed safely on the emergency runway at Woodbridge in Suffolk.

Five of the crew of P-Peter, which was lost on 16th December, survived. One of the gunners was killed in a night fighter attack, a second when his parachute failed to open. A week later six members of Pilot Officer Moulton-Barnett's crew survived when shot down en route for Berlin.

Four raids in January were to cost the squadron six Lancasters and 36 men. One of the aircraft lost was 207's T-Tommy, a Lancaster which had started life with 1662 HCU at Blyton and been delivered to 207 in mid-November 1943. It was on its eighth raid on Berlin when it was lost early in January 1944 with an eight-man crew. Two of the men on board were on secondment from the USAAF.

Spilsby's worst night in the Battle of Berlin came on 30th/31st January 1944 when three aircraft failed to return. One was shot down by a night fighter over Berlin. The rear gunner was killed but the other six members of the crew parachuted to safety. There were no survivors from the other two aircraft, one of which was a veteran Lancaster which had previously served with 57 Squadron.

Back at Spilsby, young WAAF Fay Hill (now Mrs Fay Wilson of

Boston, Lincolnshire) had the job of sending telegrams to a long list of addresses. The wording was the same on each ... 'We regret to inform you ... missing ...' and she had to fight back the tears as she went about her work. But, as the weeks and months went by, she became hardened to the task and barely gave it a thought, even if she remembered the young man concerned from an exchange in the mess or from the dances at the Shades pub in nearby Spilsby.

Spilsby lost two more aircraft in the final raid of the Battle of Berlin on 24/25th March, one shot down by a night fighter over Berlin itself and the other crash-landing on the airfield with a dead gunner on board, the victim of another combat at 18,000 feet with the Luftwaffe.

Two of Spilsby's Lancasters were amongst the 96 aircraft lost by Bomber Command in the attack on Nuremberg at the end of March 1944. One was flown by New Zealander Pilot Officer Brian Riddle. He and his crew were on their fifth operation. The second aircraft lost was flown by Pilot Officer Jack Thornton, a Canadian who, with his crew, were on their eleventh operation. Thornton's Lancaster was shot down by a night fighter just before the target and the brilliant orange glow it made as it exploded illuminated an industrial town which many crews took to be Nuremberg. It was actually Schweinfurt and this helped account for the scattered bombing on a night of unfolding disaster for Bomber Command.

207 Squadron played a significant role in the bombing operations both before and after the D-Day landings, its crews and aircraft directed against tactical targets in northern France, against V-weapon sites and rail targets. It was on one of the latter, the attack on Revigny, which is described in more detail in the chapter on Dunholme Lodge, that it lost three aircraft in one night. The raid caught 207 at a bad time and it was able to contribute only twelve of its 20 Lancasters to an all-5 Group attack on the railway marshalling yards, which had already been attacked twice before with inconclusive results. That night the squadron, then led by Wing Commander John Grey, was to lose a quarter of its attacking force.

Of the 21 men on board the three Lancasters, only two men survived, Flight Sergeant Les Aitken and Sergeant Jim Chapple. Aitken was the bomb aimer in Flying Officer Dallen's crew. He baled out when the aircraft was hit by a night fighter, returning to England in September that year. Dallen's body was never found. Chapple was the wireless operator in Flying Officer McNaughton's crew and, coincidentally, he also evaded capture and returned to England in September.

207 had one of the best safety records in 5 Group but it too lost

LACW Fay Hill, one of the first members of 207 Squadron to arrive at Spislby. (Mrs F. Wilson)

Lancasters over England. One veteran aircraft, EM-C, was written off after a heavy landing following the attack on Augsburg on 26th February 1944. Another collided with a 57 Squadron Lancaster over Ruskington during a fighter affiliation exercise in March 1944. A third was lost in a collision with a Lancaster from 49 Squadron (then at Fulbeck) in November that year as they returned from a raid on Hamburg.

Spilsby's proximity to the gunnery range at Wainfleet made it the ideal base for 5 Group's anti-aircraft school, which opened there on 15th May 1944. The school was used to train gunners on the Hispano 20mm cannon, which had been adopted as the standard close-range weapon on airfields throughout Lincolnshire. On the range, trainee gunners had the opportunity to fire at towed and fixed targets and during the months ahead many men went through the courses operated from Spilsby.

By this time the airfield had become a sub-station within 5 Group's 55 Base, the headquarters of which were nearby at East Kirkby. There were further changes later in the year when the reorganisation of 1 and 5 Groups led to the transfer of Dunholme Lodge to 1 Group and the squadron that was dispersed, 44 (Rhodesia), moving to Spilsby.

Spilsby was now home to two of the outstanding squadrons in Bomber Command. 44 had been in action from the very first day of the war (and was to be the only squadron in continuous service in 5 Group) and the first to receive the new Lancaster during its time at Waddington (207 Squadron had been the third).

Shortly after 44 Squadron arrived Spilsby was the scene of what could have been a major disaster. Following the second of two raids in 24 hours on Cologne a number of Halifaxes from 429 (Bison) Squadron based at RAF Leeming were diverted to Spilsby because of bad weather. At the same time Lancasters from its own squadrons were also returning. One of them, a 207 Squadron Lancaster, crashed on landing and spun into four of the 6 Group Halifaxes, wrecking them all.

44 and 207 Squadrons were to operate together throughout the winter of 1944 and the spring of 1945, flying their last raid together on 25th April 1945 when ten aircraft from 207 and eight from 44 took part in the raid on Berchtesgaden.

After the war, Spilsby was retained by the RAF until the mid-1950s when it was allocated to the USAF who strengthened and extended the main runway, only to leave almost as soon as the work was completed. The airfield itself was sold for agricultural purposes, the runways were taken up and the majority of the buildings removed or demolished.

31
STRUBBY

Strubby was closer to occupied Europe than any other Lincolnshire airfield, yet it did not see its first bomber operation until 4th October 1944, by which time most of France and large parts of the Low Countries had been overrun by the Allies.

Brief though Strubby's operational history is, it was unique amongst Lincolnshire airfields in that it was used both by Bomber and Coastal Commands, the latter operating first an air-sea rescue service and later a strike wing of Beaufighters from this most easterly of Lincolnshire stations.

It was early in 1943 when a team of contractors moved onto the site, which lays a few miles inland from the town of Mablethorpe. This is flat, fertile country, liable to inundation from the sea and conditions for the builders, and later for its occupants, must have been bleak during wartime winters. Although allocated to 5 Group, it was surplus to requirements when it was ready for occupation in April 1944. Planned changes, however, meant that it would be needed in the autumn of 1944 and, for the intervening period, it was loaned to 16 Group Coastal Command.

During this period 16 Group was at its most active, operating strikes by wings of Beaufighters against Axis shipping in the North Sea and along the Norwegian coast. Further north in Lincolnshire the North Coates Wing was proving particularly effective in its section of operations and it was agreed to base a second Lincolnshire strike wing at Strubby to maintain the pressure on the Germans immediately after the Normandy landings.

Two squadrons of Beaufighters, 144 and 404 (RCAF), moved in from Davistow Moor and formed the Strubby Strike Wing, beginning operations from the new airfield in July 1944.

Their first strikes were against shipping off Norderney and they helped sink a 3,000-ton merchant ship and damage another. Two days

The watch office at Strubby in 1980. The 'greenhouse' was added by the RAF some time after the war. (Grimsby Evening Telegraph)

later the Strubby and North Coates Wings combined for an operation against a big convoy off Heligoland. In one of the best co-ordinated operations of its kind in the war, the Lincolnshire Beaufighter squadrons sank three merchant ships, the *Tannhauser, Siff* and *Miranda*, along with a minesweeper and an air-sea rescue launch. A week later the Strubby Beaus helped sink a 4,000-ton cargo ship and a German minesweeper off Wangerooge and, in a separate operation, left an oil tanker on fire.

Often Strubby's torpedo squadron, 404, would operate with North Coates' bomber squadron, 236, in anti-shipping strikes and during August they accounted for a number of vessels in attacks on ports along the French and Belgian coasts.

During this time the Beaufighters had been sharing Strubby with a third Coastal Command squadron, 280, which flew Warwicks in an air-sea rescue role. The Warwick was a variant of the Wellington bomber and was to give sterling service in its new role. It could stay airborne for a considerable time and carried a lifeboat in its bomb bay. This contained food and water and could be dropped into the sea for downed aircrew. Its arrival was to save the lives of many airmen who would otherwise have perished in their small dinghies.

A Warwick ASR Mk1, fitted with double Wasp engines. (Peter Green)

By late August the Coastal Command squadrons were under notice to move from Strubby. The Beaufighters went first early in September with the Warwicks following the next day.

Despite its Coastal Command role, heavy bombers were a familiar sight at Strubby. Its proximity to the coast made it the first airfield after landfall for many aircraft and, for those low on fuel or suffering from battle damage it could provide a haven. Some didn't quite make it, including a 51 Squadron Halifax from Leconfield which crashed at Strubby following a raid on Dutch airfields.

619 Squadron had been operating from Dunholme Lodge before its move to Strubby in mid-September 1944. It was not a particularly popular move with members of the squadron who had been willing to ignore the rudimentary facilities at Dunholme for the proximity of the pleasures of Lincoln. Strubby had all the austerity of Dunholme and none of the advantages. Add to that the cold and damp winter they were to spend close to the North Sea and it is easy to understand their feelings.

619 carried out its first operation from Strubby on 4th October, when five Lancasters took off to drop mines in Oslo fjord, one aircraft failing to return. By a strange irony, 619's last operation of the war on 24th April 1945 was also to lay mines in the same area. This time all the aircraft returned.

Three days after that opening mining operation, several 619 Squadron aircraft and crews were detached to help reform 227 Squadron, which had flown Beaufighters from Malta earlier in the war before being disbanded. It now reformed as a Lancaster squadron and A-flight was created at Strubby on 7th October and, simultaneously, B-Flight was formed at Bardney, with both flights moving to Balderton, near Newark at the end of the month. 227 was to return to Strubby in the final weeks of the war.

Strubby also hosted 5 Group's Anti-Aircraft School, which had moved in from East Kirkby and used the nearby Anderby Creek firing range for its training purposes.

619's losses while operating from Strubby were low. The squadron had suffered badly since being formed in April 1943 at Woodhall but losses dropped dramatically in the closing months of the war. Not all crews, however, were lucky.

On 8th January 1945 619's Lancasters were returning from a raid on Munich when one simply broke up and crashed. Whether it had suffered battle damage or structural failure (it was barely six months old, having previously operated with 49 Squadron) is not known. Another ex-49 Squadron Lancaster was written off in a heavy landing at Strubby in February 1945 while the last of the squadron's 77 Lancasters lost on operations was shot down in a raid on Leipzig on 10/11th April 1945.

During its time at Strubby, 619 was credited with a Bomber Command 'first', Wing Commander Birch and his crew shooting down a V1 flying bomb during an attack on the Dortmund-Ems canal on 3rd/4th March, one of many of these weapons aimed at Antwerp.

227 Squadron returned to Strubby on 5th April 1945 and joined 619 in flying home former British prisoners of war from northern Europe.

Strubby was used by the RAF as a satellite of nearby Manby until its closure in 1974, after which some of the facilities continued to be used by helicopters servicing North Sea gas rigs off the Lincolnshire coast.

32
SUTTON BRIDGE

If Waterloo was won on the playing fields of Eton, then a significant part of the Battle of Britain was won from the bumpy grass runways at RAF Sutton Bridge.

It was here that many of the RAF's Hurricane pilots were trained in the spring and early summer of 1940, the fledgling pilots who acquitted themselves so well when they were pitched into the great air battles over Kent and Sussex in August and September of that year.

Sutton Bridge was one of a number of Lincolnshire RAF stations which owed their existence to the East Coast bombing and gunnery

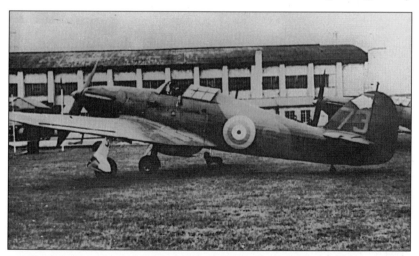

A Mk I Hurricane of 73 Squadron pictured at Sutton Bridge during an armament practice camp in the summer of 1938. (73 Squadron via Peter Green)

ranges. The airfield was established in the mid-1920s as a summer training camp for fighter squadrons from both the RAF and the Fleet Air Arm who used the vast open spaces over the Wash to practise their skills. Over the years the bell tents gave way to more permanent accommodation, wooden hangars were built and by 1936 RAF Sutton Bridge had been established as an airfield in its own right, later to become the home of 3 Armament Training School.

The airfield straddled one of those geographic points where three English counties converged. Aircraft actually landed in Norfolk but were serviced in Lincolnshire while some of the men stationed there lived in Cambridgeshire. The station headquarters, however, was in Lincolnshire and therefore falls within the purview of this book.

The day before war broke out 3 Armament Training School was dispersed to the west coast of Scotland and Sutton was to go to war as a recruit training sub-depot, providing the first taste of RAF life for the recruits then flooding into the service.

At the end of October 1939 Sutton was transferred to 12 Group of Fighter Command and, for a few months at least, was nominally an operational fighter station. The problem was, however, that it had very few aircraft. 264 and 266 Squadrons were formed at Sutton, the former being quickly moved to Martlesham Heath where it was the first RAF squadron to be equipped with Defiants, while the latter received a few Fairey Battles for use as stop-gap fighters. These were eventually replaced by Spitfire Mk 1s and the squadron took these aircraft to its

A Westland Wallace at Sutton Bridge. (M J F Bowyer via Peter Green)

new home, again at Martlesham Heath, early in 1940. 254 Squadron also had a brief spell at Sutton Bridge before it moved to Bircham Newton to receive its first aircraft.

Sutton's role was to be one of training and in March 1940 the 11 Group Fighter Pool was moved from St Athan and renumbered 6 Operational Training Unit. It was to be the half-way house for newly-trained fighter pilots, providing the vital link between primary training and squadron operations. 6 OTU quickly grew into one of the biggest RAF units of any kind then operating in Lincolnshire. Its equipment included in excess of 100 aircraft, the majority of them Hurricanes.

Flying training at Sutton was intensive and, inevitably, there were numerous accidents. Over the next three years the station was to lose in excess of 50 aircraft with many more damaged in less serious and largely unrecorded accidents.

The first aircraft recorded as lost from Sutton was a Battle of 264 Squadron which crashed near the airfield on 4th January 1940 and it was followed by many more, including several in mid-air collisions from which there were few survivors. The village churchyard in Sutton bears testament to the price paid by the trainees and their instructors.

Sutton Bridge's proximity to the Wash and the North Sea made it an

Sutton Bridge from the air looking north-west in either 1940 or 1941. Note the camouflaged hangars. (Bircham Newton records via Peter Green)

occasional target for Luftwaffe attacks. What attacks there were, however, seem to have caused little damage although in one, on 13th May 1941, a Hampden bomber was destroyed. Sutton was deemed important enough at this time to have its own decoy site, which was set up on nearby Terrington Marshes and this was bombed a number of times. It was so successful at luring away German aircraft that people living nearby complained to the Air Ministry about the danger it posed to them.

One raider fell to the guns of 6 OTU's Hurricanes. At least two aircraft were scrambled during the night of 13/14th June 1941 when there was considerable German air activity over southern Lincolnshire and one of the pilots intercepted a Ju88 which he shot down, the bomber coming down in the Wash. The Luftwaffe pilot's body was later recovered and was buried with full military honours at Sutton.

In November 1941, 6 OTU was renumbered 56 Operational Training Unit as part of a reorganisation but its work went on as before until it was transferred to Scotland in the spring of 1942.

Control of Sutton Bridge transferred to 25 (Armament) Group and its Central Gunnery School was established there. It was divided into two elements, one having responsibility for training gunners for Bomber Command and one for Fighter Command. The Bomber Wing was equipped with an assortment of well-used Hampdens and Wellingtons and the Fighter Wing with Spitfires and a few North American Mustangs. This was to continue operations from Sutton Bridge until February 1944 when the Central Gunnery School moved to Catfoss in East Yorkshire.

By now pressure on training was easing and Sutton Bridge was passed to the control of 7 (Pilot) Advance Flying Unit, which had its headquarters at Peterborough. The unit's flying element was moved some weeks later from Sibson to Sutton where it was renamed 7 Service Flying Training School. It operated some 40 Airspeed Oxfords, training mainly French pilots before the war in Europe ended. 7 SFTS remained at Sutton until the spring of 1946 when it moved to Kirton-in-Lindsey and flying ceased.

The RAF retained some of the buildings at Sutton until 1958 when the last service personnel moved out. Today a memorial in the shape of a propeller blade mounted on a brick arch stands alongside the busy A17 Nene bridge dedicated to all those who served at RAF Sutton Bridge.

33
SWINDERBY

RAF Swinderby stands alongside the A46 almost on the county boundary with Nottinghamshire. It was one of the second phase of airfields planned for the county during the expansion programmes of the 1930s and construction had still not begun when war broke out. It eventually got under way in the first weeks of 1940 and by the early summer the main contractors, John Laing, were ready to hand over part of the airfield to the Royal Air Force.

Swinderby had been built as a bomber airfield and it was allocated to 1 Group, in the process of reforming from the Advanced Air Striking Force, which had received such a battering in the Battle of France. When it finally opened in August 1940, it was 1 Group's second Lincolnshire airfield, Binbrook opening a few weeks earlier.

Swinderby's first occupants were no ordinary airmen. Sizeable elements of the Polish air force had escaped from both German and Russian invaders and had arrived in Britain, via France, ready to continue the fight against Nazism. 300 (Masovian) Squadron had been formed at Bramcote in Nottinghamshire the previous month and equipped, temporarily, with Fairey Battle light bombers, moving to the new airfield on 23rd August. It was not immediately to their liking. 300 Squadron was led by Wing Commander Waclaw Makowski, a 43 year old vastly experienced airman who had been general manager of LOT, Poland's state-run airline before the war. His complaint was the station was not finished. There were, he said, no chairs, no beds, no bar and no vodka. By the time the second Polish squadron 301 (Pomeranian) arrived from Bramcote a few days later, the station commander at Swinderby, Wing Commander Lewis, had done his best to make life easier for the Poles. There was, now, a makeshift bar (with vodka) and Makowski, and his counterpart in 301, Roman Rudkowski, declared their units were ready to go to war.

Each squadron had 16 Battles together with an Avro Anson, used for training and communication. They had a strength of some 30 aircrew and 180 ground crew, and were immediately made welcome by the people living in the Swinderby area.

The Polish squadrons went into action for the first time on the night of 14th September 1940 when three aircraft from each squadron bombed invasion barges massed in the harbour at Boulogne. The invasion ports of Boulogne, Calais, Dunkirk and Ostend were to be their targets on a number of nights in the coming weeks. One aircraft was lost to a German night fighter and two more crashed at Blidworth in Nottinghamshire on their way back to Swinderby from an attack on Boulogne.

The Fairey Battle was always intended as a stop-gap until the arrival of something more suited to the task but this did not stop the Poles carrying out experiments with the Battles as dive-bombers, even to the extent of fitting them with a siren, similar to that used so successfully by the Germans in the Ju87. They had a couple of sirens made at Robey's engineering works in Lincoln and tried them out in a simulated attack on the 1 Group HQ at Hucknall. There is no record as to the views of those inside the building at the time, but the Poles were not to keep their Battles for much longer. The first twin-engined Wellingtons began arriving in mid-September and within two months both squadrons had converted to what was the best bomber in the RAF's armoury at the time.

Both squadrons were stood down from operations in mid-October for conversion and it was during this time that the airfield was bombed by the Luftwaffe. The attack was scattered and unco-ordinated but two Battles were damaged and one man slightly injured. More crucially, the bombs cut communications from Swinderby and, until repairs could be carried out, the station took over the village post office and used the telephone there to maintain communications with the outside world.

300 and 301 used their Wellingtons in anger for the first time on the night of 22nd December when they attacked an oil refinery near Antwerp.

Swinderby had been built without hardened runways and its squadrons found it increasingly difficult to operate with fully-laden Wellingtons from the marshy grass surface. Help was at hand, however, with the opening of Winthorpe on the outskirts of Newark. It had concrete runways and it was from here that the Poles operated when conditions at Swinderby deteriorated.

There was a cruel reminder of the dangers the weather posed to night-time bomber operations on the very first day of 1941. Wellingtons from both Polish squadrons at Swinderby were among 140 aircraft which attacked Bremen and targets in Holland, Belgium and northern France. No aircraft were lost but when the Poles returned to Lincolnshire they found fog beginning to gather over the airfields. Most of the aircraft landed safely but one crashed attempting to land at Winthorpe and two more crashed at Waddington, only one man surviving.

In July both Polish squadrons left for Hemswell, which had just been transferred from 5 to 1 Group and Swinderby was passed to the control of 5 Group. Its new occupants were to be 50 squadron, which moved from Lindholme, near Doncaster, another airfield to be taken over by 1 Group. It meant a return to Lincolnshire for 50, one of the original 5 Group squadrons and they arrived on 19th July 1941, a move marred by an accident at Lindholme where one of their Hampdens crashed soon after take-off, killing all four men on board.

An historic moment at Swinderby on 16th June 1941 as General Sikorski and Air Chief Marshal Sir Charles Portal are presented with a Polish Air Force standard smuggled out of Poland. (Peter Green)

The Hampden was notorious for running out of fuel and several 50 Squadron aircraft were lost in this manner, including one machine at Wittering where it attempted to make a forced landing on its way back from Berlin in September 1941.

When 50 arrived it joined the nucleus of another squadron, 455 (Australian), which had begun forming in Australia in May, with an advance party arriving at the Lincolnshire airfield before the Poles of 300 and 301 had left. 455 had no aircraft of its own and gradually began 'inheriting' Hampdens from 50 Squadron until, by the end of August, it was deemed operational and a single aircraft, believed to be flown by the squadron's commanding officer, Wing Commander Gyll-Murray, took part in an attack on Frankfurt.

Both squadrons were to mount attacks on a number of German cities in the autumn of 1941, as well as 'gardening' operations to drop mines off the Norwegian, German, Dutch and French coasts. But it was obvious that Swinderby was unsuitable for another winter of bombing operations and preparations were made for them to move up the Fosse Way to Skellingthorpe. Before they did so there was one astonishing incident when a Hampden was reported to have made a perfect landing on the main Newark-Lincoln road which runs to the north of

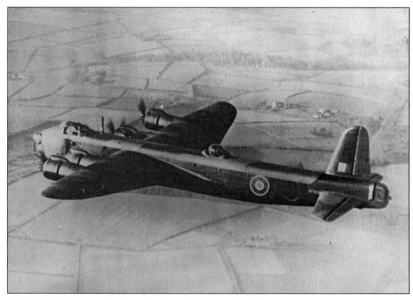

A HCU Stirling in 1944, a familiar sight at Swinderby.

236

the airfield. It was only when the pilot realised his mistake that he is reported to have run the bomber into a ditch.

Once the squadrons had moved, runway contractors moved in to begin work. Personnel from 455 Squadron continued to use the accommodation at Swinderby until February 1942 when the squadron moved to the new airfield which opened just across the Nottinghamshire border at Wigsley.

At this stage it was still intended to use Swinderby in an offensive role and 144 Squadron, which had moved from Hemswell to North Luffenham the previous summer, was put on notice to return to Lincolnshire. However, it was becoming apparent that training crews was the key to successful operations within Bomber Command. In the early days it had been a largely ad hoc affair but, with the advent of the new breed of heavy bombers and the tactics which were becoming so important to bomber operations, more facilities needed devoting to training.

5 Group was in the process of converting to Lancasters and this was being done by squadron conversion flights which were operating side-by-side with their parent squadrons. This was not the best way to train crews and thus was born the idea of heavy conversion units, on which new crews trained in a largely non-operational environment on the new aircraft. Swinderby was selected as the airfield where heavy

Reclaiming a wreck. A recovery team with Stirling III EF209 of 1660 HCU after it crashed near Stapleford Woods in June 1944. (Peter Green Via M. Hodgson)

conversion training within 5 Group would be concentrated.

1654 Heavy Conversion Unit was formed on 19th May 1942 with a mixed bag of Lancasters and Manchesters. It was to move within a month a few miles north to the new airfield at Wigsley. In August 61 and 207 Squadron Conversion Flights arrived at Swinderby, soon to be joined by similar flights from 97 and 106 Squadrons. Together they were combined to form 1660 Heavy Conversion Unit. Ironically, the very aircraft the crews were being trained for, Lancasters, were in short supply and this problem was later solved by the creation of the 5 Group Lancaster Finishing School at Syerston, near Newark, where crews completed their training. 1660 was to train thousands of young men in the complexities of flying heavy bombers. Its Manchesters gave way to a mixture of Short Stirlings and Handley Page Halifaxes, neither of which were 'indigenous' Lincolnshire aircraft. A few Lancasters did operate with the unit early in 1943, mainly those brought into Swinderby by the various squadron conversion flights which led to the creation of 1660 HCU, but the growing losses suffered by 5 Group soon saw those that survived a spate of early accidents allocated to operational squadrons.

Manchesters, Stirlings and Halifaxes were never easy aircraft to fly and soon the Lincolnshire landscape was scattered with the remains of 1660 HCU aircraft. A Manchester went down at Waddington, a Halifax at Leasingham, another Manchester and a Lancaster at Swinderby, all these in the first few weeks of 1943.

Training reached its peak during 1944 when Swinderby became grossly overcrowded. At times there were around 3,000 aircrew on conversion courses. Double bunks were fitted to many of the Nissen huts and the pressure inevitably led to more accidents and more crashes. Among the aircraft written off was the very last Avro Manchester built. It made a heavy landing on the airfield in April 1943 and never flew again.

The Stirlings and Halifaxes continued to operate from Swinderby until the beginning of 1945 when a surfeit of Lancasters enabled 5 Group to fully re-equip 1660. Training continued after the war, 1660 eventually moving to Lindholme as part of 7 Group in 1946. Swinderby was to retain its training role in the post-war years, becoming the home of the RAF School of Recruit Training before it closed some years ago.

34
WADDINGTON

At 6.35 pm on the evening of Sunday 3rd September 1939 nine Hampden bombers from 44 Squadron began taking off from the grass runways at RAF Waddington, five miles south of Lincoln. Their mission was to look for German shipping on this, the first day of the Second World War. Fifteen minutes before midnight the Hampdens began to land. They had not spotted anything which remotely resembled a German warship, but that was of little consequence. Lincolnshire's air war had begun.

It was to end as it began five years and eight months later when Lancaster bombers left a number of Lincolnshire airfields to attack an oil refinery at Tonsberg in southern Norway in what was the final operation by Bomber Command of the war. The only Lancaster which failed to return that night was from 463 (RAAF) Squadron, then based at Waddington. The crew were safe in Sweden; their aircraft was the last of some 3,314 Lancasters lost, the majority from Lincolnshire-based squadrons.

It was 1916 when the Royal Flying Corps first used the flat fields off the Ermine Street south of Lincoln as a training airfield. One of the very first units stationed there was 44 (Training) Squadron. The histories of Waddington and 44 Squadron were to be interlinked for the next 65 years.

The airfield was used briefly by the Americans before the First World War ended and closed between 1920 and 1926 when it was reopened as part of the first phase of RAF expansion between the wars. It was the home of all those weird and wonderful aircraft the RAF was equipped with during this period, including those whose names betrayed the perceived role of the RAF as guardians of the empire – Hyderabad, Hinaidi and Wapiti. Waddington had retained its buildings and hangars from the Great War but was extensively rebuilt in 1936, much of present-day Waddington being built by a small army of craftsmen who spent almost a year on the airfield.

It had already been earmarked as a bomber airfield and in 1938 was transferred from 3 to 5 Group, in whose care it would remain. Its resident squadrons were 44, 50 and 110. A fourth squadron, 503 (County of Lincoln), was disbanded, its officers and men moving to Doncaster where they formed the nucleus of 616 Squadron. 44 (which was led at the time by Wing Commander J. N. Boothman of Schneider Trophy fame) and 50 exchanged their Blenheims for Hampdens and before the year was out 110 moved to Wattisham in Norfolk. Waddington was ready for war.

After that first inconclusive offensive sweep, the Waddington squadrons had to wait until 21st December before seeing action again, providing more than half of the 24 Hampdens which again failed to find any worthwhile targets. Unfortunately, on the way home, the Waddington aircraft were intercepted by Spitfires from 602 Squadron off the north-east coast. They were mistakenly identified as German and two 44 Squadron Hampdens were shot down into the sea off Berwick-on-Tweed. Seven of the eight men on board the two aircraft were picked up by fishing boats. Gunner LAC T. Gibbin was killed in the attack, the first Waddington airman to die in action in the Second World War.

Despite this, training was still far more dangerous than the Luftwaffe. Five men were killed when a visiting 49 Squadron Hampden crashed into a hangar at Waddington and four 50 Squadron men were killed when their aircraft crashed on take-off for a night flying exercise.

With the war stalled in its 'Phoney' stage, the Hampdens' primary offensive tasks were minelaying and reconnaissance. The former was a particularly dangerous occupation. Fighters made daylight operations hazardous and flak ships did the same at night. The opening of the Norwegian campaign saw the Waddington Hampdens despatched to attack German shipping. On 12th April 1940, 44 and 50 Squadron sent twelve aircraft to the Kristiansand to search for a reported German battleship and cruiser. They found a concentration of German shipping in Kristiansand Bay and bombed in sections of three from 5,000 feet.

Accurate anti-aircraft fire inflicted some damage and then the Hampdens were set up by Me109s. Six of the Hampdens were shot down and most of those that did survive were damaged. Had the German fighters not been short of fuel the losses would have been much higher. Despite the overwhelming superiority of the Luftwaffe fighters, the Hampdens fought back and German records later showed

Hampdens of 44 Squadron over Lincolnshire in 1941. The aircraft nearest the camera, AE257, was lost on a raid on Bremen with her crew on 21st/22nd October 1941. (Via Grimsby Evening Telegraph)

that five of their fighters were lost. In one incident, the navigator of one Waddington Hampden took the Vickers K gun from the nose of the aircraft and fired it, from the shoulder, from the astro hatch to deter beam attacks from the German fighters. He earned his DFM that day.

The following day 50 Squadron's Anson (which it used as a communication aircraft) crashed in the sea near Grimsby when it ran out of fuel after a fruitless search for Hampden survivors in the North Sea. There was further tragedy that day at Waddington when a Hampden flown by Flight Lieutenant Cosgrove, the son of the Premier of Tasmania, was seen to crash off Mablethorpe after a minelaying operation. There were no survivors.

50 Squadron moved to Lindholme, near Doncaster in June 1940, its place being taken, albeit briefly, by 142 Squadron, which had been badly mauled in France. It received replacement Fairey Battles at Waddington before moving to the newly-opened airfield at Binbrook. 44 Squadron, in the meantime, found themselves in the thick of the action, bombing targets in the Low Countries, the Channel ports and

241

Germany itself. After the massacre over Kristiansand Bay, most operations were switched to night attacks. On 25/26th August the Lincolnshire Hampdens went to Berlin for the first time in an attack which was to have far-reaching consequences for the Luftwaffe and the ensuing Battle of Britain. It so angered Hitler, he ordered his bombers to switch from attacking RAF fighter airfields to London. The respite was just what Fighter Command needed and the course of history was changed.

It was a bloody autumn for 44 Squadron at Waddington. It was in action almost continuously and in the final four months of the year lost 22 aircraft. The Hampden, loved though it was by its peace-time crews, was proving to be inadequate for the task of long-range bombing. Crews feared fuel shortages as much as they did the German defences and the bottom of the North Sea is today littered with the remains of dozens of Lincolnshire-based Hampdens which ditched on their way home from distant German targets. Many of them were from 44 Squadron, which was to persist with its Hampdens throughout 1941, though there were those on the squadron who believed, with some justification, they were the lucky ones.

In November 1940, 207 Squadron had reformed at Waddington and became the first to be equipped with the new Avro Manchester (see Scampton for a more detailed description of this aircraft).

Waddington still had grassed runways and this, together with the problems the crews were experiencing with the Manchester, meant it was late February 1941 before the new aircraft finally made its operational bow, six taking part in a bombing raid on shipping at Brest. One of the Manchesters crashed on its return.

It was an unhappy aircraft from start to finish, beset with engine and hydraulic problems. 207's EM-D was a typical example. On 15th May 1941 it turned back from a raid on Berlin with jammed bomb doors. The same thing happened en route to Hamburg the following month. Engine trouble forced it back from a mining trip to St Nazaire on 2nd January 1942. A week later it failed to return from a trip to Brest.

207 Squadron did have some successes with its Manchesters. EM-G dropped the RAF's first 4,000lb blast bomb, later known by all as the 'cookie', in an attack on Hamburg on 2nd/3rd May 1941. The Manchester may have been underpowered and mechanically unreliable, but it could haul big bomb loads to targets right across Europe.

The squadron also provided eight crews as the nucleus of 97 (Straits Settlement) Squadron, which was reformed at Waddington in February 1941, worked up on its Manchesters before moving to Coningsby.

Avro Manchester L7284 of 207 Squadron at Waddington. This aircraft took part in the first Manchester operation of the war. (Via Grimsby Evening Telegraph)

Waddington itself was attacked by a German raider in May 1941 and, in what was one of the most serious Luftwaffe attacks on a Lincolnshire airfield, six bombs hit the airfield and two parachute mines fell in the adjacent village of Waddington. The mines caused widespread damage, destroying the village church and 19 houses and killing one person and injuring another 49. The bombs that hit the airfield destroyed a number of buildings, including the station Naafi. Ten people were killed, including seven members of the Naafi staff.

44 and 207 Squadrons were joined by 6 BAT Flight that summer. It was initially equipped with a mixture of Blenheims and Hampdens, but later in the year began operating Oxfords and was renumbered 1506 BAT Flight.

44 Squadron, in the meantime, was renamed 44 (Rhodesia) Squadron in recognition of the donations made by Rhodesia to the cost of the war effort and of the fact that some 25 per cent of its aircrew were Rhodesian or South African.

It was no secret among Bomber Command squadrons that the Manchester had proved a failure. It was potentially a good aircraft, but the events of 1941 had proved it was underpowered and unreliable, neither of which was acceptable in the dangerous business of night bombing. The redesign and re-engine programme instigated by Avro in the summer of 1941 and the aircraft which resulted from it is now part of aviation history. 44 Squadron at Waddington was the unit

243

chosen to prove just how successful Avro's work was to be.

The squadron received its first three Lancasters on Christmas Eve 1941. They had been built at Newton Heath in Manchester, the first of a batch of 43 to be produced there. Four more arrived on 28th December and three more early in January. Despite the losses suffered by Lancasters over the years to come, one of the aircraft delivered to Waddington on 28th December 1941, L7541 which was first registered with the squadron as KM-O, survived the war before being scrapped in July 1945.

That initial batch of aircraft was used for conversion training, the squadron handing its Hampdens over to 420 (Snowy Owl) Squadron of the Royal Canadian Air Force, which was formed at Waddington in November 1941 and flew its Hampdens from there until the summer of 1942 when it moved to 4 Group at Skipton-on-Swale in North Yorkshire.

Four of 44 Squadron's Lancasters flew on a mining operation close to the Frisian Islands on the night of 3rd/4th March 1942, the first time the new aircraft had been used in anger. The operation was led by a young South African pilot who had been with the squadron since the previous summer, Squadron Leader John Dering Nettleton. Within six weeks Nettleton was to become the first man to win a Victoria Cross in a Lancaster. A week after that mining trip 44 took its Lancasters to Germany for the first time, all the aircraft returning from a raid on Essen.

97 Squadron at Coningsby had been selected as the second to receive Lancasters and a number of its crews went to Waddington for conversion training. It was there one of their aircraft crashed in February 1942, the second Lancaster crash in Lincolnshire. The first operational loss came on the night of 24/25th March when an aircraft flown by South African Flight Sergeant L. Warren-Smith failed to return from a mining operation in the Bay of Biscay.

For some time Bomber Command's hierarchy had wanted to experiment with a deep-penetration daylight attack by a small force of bombers against one of a number of strategically important targets. The immediate success of the Lancaster prompted just such an attack on 17th April 1942 on the MAN vehicle factory at Augsburg in southern Germany, a round trip of almost 2,000 miles from Lincoln-shire. The attack was mounted by six Lancasters from 44 Squadron and six more from 97 Squadron, which had recently moved again, this time to nearby Woodhall Spa. The attack was led by Nettleton, each aircraft carrying four 1,000lb bombs with eleven-second delay detonators and a

Sqdn Ldr John Nettleton VC, 20th August 1942.

maximum fuel load of 2,154 gallons.

An elaborate operation involving 80 Boston light bombers and hundreds of fighters was already in progress over northern France in an attempt to engage the Luftwaffe fighters as the twelve Lancasters dropped to 50 feet over the Channel. The diversion appeared to have

245

worked well but then the Waddington element, which had drawn ahead of the 97 Squadron aircraft, had the bad luck to fly close to a fighter airfield just as Fw190s were returning after a fruitless chase of the fleeing Bostons. Four of the Lancasters were shot down and the remaining two, including Nettleton's aircraft, were damaged. Both made it to Augsburg but the second surviving Lancaster crashed after bombing the target, leaving Nettleton to make the long journey back to England alone in the only surviving 44 Squadron aircraft. The 97 Squadron Lancasters fared slightly better, one falling to flak before it could attack and a second crashing after bombing the target. The remaining four all returned to Woodhall Spa.

Ten days after the raid Nettleton was awarded the Victoria Cross. After a six-week tour of the United States he later commanded the 44 Conversion Flight at Waddington before becoming the first commanding officer of 1661 HCU, which was formed at Waddington and later moved to Winthorpe. In January 1943 he was promoted to wing commander and returned to Waddington to take command of 44 Squadron. On the night of 12th/13th July 1943 Nettleton's Lancaster failed to return from a raid on Turin. It was later discovered the aircraft had been shot down over the Channel by a night fighter. His body was never found.

44 Squadron was joined at Waddington by 9 Squadron which arrived with its Wellingtons from Honiton in Suffolk, from where it had operated as part of 3 Group. It quickly began converting to Lancasters, via a handful of remaining Manchesters, and flew its first operation from Waddington to Bremen in September 1942.

There was a double tragedy at the airfield in November when a 44 Squadron Lancaster and a second from 9 Squadron collided in the circuit on their return from Genoa and all 14 men on board were killed. Three weeks later the same thing happened again, this time the collision occurring as the Lancasters took off for Duisburg.

Waddington was high on the list of airfields needing concrete runways and these were laid in the late spring and summer of 1943. 9 Squadron went to Bardney and 44 to Dunholme Lodge, just two of the crop of new airfields then springing up around Lincoln. Waddington now prepared itself for a new era in its history – home to Australian bomber squadrons.

In November that year 467 (RAAF) Squadron was formed at Bottesford in Leicestershire and moved into Waddington and later that month a second squadron, 463 (RAAF), was formed from elements of 467 at Waddington. The airfield had also become 53 Base HQ with its

Waddington's most famous Lancaster, R5868, seen here as 467 Squadron's S-Sugar during the late summer of 1944 and today preserved in the RAF Museum at Hendon. (Via Grimsby Evening Telegraph)

sub stations at Bardney and Skellingthorpe.

463's first Lancaster operation from Waddington was to Berlin on the night of 26/27th November 1943. The first aircraft off that night from the new runway was the squadron's JO-E (which formerly had the unfortunate squadron codes PO-X while with 467 Squadron). This veteran Lancaster was to fly from Waddington until the following spring when, on its return from a raid on Stuttgart, it collided with a Lancaster from 625 Squadron at Kelstern over the village of Branston and crashed not far from Waddington. There were no survivors.

Both squadrons suffered heavy losses in their time at Waddington. 463 recorded the highest percentage loss of any of the three Australian squadrons in Lincolnshire (the third was 460 at Binbrook). Not all their losses came over Germany and occupied Europe. Two 467 Lancasters collided during an air test over Swinderby in October 1944. One managed to land safely at Waddington (it was lost in action two weeks later) while the second was diverted to the emergency airfield at Carnaby, near Bridlington, where it managed to land but was destined not to fly again. Another Lancaster from 463 was lost when it collided with a Hurricane on a fighter affiliation exercise over Metheringham in March 1945.

One of 463's veterans was ND733, which had already served with both 9 and 550 Squadrons by the time it arrived at Waddington. It had been badly damaged over Mailly-le-Camp while serving with 550 and virtually rebuilt before being issued to 463. It was lost on the Dresden raid in February 1945, the aircraft being abandoned over France by its crew after being attacked and severely mauled by a night fighter.

Many damaged Lancasters were repaired at the Avro factory at Bracebridge Heath, which lay between Lincoln and Waddington. Once repaired, the aircraft were taken by road to Waddington where Avro had been allocated a hangar. Here, the aircraft were reassembled, air tested and allocated to squadrons. This practice may explain why so many 'second-hand' Lancasters were flown at various periods by the two resident squadrons.

463 Squadron also had the task of supporting the RAF Film Unit and in November 1944 an aircraft from the squadron, the appropriately coded JO-Y, filmed the capsizing of the German battleship *Tirpitz* following attacks by Lancasters from 617 and 9 Squadrons.

After the war, Waddington became one of the cornerstones of Britain's aerial defences. It operated Lancaster, Lincoln, Washington (the name given by the RAF to the American B29), Canberra and Vulcan bombers. It was Waddington-based Vulcans of 44 Squadron which attacked the airfield at Port Stanley in the Falkland Islands. It was later to be one of the airfields used for staging aircraft through to the Middle East as part of the preparations for Operation Desert Storm.

Today Waddington is home to a squadron of E3A Sentry early warning aircraft. At its gates stands one of the Vulcan bombers which took part in the Falklands raids in 1982.

35
WALTHAM

No one who served at RAF Grimsby knew it by its official title. To everyone who worked there or flew from there it was simply 'Waltham'. The camp gates were not far from the village pub, the flight path was directly over the village school and, although some of the dispersals lay in the neighbouring parish of Holton-le-Clay, it was, and still is, referred to by the name which predated the RAF's acquisition of the site.

There had been flying at Waltham since 1933 when a large grassed area alongside the Grimsby-Louth road just south of Waltham Toll Bar was opened as Grimsby's municipal airport. This was at the time when local authorities around the country were being encouraged to create facilities for 'bus stop' airfields for regional air services. Some limited services were provided (including one to Hull, using the airfield at Brough as its northern 'terminal') but the idea of an inter-city air service never really caught on. The idea of flying did, however, and Waltham was soon supporting its own aero club.

Waltham's military links began in 1938 when Bomber Command's 5 Group set up 25 Elementary and Reserve Flying Training School to provide tuition for the weekend flyers of the RAFVR. A branch of the Civil Air Guard was also established and between them the units helped train many men who would later serve with distinction as aircrew with both Bomber and Fighter Commands.

The airfield was requisitioned by the Air Ministry in May 1940 and work started the summer on building a bomber airfield for 1 Group. It was to have concrete runways, the first on a bomber airfield in north Lincolnshire, and was ready for occupation by the summer of 1941.

Waltham had been built as a satellite of the nearby bomber airfield at Binbrook, then the home of two Wellington squadrons, 12 and 142. Binbrook was a big airfield, planned and largely built before the war, but it lacked the concrete runways now laid at Waltham. In that second winter of war its Wellingtons were grounded for long periods simply because the airfield was too soft from which to operate so the new runways at Waltham provided something of a welcome relief to them. The Binbrook Wellingtons would, when necessary, fly to Waltham where they were bombed up, take off for the designated targets and, on return, land again at Binbrook. In November 1941, 142 Squadron officially moved into Waltham, bringing with it two Flights of Wellingtons and their ground crews. The airfield remained a satellite of Binbrook and was administered from there.

142 stayed at Waltham for over a year before moving to North Africa. It was a tough year for the Wellington crews. Arthur Johnson was then a 19 year old rear gunner, who had already seen action in North Africa before he was posted to Binbrook where, after just two days, he was told to report to Waltham.

He arrived on the back of a lorry and was directed to his living quarters, one of the wooden huts off Cheapside. There he found orderlies removing the belongings of the other occupants who had all gone missing the night before.

His spirits revived when he met his new crew (he was a replacement for a gunner who had lost his nerve and was ultimately discharged on medical grounds from the RAF). They had already completed six ops and his first trip with them was an unsuccessful mining operation. The weather off Heligoland was so bad, with the cloud base down to 700 feet, they brought the mines back.

Later that month Johnson's Wellington Z1469 was one of the 15 sent by 142 Squadron to Kassel in the Ruhr. It was a horrifying night. They were coned in searchlights for almost 20 minutes and his skipper, Pilot Officer Ron Brooks, eventually dived down to 1,000 feet to shake off the lights. The Wellington was hit numerous times by both heavy and light flak and Brooks did well to get the damaged aircraft back to Harwell in Berkshire. When the crew returned to Waltham they found they were the only survivors of 142's B-Flight. Five other Waltham Wellingtons had been shot down over the Ruhr. Pilot Officer Brooks was awarded an immediate DFC for his actions that night.

Their final operation from Waltham was a daylight attack on Essen on 7th November 1942, their Wellington being one of 20 aircraft sent by 1 and 2 Groups on a series of nuisance raids in thick cloud over Germany. A month later 142 was on the move. Ground crews were ordered to modify twelve of the squadron's aircraft and, on 11th December, they left for Blida in North Africa. The remaining aircraft went to the new north Lincolnshire airfield at Kirmington to help

A rare view of Waltham in its pre-Lancaster days, with Pilot Officer Ron Brooks and his 142 Squadron crew sitting astride a 4,000lb HC bomb.

reform 166 Squadron. Waltham, for just four days, was quiet.

100 Squadron had formed part of the RAF contingent in the Far East, where it had been posted in 1939 to operate the obsolete Vickers Vilderbeest torpedo bombers. They continued to fly these lumbering biplanes from airfields in Malaya and Java against the fast, modern fighters of the Japanese during the first few months of 1942 until they were almost wiped out. Now they were to be reformed to fight a different war with a vastly different aircraft, the Avro Lancaster.

The squadron was at Waltham in late January to see the first of its new Lancasters flown in by ferry pilots. Six weeks later they were operational, eight aircraft taking part in a mining operation off the French coast. One Lancaster was shot down and another crashed on return. It was not a happy start for 100 Squadron. Between then and April 1945, the squadron was to fly almost 4,000 Lancaster sorties from Waltham, losing 92 aircraft with another 21 being destroyed in crashes.

The squadron was in the thick of the action in what was to become known as the Battle of the Ruhr in its first spring and summer at Waltham. Its commanding officer, Wing Commander R. V. McIntyre, set an example to all his crews when his aircraft was badly damaged on a raid on Bochum in May but, despite losing two engines, he bombed the target and brought his aircraft back for a crash-landing at Coltishall. It earned him the DFC. In the same raid another 100 Squadron Lancaster was coned by the Bochum searchlights and only a desperate 10,000 feet dive by the pilot managed to shake them off.

The fact that it was equipped with Lancasters gave 100 Squadron a big advantage over many other squadrons operating over the Ruhr in 1943. In an attack on Düsseldorf in June, 100 Squadron crews watched in awe as the weight of the Happy Valley flak was concentrated on the Wellingtons and Stirlings flying many thousands of feet below them. Height advantage or not, 100 Squadron suffered badly that summer, losing nine aircraft, almost half the squadron's strength, in just one month.

After the Ruhr came the Battle of Berlin, the series of raids through the winter of 1943–44 which were to cost 100 Squadron 20 Lancasters and almost break the back of Bomber Command.

Four of those aircraft were lost in the most tragic circumstances on the night of 16/17th December. Bomber Command had lost 25 aircraft over Berlin that night but worse was to follow on what came to be known in Bomber Command as 'Black Thursday'.

While the bombers had been attacking Berlin, the weather changed dramatically back in England and when the weary Lancaster crews returned they found a blanket of fog rapidly enveloping Lincolnshire and much of East Anglia.

The rest was little short of carnage, 36 aircraft crashing with the loss of 130 aircrew killed. Thirteen were 1 Group Lancasters and four of those were from 100 Squadron. Two collided in thick fog right over the airfield, all 14 men on board being killed instantly. A third crashed three miles away at Barnoldby-le-Beck with four of the crew killed and the fourth, piloted by 100 Squadron's commanding officer, Wing Commander David Holford, crashed while attempting to land at nearby Kelstern. Two of the crew survived. Wing Commander Holford's wife was staying at a nearby pub when the accident happened and the news was broken to her by Wing Commander Jimmy Bennett, who was just in the process of forming a new squadron at Waltham.

The new squadron formed from 100's C-Flight was 550 which operated briefly from Waltham before moving to the newly-opened airfield at North Killingholme. 550 flew a few sorties from Waltham and, after one of these to Berlin on Christmas Eve, two aircraft from the squadron collided in mid-air over the village of Fulstow, just south of

E-Easy of 100 Squadron at dispersal early in October 1944 after completing its 84th operation. It was eventually lost on its 112th, a raid on Hanover on 5/6th January. (Via Grimsby Evening Telegraph)

Waltham. Fourteen men died and it brought back tragic memories of Black Thursday to everyone.

100 Squadron lost another commanding officer early in the new year when Wing Commander John Dilworth was killed in a raid on Schweinfurt. It was during this time that a Waltham Lancaster crew is believed to have been the first to have reported the existence of a hitherto unknown weapon in the German night fighter armoury – the upward firing cannon. 'Schrage Musik' was a devastatingly simple way of dealing with heavy bombers. The night fighter simply slid underneath its unsuspecting prey and fired upwards into the bomber. Experienced fighter crews aimed for the wing-mounted fuel tanks for they knew only too well the perils of hitting the bomb bay of a heavily laden aircraft on its way to the target. Ironically, the night when Schrage Musik was at its most deadly, when 96 aircraft were lost on the Nuremberg raid, all 100 Squadron aircraft returned unscathed.

The summer of 1944 saw 100 Squadron heavily engaged in bombing raids on French targets in the run-up and the aftermath of the Normandy invasion. The squadron also played its full part in the 'No Ball' attacks on suspected V1 sites in northern France.

Remarkably, only one aircraft was lost between early September and Christmas Eve 1944, an extraordinary record for an airfield providing maximum effort on every Main Force raid it was involved in.

Crews who were at Waltham at the time remember this period clearly and many link it with Betty Lancaster, a little girl whose family lived near the camp. She used to give hand-knitted dolls to aircrew as good luck tokens and they seemed to work remarkably well. It was that spell of good fortune for the squadron which helped it become one of only four Lancaster squadrons in Bomber Command to have four aircraft which were to fly more than 100 operations: JB603 *Take It Easy* (lost on its 112th operation over Hanover in January 1945); ND458 *Able Mabel* (it survived the war and was the Lancaster later built by generations of Airfix modelmakers); ND644 *Nan*, which was lost over

A hundred up for Able Mabel, one of 100 Squadron's veteran Lancasters at Waltham. Flt Lt Jack Playford is shaking hands with the groundcrew chief, Sgt W. Hearn. Looking on are other members of her ground crew, LAC J. Cowls, Cpl R. Withey, LAC J. Robinson and AC J. Hale. Mabel completed 130 operations before being retired. (Via Roland Hardy)

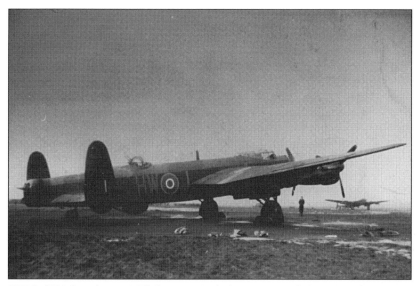

HW-J of 100 Squadron's A-Flight at rest in the late summer of 1944. Note the scattered parachute packs and cycle. The aircraft was known as J-Jug and Bottle and today a public house stands on this very spot and bears the same name. (Arthur White)

Nuremberg in March 1945; and EE139 *Phantom of the Ruhr*, which flew on 29 operations with 100 Squadron and a further 92 with 550 Squadron.

The war ended quietly at Waltham. Early in April 1945 100 Squadron moved out, going to Elsham Wolds, and flying ceased. The airfield itself is almost intact today. Some of the buildings, including two of the hangars, are still in use by commercial organisations. Two of the original Nissen huts which stood in one of the accommodation sites alongside the village's famous windmill are still complete, housing a museum of rural life which, as it reflects Lincolnshire's past, naturally includes some aviation artefacts. In addition, parts of the runways and several of the dispersal pans are still visible. On one of these, inside the parish of Holton-le-Clay, a new public house stands. It is named the Jug and Bottle after a 100 Squadron Lancaster, HW-J, which used to stand on the very spot more than half a century earlier.

36
WICKENBY

RAF Wickenby has a special place in the hearts of the men and women who served there during the years it was an operational bomber station. Talk to them now and they'll smile and tell you about the lack of coke for the stoves, the bitterly cold mornings, the trouble they had getting a train from Lincoln. But among those who served at Wickenby is that kind of comradeship, that sense of belonging you can only find among people who shared something special, in their case serving at an outstanding airfield in one of two outstanding bomber squadrons.

One man who served there was Michael Bentine, later to become one of Britain's favourite funny men and a member of the Goons. He was an intelligence officer with 12 Squadron and has made a number of return visits to his old camp, where he admits the memories still come flooding back. He remembers particularly the young faces at briefings, when targets were revealed for the first time and men had the opportunity to assess their chance of getting back alive.

'I could always tell those who were not going to come back,' he said recently. 'There was a special look in their eyes as though they were preparing themselves for what lay ahead for them that night.'

It took the Irish navvies employed by McAlpines only a few months to build RAF Wickenby for Bomber Command's 1 Group in the winter of 1941-42. There was some urgency about the £1-million contract as the RAF desperately wanted the airfield open and McAlpines had plenty of other airfields to build nearby.

It was built on a large site which lay almost in the centre of an area bordered by the villages of Wickenby, Snelland, Fulnetby and Holton Beckering, a site so rural that one of the first people posted there, a Lincolnshire-born WAAF, had never heard of it. Wickenby had its compensations. The White Hart in Lissington was one, nearby Lincoln with its pubs, cinemas and railway station, which ensured a quick getaway when leave was granted, was another.

The two squadrons which were to operate from Wickenby, 12 and 626, lost 160 Lancasters between them during the time they spent at the airfield, but despite all the hardships, despite the terrible losses its squadrons suffered, it was a happy, well-run station where morale was never allowed to drop too far for long. Much of the credit for that spirit was down to the first station commanding officer, Group Captain Basil Crummy, a cricket-loving airman who was universally liked and respected by all who served with him.

Wickenby had officially opened in the late summer of 1942, but it was September before the first aircraft began to arrive, Wellingtons of 12 Squadron, which had been flying from Binbrook since 1940, moving out to make way for runway construction.

Two of the war's first Victoria Crosses had gone to 12 Squadron men, Donald Garland and Thomas Gray, who had won them in a vain attempt to bomb the Maastricht bridges in May 1940. Since then the squadron had helped recreate 1 Group and had been flying its Wellingtons with great determination from Binbrook and Waltham. Now it was entering a new chapter in its history.

12 flew only a handful of operations in its Wellingtons before orders came through that the squadron was to get the new aircraft which everyone wanted, the Lancaster. 1 Group crews had been looking on with envy as neighbouring 5 Group Lancaster-equipped squadrons flew thousands of feet higher on operations. Now it was 12's turn, the second squadron in 1 Group to be equipped with the four-engined bomber. The first aircraft arrived early in November and conversion work began immediately so that, on 12th January 1943, 12 Squadron was able to provide nine of the 72 Lancasters which took part in an attack on Essen.

There was rapid expansion of both flying activity and the airfield itself that spring. On the day 12 Squadron was expanded to three flights, the new accommodation sites at Fulnetby opened, although the station records speak of spartan conditions, with no electricity or running water. It was mid-September before the contractors handed over the remaining facilities at Wickenby.

The Ruhr was the target of Bomber Command's attention in the spring and summer of 1943 and 12 Squadron was heavily engaged in the raids on Germany's industrial heartland.

Minelaying or 'gardening' as it was referred to, was an important part of Bomber Command's operations. It was dangerous work and there was a near-disastrous end to a sortie over the Baltic on 28th April 1943 for Laurie Lawrence's 12 Squadron crew. It was the largest

All in a night's work. This was a typical bomb load for a Lincolnshire Lancaster squadron in the spring of 1944. It was taken at Wickenby during a visit by the national press to a bomber station 'somewhere in eastern England'. Their visit was actually to 101 Squadron at Ludford Magna but, so secret were the squadron's ABC-equipped Lancasters, all the photographs were taken at Wickenby, which was then one of Ludford's sub-stations. (Redfearn collection)

concentrated minelaying operation of the war, with over 200 aircraft taking part. Lawrence's Lancaster was so badly shot up it was forced to land in Norfolk, where both gunners needed hospital treatment. Later the wireless operator, Sergeant Albert Jackson, discovered an un-exploded cannon shell lodged in the Lancaster's hydraulic reservoir, just above his head. He recovered it and gave it to the crew's Canadian bomb-aimer, Flight Sergeant Bert Cruse, as a keepsake.

Some weeks after this incident Lawrence's crew was one of two selected from 12 Squadron to be presented to the King and Queen during a visit to Binbrook. Cruse took along his cannon shell with him. During the inspection, the Queen noticed the shell and, naturally, asked Cruse about it. After the bomb-aimer had related the story, Her Majesty remarked: 'What a terrifying object.' Bert immediately replied: 'Well, Ma'am, it certainly put the shits up me.' The Queen replied: 'I can well imagine it did, young man.'

A vital part of the bomber's equipment was still the homing pigeon, an object of amusement to some airmen but one which could still prove to be a lifesaver, as 12 Squadron found out in May 1943.

Two of the 14 aircraft sent from Wickenby on a raid on Bochum on the night of 13th May failed to return and the following day preparations were under way to inform the relatives of the crews of Sergeants Scott and Morgan that they were missing when a lone pigeon flew into Wickenby. It was the one taken by Scott's crew. A major search of the North Sea began and five days later the crew of the 12 Squadron Lancaster were found by a minesweeper and landed at Dover, where they were treated for exposure. But for that pigeon, the chances are that they would have died in their dinghy.

Wickenby suffered its worst night of the war so far on the night of 11/12th June when four of the 24 Lancasters sent to Düsseldorf failed to return. One of these was flown by Sergeant Danny Thompson, an Australian, who was on his third operation. After bombing the target, his Lancaster was attacked by a fighter over Holland, which raked the aircraft with cannon fire. Thompson ordered his crew to bale out. Only two managed to escape, the gunners Bill Pingle and 'Sparky' Sparling. They were picked up by a Dutch barge and spent the rest of the war as prisoners of war. Their story had a sequel 21 years later when, during reclamation work in the Zuider Zee, the remains of their aircraft was found and a propeller from the Lancaster was later mounted on a memorial in the town of Dronten where seven streets were named after the crew members.

It was a hard summer for 12 Squadron. Losses continued to mount on the Ruhr raids and, for the first time, there was a noticeable drop in morale. In June the medical officer at Wickenby reported five cases of LMF – lack of moral fibre, for which the 'cure' was humiliation and a spell at a punishment centre. There was also an incident at the end of June when one aircraft crashed on take off for a raid on Cologne and three hours later the wireless operator was hospitalised with 'acute emotional disorder'.

As the attention switched from the Ruhr and the nights became longer, losses started to fall, but crews were only too aware their chances of surviving a tour of 30 operations were slim. One crew was rescued from the North Sea by the rescue launches from Grimsby only to be killed a few nights later on the final trip of their tour when their Lancaster went down over Schweinfurt.

In November, a second squadron, 626, was formed at Wickenby from 12's C-Flight. 626 was to have a brief but eventful life, losing 49 Lancasters in the 19 months it was operational at Wickenby.

The airfield, which was now a sub-station of 14 Base at Ludford

Magna, was busier than ever before, with up to 28 aircraft a night being sent out on raids during the Battle of Berlin. Losses began to mount again, but the Wickenby Lancasters were capable of hitting back. Flight Sergeant Stavant and his crew survived a mauling at the hands of a night fighter over Berlin on their first operation. Two nights later, over the same target, they were attacked again but this time shot down their attacker.

One badly-damaged 626 Squadron aircraft which made it back from a Berlin raid to crash-land at Wickenby was piloted by Flying Officer Breckenridge. His aircraft had been attacked by a night fighter as it approached the German capital. The initial attack killed the wireless operator and badly wounded the rear gunner, Pilot Officer Baker, who was struck in the face by a bullet and lost consciousness. Breckenridge 'corkscrewed' the bomber and finally threw off his attacker and continued on to the target. Within minutes of dropping its bombs, the Lancaster was attacked again and this time the Canadian navigator, Warrant Officer Dick Meek, was severely wounded, one bullet hitting him in the chest, another in the shoulder.

Breckenridge again threw off his attacker, despite the damage to his aircraft. Baker, in the meantime, had regained consciousness and, despite his wounds, returned to his damaged turret, only leaving its intense cold briefly to put out a fire which had started in the aircraft. Meek, despite his injuries and the pain he was in, refused to leave his post and, although without most of his navigational equipment, plotted a course back to Lincolnshire for his pilot. There were immediate DFCs for both Breckenridge and Baker while Meek received a Conspicuous Gallantry Medal.

By mid-March Wickenby was sending 36 aircraft a time on raids, the station record of 42 being set during an attack on Gelsenkirchen. The weight of bombs also went up sharply as Bomber Command switched its emphasis to France on the run-up to the invasion. Some of these, however, were just as punishing as the Ruhr or Berlin had ever been: Wickenby's squadrons lost seven Lancasters in the attack on Mailly-le-Camp in May with another seven badly damaged.

Five aircraft failed to return from a raid on Orleans and three each from attacks on Courtrai and Karlsruhe, while two attacks in a day on Duisburg in October cost Wickenby six aircraft. One of these was 12 Squadron's Q-Queenie, the mount of New Zealander Colin Henry and his otherwise all-British crew. An engine caught fire on take off on the first of the two attacks. They were refused permission to land again and told to head out to sea, dump their bombs and ditch the aircraft. This they did, the bombs shattering windows in nearby Mablethorpe, and within half an hour they were picked up by an air-sea rescue launch from Grimsby.

In that same month the Wickenby squadrons dropped almost 2,400 tons of bombs, mainly on German targets. One exception was a low-level attack on the island of Walcheren, so low-level that some aircraft came back bearing damage from bomb splinters.

There was a grim reminder for all at Wickenby what a Lancaster's bomb load could do when a 626 Squadron aircraft developed engine problems on take off and dived out of control into the bays alongside the station bomb dump, killing all on board. That same bomb dump was the scene of a serious accident in January 1945 when a bomb exploded prematurely, killing three armourers, just three of the 8,000 RAF ground crew killed in airfield accidents and through enemy action.

Although the Allies were across the Rhine, March was still a costly month for the Wickenby Lancasters. Eight of 12 Squadron's aircraft

12 Squadron's N-Nan at the end of the war, by which time she had clocked up 108 bombing operations and six Manna drops. With her are the crew which took her on the last of these. Back row: W/O L. Bratby, Sqdn Ldr Huggins DFC, W/O Len Laing, Flt Sgt Geoff Robinson; front: W/O B. Jackson, W/O S. Petchett, F/O T. Thompson. (Geoff Robinson via Peter Green)

failed to return, two landing safely in France, from a series of operations. Six were lost in a single raid on Nuremberg, which also cost 626 a Lancaster and its crew.

The final losses of the war occurred in the same raid, against the refinery at Lutzendorf on 12th April, two 626 and one 12 Squadron aircraft failing to return. Both squadrons were involved in a repeat attack on the same target the following night.

Wickenby was to contribute towards two further raids, sending 41 aircraft for an attack on Heligoland on 14th April and 30 more in the last Main Force operation of the war, against Berchtesgaden on 25th April.

In between, the Wickenby Lancasters were involved in 'Spam' drops in Holland, delivering food to the starving Dutch population. The station records note that the roads around Wickenby were almost blocked by RASC lorries waiting to deliver loads of food which were packed into the Lancaster bomb bays.

One of the aircraft taking part in Operation Manna was N-Nan of 12 Squadron, the only Lancaster at Wickenby to record 100-plus operations. It had been delivered in the spring of 1944 and, in a total of 106 operations, it was only damaged once, hit by light flak in a daylight attack on Normandy in July 1944. Lucky though it may have been, it did not survive long after the end of the war, being scrapped in October 1945, just 18 months after it was built.

Soon after the war ended 12 Squadron moved back to Binbrook while 626 was disbanded. Wickenby was to remain in RAF hands for the next ten years. Some limited civilian flying did continue and today a number of the airfield's wartime buildings remain.

37

WOODHALL SPA

Mention the RAF's most famous squadron, 617, and everyone immediately thinks of Scampton. But their true wartime home in Lincolnshire was not the big pre-war station just north of Lincoln from where they mounted the Dams raid, but a wartime airfield near the pleasant town of Woodhall Spa.

It was from Woodhall that 617 operated for the bulk of its wartime career when it became the precision arm of Bomber Command, inflicting enormous damage on the German war machine and the infrastructure of Nazi-occupied Europe. And it was from Woodhall that 617, aided by 9 Squadron from nearby Bardney, mounted the raids that led to the sinking of the *Tirpitz* in a remote Norwegian fjord.

A site for a bomber airfield was identified by Air Ministry surveys midway between the town of Woodhall Spa and the village of Tattershall Thorpe early in 1941 and construction began towards the end of the year, the contractors having to clear many trees during their work before the airfield finally opened as a satellite of Coningsby on 1st February 1942. Coningsby at the time was still without hardened runways and the Hampdens of 106 Squadron operated from Woodhall whenever conditions prevented them taking off with full bomb loads.

A month after the station opened, 97 Squadron, which had just re-equipped with Lancasters, moved in from Coningsby, mounting its first operation from the airfield on 20th March. It was to end in disaster. Six aircraft took off on a daylight 'gardening' operation, dropping sea mines in shipping lanes off the Frisian coast. Bad weather dogged the operation and on their return one aircraft, OF-B, clipped a building in Boston and crashed at Freiston Shore, the crew of seven escaping injury. Two others were diverted away from Woodhall because of the weather and they, too, crashed.

97 was to remain at Woodhall for another year before moving to Bourn in Cambridgeshire as part of the new Pathfinder Force. During its time at Woodhall, however, it earned a formidable reputation as a

squadron which could find targets and deliver bombs. It joined 44 Squadron in the Augsburg raid in April 1942 in which John Nettleton won his Victoria Cross, six of its aircraft taking part in the daring daylight attack on the MAN factory. The 97 Squadron aircraft were led by Squadron Leader J. S. Sherwood, whose aircraft was hit by flak as it flew almost at street level after dropping its bombs. The burning aircraft flew into the ground and exploded, Sherwood miraculously escaping. Most of the other Woodhall aircraft were hit but only one other crashed.

97 Squadron moved out in early March 1943, leaving behind just three crews who were to form the nucleus of a new squadron, 619, on 18th April, flying its first operation on 11th June with an attack on Düsseldorf. 619 played its full part in the summer's offensive, mainly against targets in the Ruhr. Its first operational loss came on the night of 14/15th June when Pilot Officer McCulloch and his crew failed to return from Oberhausen. Exactly a week later another Lancaster was lost in a raid on Krefeld. After that, 619 led a relatively charmed life over the Ruhr and in the series of Hamburg raids. Casualties were light, but the squadron was not to fare so well in the months to come.

Woodhall's worst night of the war so far came in August 1943 when 619 Squadron provided twelve of the 596 aircraft which raided the rocket research works at Peenemunde on Germany's Baltic coast. Three aircraft were shot down and 22 men killed, including one of the squadron's flight commanders, Wing Commander I. J. McGhie.

Coincidentally, McGhie's wife and family, who were living in Woodhall Spa at the time, narrowly escaped injury themselves that same night when the town was bombed. Two parachute mines destroyed a hotel and badly damaged a block of flats and eight other buildings. Three people died in the attack and 66 others were injured, almost all civilians.

619 lost another ten aircraft in the Battle of Berlin, plus another five in crashes and with them the lives of 72 men. On two of the raids 619 lost two aircraft, losses that were keenly felt in what was still a small, tightly-knit squadron. Two Lancasters went down on the night of 2nd/3rd December, five men surviving to become prisoners of war. A month later two more were lost, one over Berlin and a second shot down in the Zuider Zee by a night fighter. Two men survived from this aircraft.

A week later 619 left Woodhall for the last time, moving the few miles to Coningsby where they were to change places with 617 Squadron, which brought 34 Lancasters with them to operate in a new

Group Capt Leonard Cheshire, who was awarded his Victoria Cross while serving as 617's CO at Woodhall Spa.

role as a precision bombing squadron, usually acting independently of the Main Force squadrons. They were, quite simply, the elite of Bomber Command; part of 5 Group yet very much a squadron which went its own way. They were led by Group Captain Leonard Cheshire, a vastly experienced pilot and commander who was one of the outstanding men of Bomber Command. He eventually amassed 100 operations before he was ordered to stop operational flying and was one of the few men in history to win his nation's highest bravery award, the Victoria Cross, for a sustained period of the highest service rather than a single act of courage.

It was Cheshire who almost became 617's first Woodhall casualty. On 13th January 1944 he took off to air test his Lancaster only to hit a flock of plover. One bird crashed through the windscreen, narrowly missing Cheshire while another struck his flight engineer, injuring him. Cheshire managed to land his damaged aircraft and that night, legend has it, 20 plover were served at dinner in the officers' mess.

The first casualty was not long in coming, Flight Lieutenant O'Shaughnessy and another man of his crew being killed when his Lancaster hit a sea wall during a low level exercise over the Norfolk coast.

The following day 617 went to war from Woodhall for the first time, bombing a suspected V1 ski-site in northern France. A second attack followed 24 hours later.

Early in February 617 hit the Gnome-Rhome aircraft engine at Limoges. The target was marked by Cheshire and Squadron Leader Mickey Martin, whose early arrival over the target allowed the civilian workers to take shelter before the bombing began. Damage was very severe, the factory being hit by one 12,000lb and numerous 1,000lb bombs.

Four nights later 617 attacked the Antheor viaduct, which carried much of the rail traffic between southern France and Italy. One aircraft was damaged and forced to land in Sardinia while a second crashed after landing to refuel in Hampshire, killing Squadron Leader Bill Suggitt and his crew, which included John Pulford, Guy Gibson's flight engineer on the Dams raid.

An aircraft factory at Albert followed, then a factory at St Etienne and an aero engine plant near Metz. During the latter, one 617 Lancaster shot down two night fighters and is believed to have damaged a third. 617 was joined by six Lancasters from 106 Squadron from Metheringham as target illuminators for a successful attack on the Michelin factory at Clermont-Ferrand.

A powder works and ammunition dump at Bergerac followed, then a factory at Angoulême and a vehicle plant near Paris. Two raids on factories in Lyons followed before an aircraft factory in Toulouse was attacked early in April. This was the first time 617 had used Mosquitos to mark the target and so concerned was the aircraft's designer, John de Havilland, that he travelled to Woodhall Spa before the raid and remained at the station until all the 617 Squadron aircraft were safely home.

Cheshire was delighted with the Mosquito as a low-level marking aircraft and he used it to good effect five nights later when a military depot next door to the French military academy at St Cyr was accurately bombed.

617 was joined by the two 5 Group Pathfinder squadrons, 83 and 97 (both of which had recently moved to Coningsby) for an attack on Juvisy, a raid which saw Flight Lieutenant Bill Reid VC, formerly of 61 Squadron, operate for the first time with 617.

Following a raid on La Chapelle, 617 used its marker technique for the first time on a German target when it bombed a factory in Brunswick. Two nights later the squadron went to Munich and suffered its first operational loss from Woodhall when Flight Lieutenant Cooper's aircraft was shot down. Cooper and five of his colleagues got out of the aircraft but the bomb aimer was killed.

The squadron had been earmarked for a vital, though unglamorous, task on D-Day: it was to simulate an invasion force as part of Operation Taxable. The crews trained for a month, flying regular box patterns at a predetermined height across an area of sea off Flamborough Head dropping bundles of 'window', thin strips of aluminium foil. The results were monitored at the radar station at Bempton and were so impressive that 617 was given the task of simulating an invasion force in the Straits of Dover in the early hours of D-Day. The ruse carried out by 16 Lancasters from Woodhall so foxed the German defenders that reinforcements which could have been sent to Normandy were ordered to remain in the Pas de Calais.

Two nights later 617 was back dropping bombs again, this time its 12,000-pounders blocking the Samur tunnel. A series of raids were then mounted against U-boat pens on the Channel coast. In the attack against Le Havre, the first daylight operation carried out by 617, 22 Lancasters, each armed with a 12,000lb Tallboy, hit the target ahead of a further 199 Lancasters from 1 and 5 Group. The 617 bombing was particularly accurate, several bombs hitting the pens and one penetrating the thick concrete roof.

The squadron then turned its attention to flying bomb sites along the French coast. It was in one of these, a highly-accurate attack on a site at Wizernes, that Flight Lieutenant Edwards' Lancaster was shot down by flak, 617's first loss for some two months. Four of the crew managed to survive. The following day 617 were ordered to attack a site at Siracourt. They were still using Mosquitos for marking but that morning a crated P51 Mustang arrived at Woodhall, a gift to Leonard Cheshire from his admirers in the US 8th Air Force. Cheshire had the single-seat fighter unpacked, assembled and the engine tested. 617 took off without him but Cheshire, determined to test the possibilities of the Mustang as a marker aircraft, took off sometime after the squadron and, in what was his first flight in the aircraft, overhauled them over the French coast and proceeded to mark the target, a V1 storage depot, accurately for the squadron which landed at least three Tallboys on it. Later, Cheshire landed his Mustang in the dark at Woodhall.

Less than two weeks later, after an attack on what was believed to be the site of the V3 gun at Mimoyecques, Cheshire completed his 100th operation. He was immediately ordered to stop operational flying, along with three other 617 veterans, Dave Shannon, Les Munro and Joe McCarthy. Cheshire's place as commanding officer passed to Wing Commander Willie Tait. At the end of July Cheshire was awarded his Victoria Cross.

The V-bomb site attacks went on. In one, the Lancaster flown by Bill Reid VC was struck by a bomb dropped from another Lancaster. Reid was one of the two survivors from the aircraft. In August the emphasis switched to attacks on U-boat pens with raids on Brest (four times), La Pallice (three), Lorient and Ijmuiden.

Then came the *Tirpitz*. The 45,000-ton German battleship, the last of Hitler's major capital vessels, had been posing a threat to Allied shipping in the North Atlantic for some years. Attempts had been made before to sink the *Tirpitz* and now it was the turn of 617. The squadron had been operating with 9 Squadron from nearby Bardney on precision attacks during the summer and both units were ordered to mount a special operation to attack the *Tirpitz*, which was moored in Kaa fjord in northern Norway. Long-range tanks were fitted to the Lancasters, and 38 aircraft set off from Lincolnshire for the 2,100 mile journey to their operating base at Yagavik. One Lancaster turned back and six more were to crash-land in Russia, but the remainder, carrying 21 Tallboys and six anti-shipping 'Johnny Walker' mines, attacked the *Tirpitz* on 15th September. The attack took the Germans by surprise and at least one Tallboy exploded close to the battleship's bows, causing severe damage. From the air, however, the damage was not apparent and it appeared that the *Tirpitz* had escaped yet again. The Lancasters all returned to their Russian base to refuel before flying back to England, one 617 aircraft crashing in Norway on the return flight.

Back in England, 617 was ordered to attack the Dortmund-Ems canal, a seemingly evergreen target for Bomber Command. With 627 Squadron providing the marking, it was a successful operation, although one Lancaster was lost.

There was another dam for the squadron to destroy at the end of the month. A brilliantly executed raid by 617 destroyed the lock gates on the Kembs dam near Basle but cost the squadron two aircraft. The crew of one crash-landed in the lake and managed to get into their dinghy intending to head for the Swiss shore but were killed by machine gun fire from German troops.

A second attack was then ordered on the *Tirpitz*. The battleship had been moved south to Tromsö fjord and this time, the 617 and 9 Squadron Lancasters were able to operate from Lossiemouth in Scotland. With extra fuel tanks and stripped of their mid-upper turrets, 37 Lancasters (18 from each squadron plus an RAF film unit aircraft from Waddington) attacked the battleship for a second time. *Tirpitz*, however, seemed to have a charmed life. As the aircraft approached Tromsö, clouds drifted across the target and bombs had to be dropped on the battleship's estimated position. All missed.

A third raid was mounted on 12th November. Thirty aircraft made the 2,250 mile round trip from Lossiemouth and this time *Tirpitz*'s luck ran out. German fighters scrambled to intercept the Lancasters were mistakenly sent to Kaa fjord (no one had told their controller *Tirpitz* had been moved) and the Lancasters bombed in perfect visibility. She was hit several times by the Tallboys and soon after was shaken by a violent internal explosion before capsizing in the fjord with the loss of almost 1,000 lives.

617 was to spend the remainder of the war as a precision bombing squadron. Early in 1945 it began carrying the new Grand Slam bomb, a 22,000lb weapon which was so big that initial operations were mounted from the extra-long runway at Carnaby in East Yorkshire. The bombs were carried in specially-adapted Lancasters, some of which were fitted with the undercarriage of the new Lincoln bomber, and were used with devastating effect on a number of targets, including the Bielefeld and Arnsberg viaducts and a submarine plant at Vegesack.

Different codes, different jobs. Three 617 Squadron Lancasters pictured airborne, 1945. KC was then the standard squadron code while the two aircraft coded YZ had both been adapted to carry Grand Slam 22,000lb bombs. (Peter Green)

617 suffered its last operational loss of the war on 16th April when the squadron sank the pocket battleship *Lutzow* at Swinemunde, Squadron Leader Powell and his crew falling to intense flak over the target.

The squadron shared the final year of the war at Woodhall with 627 Squadron, which operated as part of 5 Group's marker force, flying Mosquitos. It was in a 627 Squadron Mosquito that Wing Commander Guy Gibson was killed on the night of 19/20th September 1944. At the time he was Base Operations Officer at Coningsby and decided to fly a 627 marker aircraft in an attack on München Gladbach and Rheydt. He was heard giving instructions over the target but on the return flight his Mosquito, which may have suffered flak damage, crashed at Steenbergen-en-Kruisland in Holland, killing Gibson and his navigator. Both are buried in the village cemetery.

627 played a key part in the operations of 5 Group during the final twelve months of the war. Apart from its marking role, some of its Mosquitos carried 4,000lb bombs and it suffered 13 operational losses during its time at Woodhall.

A number of other aircraft were lost in crashes and it was one of these which led to a Woodhall airman winning the George Medal a few

VE Night at the NAAFI at the No 1 Communal Site at Woodhall Spa. (Peter Green via Douglas Garton)

weeks after the war ended. The Mosquito involved crashed and caught fire while attempting to overshoot, killing the pilot and trapping the navigator. Corporal Stephen Cogger, who was in charge of the fire party, made repeated attempts to get to the two men and finally used a hacksaw to free the navigator from the cable trapping him by the ankle.

Woodhall closed soon after the end of the war, but was later reactivated and used to house Bloodhound missiles. Today, most of the land has been returned to agriculture but part of the site is still used by nearby RAF Coningsby.

38

THE CIVILIANS

The lives of every man, woman and child in Lincolnshire were to be touched by the influx of RAF personnel into the county, which had begun even before war was declared. There were young men and women everywhere in their uniform of air force blue, forage caps at an angle, gas masks over their shoulder. They were bright and cheerful and many took to Lincolnshire as much as Lincolnshire took to them.

It was impossible to board a bus or train without coming across them. Every pub or cinema queue seemed to be full of RAF personnel. Roads were diverted to make way for airfields and every day and

The remains of a 44 Squadron Hampden after it crashed into the Girls' High School on Lindum Hill, Lincoln early on the morning of 23rd July 1941. (Lincolnshire Echo)

A Halifax MkII of 51 Squadron from Yorkshire crashed into a cottage at Snitterby, near Brigg when an engine caught fire on take-off from Hemswell on 10th August 1943. The occupants of the cottage, Mrs G. Dickenson and her four month old son, were both killed in the crash. (Grimsby Evening Telegraph)

every night the skies were full of the sound of aircraft. Lincolnshire was, to all intents and purposes, one enormous airfield, populated by around 300,000 civilians and 80,000 airmen and women.

The RAF brought work and danger to Lincolnshire. Many people made a good living out of it, through construction jobs, factory work or from the money the airmen brought in. One factory in Lincoln alone employed 1,500 men on repairing damaged aircraft. But there was a price to pay. Many civilians were to die because of the bombing raids brought on Lincolnshire by the presence of the RAF or from crashing aircraft, always a hazard in a county where over 1,000 crashes were recorded in the war years and many more went unrecorded.

Typical of these incidents was the tragedy which occurred in July 1941 when a Hampden bomber of 44 Squadron was returning to Waddington from a minelaying operation when it crashed into the staff residence at Lincoln's Girls' High School on Lindum Hill. The crew of four were killed along with the senior French mistress, who died trying to escape from the burning building. Four other members of staff were injured and exploding ammunition peppered the surrounding area. In the same month four people died in Lincoln when two Spitfires from RAF Digby collided right over the city centre while performing aerobatics. Both pilots baled out but one of the aircraft fell onto a house in Oxford Street.

Air raids, many of them directed at airfields, were also responsible for numerous civilian casualties. One of the worst incidents was at Waddington in May 1941 when two parachute mines were dropped. One hit the airfield, killing ten people, including seven members of the Naafi staff. The other hit the village itself, killing one person, injuring another 49, destroying the village church and 19 houses.

Lincolnshire was particularly vulnerable to air attack. Though large-scale raids were few and far between and only the neighbouring towns of Grimsby and Cleethorpes saw widespread bombing during the war, the county was a favourite target for the hit-and-run raiders, bombers operating either singly or in pairs. Some attacks were at night, others in daylight when there was cloud cover for the raiders to disappear into.

All that remained of Grimsby's public library after a hit-and-run raid on the town in February 1941. (Grimsby Evening Telegraph)

An Me109, still bearing scars of a recent forced landing, on display in Grimsby's Town Hall Square. The picture is believed to have been taken in the winter of 1941 when the Messerschmitt, which had landed out of fuel in the south of England, was on display in a number of Lincolnshire towns. (Grimsby Evening Telegraph)

Most towns in the county suffered to a greater or lesser degree, although, surprisingly, the Luftwaffe almost completely ignored Scunthorpe and its vitally-important steel works.

The highest proportion of the county's casualties were in Grimsby and Cleethorpes, where 199 people were killed, half of them in a single raid in which anti-personnel butterfly bombs were scattered across the area. This particular weapon had a devastating effect on civilian life, paralysing whole areas where the bombs, so named because of their winged arming device, lay waiting for the slightest touch to detonate them. They were used in other areas of the county, notably around Louth and the Tattersall area. However, it seemed the Germans never did discover how effective they were, news censorship ensuring that no hint of their disruptive power leaked out.

The thousands of young airmen and women who were stationed in Lincolnshire were almost universally welcomed by the local residents. There are a few stories such as that related by Guy Gibson's biographer who writes of the ill-feeling which existed between some of those in the

275

village of Wellingore, near Grantham, and the men stationed on the local night fighter station. Some of the aircrew were billeted in the village and one man was ordered to leave his accommodation when he asked for another blanket.

That was the exception which proved the rule. In most towns and villages, there was a realisation of the role the RAF was playing and the losses it was sustaining and a real bond of friendship was formed between the people of Lincolnshire and the airmen who found themselves serving in the county.

Typical of that welcome were the efforts made by the inhabitants of Ludford Magna, near Market Rasen, whose village lies at the very top of the Lincolnshire Wolds. An airfield was built there in 1943 (and a cold and miserable place it was) and when its only occupants, 101 Squadron, arrived from Holme-on-Spalding Moor in East Yorkshire, the ladies of the village turned out to make sure there was a meal for them in an improvised canteen in the rectory grounds. Today some of those ladies are still serving the same men when they return to the village every year for their annual reunion.

The presence of so many airfields in Lincolnshire was particularly exciting for the county's children. Typical of them was Allen Parker, whose family home was in Church Lane, Waltham, close to what was officially RAF Grimsby. Waltham, now very much a suburb of Grimsby, was still a largely rural community and Allen, then eleven, was almost beside himself with joy at having both teams of shire horses and bomber aircraft as near neighbours. He managed to combine the two by hitching a ride on Clayton's farm cart when it went onto the airfield to pick up swill from the camp cookhouse, often returning with big tins of jam or other delicacies for the family.

He remembers, too, how the shire horses on nearby Mumby's farm were quite oblivious of the noise from the nearby airfield, but it was not the same story for the Markham family, one of whose horses bolted, towing its cart behind it, when startled by a low flying aircraft.

Allen's mother and sister both worked in the WVS canteen in the Temperance Hall in Cheapside, Waltham and it was there that his sister was to meet her future husband, who worked on the MT section at both Waltham and Kelstern. Allen himself was one of a group of keen aircraft-spotters in Waltham who would congregate in a spinney close to the end of the runway to watch the Lancasters of 100 Squadron taking off.

At the opposite end of the county Don Stewart was raised in Great Ponton, a village just south of Grantham, where his father was the

Visitors to an open day at RAF Spittlegate queueing to have a look inside Avro Anson K6167. (Ian Simpson via G. Gardiner)

village policeman. Restrictions on travel and on visiting military establishments meant that most civilians knew little of what went on behind the camp gates, but Don Stewart, through first his father and then, after 1943, his job as a trainee Post Office engineer, was able to visit most of the RAF and USAAF stations in the area and has a wonderful fund of memories of those times.

One of his father's additional responsibilities was as the local bomb reconnaissance officer, which involved investigating the sites of any bombs, 'friendly' or otherwise, which may have fallen in his area. On one occasion, he recalled his father and a civilian BRO came across something which had fallen from an aircraft near the Lincolnshire border with Nottinghamshire. They decided it didn't look too dangerous so they tied it to the back of the family's Singer Nine car and, with young Don in the back seat to keep an eye on the 'bomb', set off for RAF Balderton, near Newark, where it was recognised as an RAF smoke float.

Visits to RAF establishments were always an exciting affair and he recalled a visit to Harlaxton where an Avro Manchester had made an emergency landing. The grass runway was so short, the Manchester was unable to take off and had to be dismantled and moved by road. On the same airfield, he was also allowed to 'fly' the Link trainer, a ground training device for pilots.

One of his friends was the son of the village policeman at Byard's Leap, near Cranwell, who confided in him one day that his father had seen an aircraft without a propeller take off from the airfield. It was only some years later, when the existence of jet-engined aircraft was first revealed, that Don believed his pal.

Cranwell was a particular favourite for plane-spotters because of the wide variety of aircraft used there and one which every schoolboy wanted to see was a De Havilland 86b, a four-engined pre-war airliner which was used for navigational and W/T instruction.

The pre-war Tyresoles depot in Great Ponton was used for training ground crew in aircraft tyre maintenance and the airmen and women would usually arrive on Sunday ready for their week-long course. The reporting point was the village police station and it was Don's father whose job it was to allocate billets in the village. When he was out on other duties, however, it was left to whoever was at home at the time. One evening a young airwoman turned up unannounced and, with his father out, Don took it upon himself to be the billeting officer for Great Ponton. He consulted the list and found one house which was shown as taking two people and had a vacancy, so he directed the young woman to the house. Twenty minutes later she was back. It did take two people, she told him, but in a double bed – and the other occupant was an airman.

Later, he remembers his father had to find extra billets in the village and approached a local farmer's wife who agreed to take an airman. His father came across the airman and asked him if he was comfortable. 'Comfortable?' came the reply. 'I don't know whether I'm sleeping on bloody flocks or socks.' And what about the food? 'Rabbit,' he replied. 'It's rabbit for breakfast, rabbit for dinner and rabbit for supper. I don't want to see another ruddy rabbit in my life.' That particular billet was never used again.

Once he had joined the Post Office, young Don Stewart was to see even more of the airfields and RAF establishments in the Grantham area. Many had some civilians amongst their staff and he particularly remembers a blind civilian telephonist, Arthur Snell, who operated the switchboard at Spittlegate alongside RAF personnel, and later at other RAF sites in the Grantham area. He was a cheerful character whose ringing tones announcing 'Grantham eight-five-oh' were familiar to many in the RAF.

Many of his dealings in these days were with the Americans at Barkston Heath, South Witham and Folkingham. Post Office engineers worked in concert with American Signal Corps personnel. The PO engineers had responsibility for much of the specialised equipment, including teleprinters and VF equipment, but they also had to look after the phone boxes on the camps. One problem they had was the rapidity with which coin boxes filled up, particularly in the PX buildings, a favourite for the Americans when arranging dates with local girls.

The American forces introduced the PO engineers to much equipment which was completely new to them. Particularly memorable was a Signal Corps truck-borne machine for boring holes for telegraph posts. Don remembers this particularly because the Americans at Barkston Heath were proud of a lump of copper, all that remained of an underground electricity cable they had bored into!

The Americans also introduced their British counterparts to the 'throw-away culture'. Airfields in south Lincolnshire often used village tips for dumping their refuse, and this provided good pickings for local people, who were quite unaccustomed to good items of clothing or repairable electrical items being thrown away.

There was some discord in Grantham between American and British service personnel, particularly when sizeable airborne forces were stationed in the area, but relationships between civilians and the Americans were generally cordial. The Americans were generous almost to a fault and whenever they visited civilians in their homes they always went laden with gifts of food. Dances were held in Grantham and most of the larger villages in the area. Colsterworth was the favourite location for personnel stationed at North Witham, girls being brought in from far afield in the backs of American military trucks.

Help for the local population from the Americans took many forms. Don remembers a police sergeant enlisting the help of the Provost Marshal in solving a particularly difficult local problem – cutting the grass on the local golf course. Petrol for the old lorry which was used to tow the gang mower was in short supply and, as the Americans used the golf course themselves, they were only too happy to oblige, sending a jeep along once a week to tow the mower round the course.

In north Lincolnshire, the American presence at Goxhill was such that a large American Red Cross club was opened in a former department store in nearby Grimsby. It had an American staff but employed a number of local women. They found the Americans generous, kind and good company. What did, however, shock many people in Grimsby was their attitude to black Americans. There was a

Dancing on the lawns. Americans based at nearby Goxhill are entertained on a summer's afternoon at Thornton Hall. (Author's collection)

sizeable army detachment stationed at Immingham where black soldiers were used to unload munitions from ships arriving from the United States. They lived in tented accommodation and had their own Red Cross club quarters in Grimsby. They were not allowed to share the same facilities as the white soldiers or airmen, even being forced to use separate compartments on the trains into Grimsby.

One thing the Americans shared with their British counterparts was a love of Lincolnshire's public houses. The rural nature of most airfields meant a big upturn in trade for the publicans, most of whose premises in those days were little more than converted houses. Typical of these was the Marrowbone and Cleaver in the north Lincolnshire village of Kirmington, close to the site of the RAF station opened in 1942. It was the only pub in the village and became a natural haven for the young airmen, whose accommodation sites were scattered over a large area on the edge of nearby Brocklesby Park. Its name was shortened to 'The Chopper' and the affection with which it was held is still seen today; 166 Squadron holds its annual reunion there and the public house sign depicts a Lancaster flown by the squadron.

Every town had its favourite pubs for the RAF: the Peacock in

280

Boston, the Wheatsheaf in Louth, the White Hart in Gainsborough, the 'Mucky Duck' in Grimsby. The most famous of them all was the Saracen's Head in Lincoln's High Street, a popular haunt for the many bomber squadrons stationed around the city. It was known to all at the time as the Snake Pit and, although it closed in 1959 and was demolished some time after that, a plaque has been erected marking its approximate position as part of Lincoln's heritage trail.

Many pubs were called upon to provide accommodation, particularly for wives of married airmen. One such was the Moncks Arms at Caenby Corner, close to RAF Hemswell where rooms were particularly in demand during the time it was used by the 1 Group Lancaster Finishing School. Crews were only there for two or three weeks prior to posting to squadrons and it was a popular place for brief visits. Even when no rooms were available, the landlord was known to put up camp beds in the pub's tiny linen room to meet the demand from the nearby airfield.

Airmen and their wives were generally welcomed by people living near airfields. Joan Dickie recalls the time her husband Jack was posted to 12 Squadron at Wickenby and they set about looking for accommodation in the Wragby area. A local butcher provided them with a magnificent breakfast (for which he refused payment) and loaned them bikes to scour the countryside. Finally, he put them in touch with a family in the area who provided all-in accommodation for the two of them for £2 a week.

At Elsham Wolds Alex Temperley and his wife found accommodation in the nearby village of Barnetby in a house which was later to become one of the country's first Cheshire Homes. They became particularly attached to the governess of the house, who looked after the elderly owner. She was very kind to them but found it difficult to come to terms with the fact that Bomber Command operated on Sundays. She thought that was a wicked thing to do.

Sometimes, however, the relationship between the RAF and the civilian population, at least its civic leaders, became strained. There is a story, which may be apocryphal, of the chairman of a local council in a mid-Lincolnshire town, complaining to the RAF of the noise which emanated night after night from the local airfield. Had they no thought for what all this noise was doing to their sleep? The reply, it is alleged, came soon afterwards: a Lancaster bomber deposited most of the station's stock of toilet rolls across the roofs of the offending town early the next day.

If it is true, that story is not typical. The RAF, and particularly the

The wreckage of a Heinkel bomber, shot down by the anti-aircraft defences over Immingham, passing through Scunthorpe in March 1941 en route to a salvage depot. (Scunthorpe Evening Telegraph)

bomber squadrons, were held in the highest regard in Lincolnshire. Even the county's constabulary turned a blind eye to many (though not all) misdemeanours.

Riding a bicycle at night without lights appears to have been one offence which the police were at pains to enforce. Don Chaney, who also served at Wickenby, remembered a particularly boisterous night spent in the pubs of Market Rasen. As he and his 626 Squadron crew attempted to return to camp on their unlit bicycles, they found a line of policemen, linked arm-in-arm, across the road, blocking their way. They were all subsequently fined by a local magistrate for their offence, which may have been hard for some airmen to accept; it was all right to navigate across Europe by night without lights, but not, it seemed, from Market Rasen to Wickenby!

Apart from the huge influx of service personnel, Lincolnshire also hosted large numbers of workers brought into the county to help build the airfields. There simply wasn't enough manpower in the county to cope with the job and many of those who built the airfields were from southern Ireland. A similar situation had existed even before the war began. The expansion scheme of the late 1930s had brought a lot of work for skilled men in Lincolnshire, but much of the labouring was done by groups of itinerant workers, who lived in make-shift camps before moving on to the next airfield.

Jack Vinter had been an apprentice joiner in Boston before joining a firm based in Ruskington, near Sleaford which had contractors for joinery work on airfield sites in the county. Standards of workmanship were high. On his first job, at Cranwell, Jack's job was hanging doors in the officers' mess, heavy, solidly-built affairs. It was a job which required considerable strength as well as skill and once the doors were hung, the joiner foreman Jim Munton would check the clearance with a cigarette paper to ensure the fit was exact. If the door failed his paper test, it had to be rehung.

From Cranwell, he moved to North Coates where his employers had the joinery maintenance contract. Then he moved to Manby, where the new airfield was under construction. Most of the construction work was being carried out by teams of Irish workers, who lived in a hutted camp near the airfield. Jack, in the meantime, was lodging in Louth and remembers arriving at the site one morning to find a pitched battle going on between two large groups of the Irish workers. No quarter was being given or asked and all kinds of make-shift weapons were being used. Eventually, large numbers of police arrived from the nearby town to restore order.

Like Cranwell, the work at Manby was of the highest quality. Jack was set to work on the roof of the sergeants' mess. The man in charge of the job was Harry Bonner of Louth, who marked out every angle on each piece of wood on his steel set square. Only then was he happy for the work to begin. No expense was spared. When the sash windows were fitted in the sergeants' mess, top quality steel chains were fitted instead of the standard sash cords.

This same standard of workmanship, however, was not to be found on those airfields built during the war. Then, the emphasis was on speed, not quality, as the huge RAF build up in Lincolnshire got into its full stride.

Today, Lincolnshire is as proud as ever of its wartime association with the Royal Air Force. In recent years the county fought a united campaign to prevent the closure of RAF Scampton. It was unsuccessful but it highlighted yet again the strength of those bonds forged in wartime.

BIBLIOGRAPHY

Ashworth, Chris, *RAF Coastal Command*, Patrick Stephens.

Blake, R., Hodgson, M. & Taylor, B, *Airfields of Lincolnshire Since 1912*, Midland Counties.

Bowyer, Chaz, *For Valour: The Air VCs*, William Kimber.

Bowyer, Chaz, *Lancaster Group at War*, Ian Allen.

Clutton-Brook, Oliver, *Massacre Over The Marne*, Patrick Stephens.

Cooper, Alan, *Air Battles of the Ruhr*, Airlife.

Cooper, Alan, *Bombers Over Berlin*, William Kimber.

Copeland, Geoff, *Silksheen: The History of East Kirkby*, Midland Counties.

Falconer, Jonathan, *RAF Bomber Airfields of World War Two*, Ian Allen.

Falconer, Jonathan, *RAF Fighter Airfields of World War Two*, Ian Allen.

Finn, Sid, *Black Swan*, Newton.

Finn, Sid, *Lincolnshire Air War*, Aero Litho.

Franks, Norman, *Claims to Fame: Lancaster*, Arms and Armour.

Gardiner, Geoff, *Airfield Focus: Spitalgate*, GMS Enterprises.

Gibson, Guy, *Enemy Coast Ahead*, Goodhall.

Halpenny, Barry, *Action Stations*, Patrick Stephens.

Hancock, Terry, *Bomber County*, Lincs CC.

Haslam, E. B., *History of RAF Cranwell*, HMSO.

Ingham, Mike, *Air Force Memorials of Lincolnshire*, Midland Counties.

Jacobs, V. K., *The Woodpecker Story*, Pentland Press.

Mason, Francis K., *Avro Lancaster*, Aston Publishing.

Middlebrook, Martin, *Arnhem 1944: The Airborne Battle*, Viking.

Middlebrook, Martin, *Battle of Hamburg*, Allen Lane.

Middlebrook, Martin, *Berlin Raids*, Viking.

Middlebrook, Martin & Everitt, Chris, *Bomber Command War Diaries*, Penguin.

Middlebrook, Martin, *Nuremberg Raid*, Allen Lane.

Middlebrook, Martin, *Peenemunde Raid*, Allen Lane.

Miller, Russell, *Nothing Less Than Victory*, Penguin.

Morris, Richard, *Guy Gibson*, Viking.

Moyes, Philip, *Bomber Squadrons of the RAF*, McDonald & Jane's.

Moyle, Harry, *Hampden File*, Air Britain.

Otter, Patrick, *Maximum Effort: The Story of the North Lincolnshire*

Bombers, Archive.
Otter, Patrick, *Maximum Effort: One Group at War*, Manor Publications
Otter, Patrick, *Maximum Effort: The Untold Stories*, Hutton Press.
Reynolds, David, *Rich Relations*, Harper Collins.
Searby, John, *Bomber Battle For Berlin*, Airlife.

INDEX

Holton-le-Clay 249, 255
Hudson 175, 185, 186, 187, 188
Humberston 12
Hurricane 25, 26, 63, 82, 84, 139, 143, 160, 164, 165, 229, 231, 232

Immingham 128, 280
Ingham 19, 108, 133, 141-143
Ingoldmells 11

Jackson, Norman (VC) 180-181
Junkers Ju88 62, 79, 80, 175, 232

Keadby 57
Kelstern 19, 51, 52, 58, 144-150, 252
Killingholme 10, 23
Kirmington 19, 103, 151-159, 280
Kirton Lindsey 10, 11, 21-22, 27, 128, 132, 136, 139, 160-165

Lancaster 4, 13, 14, 15-21 passim, 24, 25, 26, 29-36, 49-53, 55, 58, 67-74, 88-99 passim, 102-108 passim, 110-118 passim, 121-122, 133-135, 140, 143-150 passim, 152, 154-158, 166-172, 175, 177-183, 191-198, 203-209, 214-218, 220-224, 227-228, 237-239, 244-248, 251-255, 257-262, 264-269
Langtoft 11
Lea 58
Leadenham 62
Learoyd, Roderick (VC) 199, 200-201

Leasingham 238
Lightning P38 25, 28, 72, 124, 126, 128, 164
Lincoln 149
Lincoln 10, 12, 210, 218, 256, 272, 273, 274, 281
Lissington 256
Little Grimsby 148
Louth 275, 281, 283
Ludford Magna 14, 16, 19, 26, 28, 52, 143, 166-172, 276
Lysander 48, 55, 188

Mablethorpe 62, 176, 225, 241, 261
Magister 87
Manby 11, 13, 24, 62, 173-176, 228, 283
Manchester 25, 30, 55, 65, 66-67, 89, 120, 178, 203, 211-214, 238, 242-243, 277
Manser, Leslie (VC) 211-214
Market Rasen 101, 282
Market Stainton 12, 51
Martinet 55, 165, 183
Master 28, 77, 140, 165
Messerschmitt
  Me109 124, 130, 161, 240, 275; *Me110* 115, 142, 155; *Me262* 126
Metheringham 19, 36, 70, 178-183, 248
Meteor 78
Minting 32
Mosquito 25, 27, 60, 70, 71, 72, 86, 111, 175, 267, 268, 270-271
Mustang P51 25, 28, 62, 86, 124, 125, 126, 189, 232, 268

Navenby 61
Nettleton, John Dering (VC) 244-246

North Coates 11, 13, 23, 27, 62, 184-190, 225, 226, 283
North Killingholme 19, 20, 25, 103, 191-198
North Witham 24, 43-44, 279
Norton Disney 12

Orby 11
Overstrand 174
Owston Ferry 57
Oxford 38, 58, 60, 69, 76, 79, 80, 81, 86, 116, 119, 120, 152, 232, 243

Parker, Donald (GC) 200
Polish squadrons 16, 44, 54, 56, 60, 92, 108-110, 132-133, 141-143, 162, 164-165, 233-235

Royal Australian Air Force 13, 18, 45, 49-53, 162, 203, 210, 236, 246
Royal Canadian Air Force 21, 59-60, 62, 82, 84-87, 185, 186, 188, 244

Sandtoft 19, 56-58
Scampton 11, 14, 15, 19, 33, 89, 90, 91, 130, 141, 199-209, 283
Scopwick 82
Scunthorpe 275, 282
Skegness 32, 62, 201
Skellingthorpe 19, 77, 171, 210-218
Skendleby 11
Sleaford 61, 283
Snitterby 273
Sopwith Gunbus 10
South Elkington 12